UNSHAKEABLE KINGDOM

Therefore, since we receive a kingdom which cannot be shaken, let us show gratitude, by which we may offer to God an acceptable service with reverence and awe; for our God is a consuming fire.

Hebrews 12:28, 29

UNSHAKEABLE KINGDOM

*Unveiling God's Mysterious Stone
and Glorious Mountain*

RUTHVEN J. ROY

REHOBOTH
PUBLISHING

Unless otherwise indicated, all Scripture quotations are taken from the *New American Standard Bible,* © 1960, 1962, 1963, 1968, 1971, 1972, 1973, 1975, 1977, by The Lockman Foundation. Used by permission.

Other versions used are
AMP - *The Amplified Bible,* © 1987, by The Lockman Foundation. Used by permission.
KJV - *The Authorized King James Version,* © 1975 by Thomas Nelson Inc., Publishers.
NIV – Scriptures taken from the *Holy Bible, New International Version.* © 1973, 1978, 1984 by International Bible Society. Used by permission of Zondervan Publishing House. All rights reserved.
NRSV – Scriptures taken from the *Holy Bible, New Revised Standard Version,* © 1989, by Division of Christian Education of the National Council of the Churches of Christ in the United States of America.

Unshakeable Kingdom: God's Mysterious Stone and Glorious Mountain
Copyright © 2010 by Ruthven J. Roy

ISBN: Paperback   978-0-9717853-5-9
                                0-9717853-5-x

Printed in the United States of America. **All rights reserved.** No part of this book may be reproduced or transmitted in any form or by any means without written permission from the publisher.

Rehoboth Publishing, LLC
P.O. Box 33
Berrien Springs, MI 49103

For additional copies of this book or for author speaking engagements write to: ruthvenroy@networkdiscipling.org,
or visit www.networkdiscipling.org

CONTENTS

Acknowledgements   9

Introduction   11

1. NOT JUST A STONE 17

   i. Daniel to the Rescue   18
   ii. A Sure Word of Prophecy   21
   iii. The Return of Elijah   25
   iv. The Coming of the Lamb-King   33
   v. In the Wilderness   36

2. LAUNCHING THE KINGDOM 43

   i. Kingdom Operative   44
   ii. Personal Invitation   47
   iii. Powerful Transformation   48
   iv. Productive Occupation   50
   v. Kingdom Concepts   52

3. MISSING THE KINGDOM 55

   i. The Nicodemus Syndrome   58
   ii. Touching the Unseen   59
   iii. Proclamation and Demonstration   61
   iv. Legacy of the Early Church   66

4 THE CHURCH AND THE KINGDOM 71

    i.   Birthing His Church   71
    ii   Signs and Wonders   75
    iii. God's Revelation   79
    iv. The Messiah   83
    v. Building His Church   90
    vi. The Mission of the Church   99

5 PENTECOST AND KINGDOM EXPANSION..........109

    i.   The Kingdom Priority   109
    ii   Ready for "*THIS*"   114
    iii. David's Kingdom Legacy   117
    iv. Kingdom Beyond Israel and Judaism   126
    v. Breaking Barriers   131

6 ATTACKS ON THE KINGDOM 145

    i.   Christ Confronts Caesar   145
    ii. A Change in Policy   155
    iii. Mystery of Iniquity   157
    iv. Deadly Alliance   159
    v. Supernatural Warfare   165

7 CONFLICTS IN THE KINGDOM 173

    i.   Tares Among the Wheat   173
    ii. In the Shadows of the Reformation   178
    iii. Reformation or Redistribution of
         Neo-Catholicism?   181
    iv. Satan's Expansion Strategy   187
    v. The Shepherd and His Sheep   189
    vi. God's Prevailing Will   198

8 PRELUDE TO THE PRESENCE 209

    i. Return of the Forerunner   209
    ii. Signs of the Approaching King   211
    iii. Kingly Indictment   227
    iv. Zealous, Corporate Repentance   234
    v. A Doomed System   239
    vi. The King's Final Call   242

9 ONE DAY WITH THE KING 251

    i. Disciples and D-Day   256
    ii. Panoramic Display   258
    iii. Snapshots of D-Day   259
    iv. Guess Who is Coming to Supper?   263
    v. Dress Rehearsal   264

10 GOD'S GLORIOUS MOUNTAIN 269

    i. An Answer to Prayer   272
    ii. Coronation of the Stone   274

Conclusion   281

Dedicated to:

*The King, my Lord, the blessed and only Potentate;
and to all kingdom seekers—the poor in spirit,
the meek, and the pure in heart . . .*

Acknowledgement

Always giving thanks to my God and Father for His goodness and grace; for the gift of my Savior, Jesus Christ; and from my Counselor, the Holy Spirit, by whose wisdom and revelation I was able to produce this work. I am always grateful and appreciative of my wife, Lyris, and our three daughters for their help and support in all my endeavors, including the writing of this manuscript. God has also brought to my assistance the invaluable editorial services of Patricia Elder and Dr. Ermine Leader, to make this book worthwhile reading material. Thanks to both of you for your excellent work. Emmerson (Emmo) Cyrille, I cannot thank you enough for your priceless contribution to this much-needed, timely volume. God bless you.

Introduction

> After this manner therefore pray ye: *Our Father which art in heaven, Hallowed be thy name. <u>Thy kingdom come</u>. Thy will be done in earth, as it is in heaven. Give us this day our daily bread. And forgive us our debts, as we forgive our debtors. And lead us not into temptation, but deliver us from evil: For <u>thine is the kingdom</u>, and <u>the power</u>, and <u>the glory</u>, forever. Amen.*
>
> Matthew 6:9-13, KJV

For many centuries, this simple model prayer has been the foundational and, if not, the primary invocation to God for countless millions throughout the world. Ever since it was spoken by Jesus to His first group of disciples in His acclaimed Sermon on the Mount, this prayer became the touchstone petition for Christians everywhere. Whenever words would fail the average petitioner, the Lord's model prayer has always proven to be an appropriate substitute for any occasion. The same is true in choosing a relevant starting point for this volume about the kingdom of God. We do not have to look very far to see that the entire prayer is held together by the imminence and immediacy of that kingdom, and the power and the glory of the King. While this volume does not allow me the time and space to delineate various truths that surface from this prayer, it is readily seen that it certainly carries very strong kingdom overtones. The Master is clearly telling His disciples, then and now, that they must live and pray with kingdom consciousness, and completely submit themselves to the will of the Father, His kingdom rule and the kingdom life.

This basic orientation formed the heart and soul of Christ's kingdom agenda, drove His life and ministry, and became the chart and compass for recruiting others into the fellowship and mission of

His kingdom. Jesus began His ministry from the shores of Galilee by preaching *the kingdom of heaven is at hand* (Matthew 4:17). This was the very message that was given by His cousin and forerunner, John the Baptist (Matthew 3:1, 2).

It is not without great significance that Christ's first official sermon, (The Sermon on the Mount) had a very strong kingdom ring. The very first blessing that fell from His lips offered the kingdom of heaven to the poor in spirit (Matthew 5:3). He also extended the kingdom to those who were unjustly persecuted for pursuing righteousness (Matthew 5:10), and denied entry to the self-righteous and those who attempted to annul any of His commandments and taught others to do the same (Matthew 5:20, 19). In that very sermon, Jesus emphasized the supreme importance of every believer making kingdom seeking the primary ambition of his/her earthly life (Matthew 6:33), but He also warned that mere lip service to His name would not qualify anyone for entry therein.

It was quite evident through Jesus' teaching and His actions that the kingdom of heaven and its advancement in the earth was the paramount focus of His ministry. The good news of the kingdom of heaven formed the central thesis of most of His parables (Matthew 13:11, 24, 31, 33, 44, 45, 47; Mark 4:26; Luke 19:12, 15). Christ's purpose was not only to proclaim the kingdom's reign but also to demonstrate its awesome power and unabashed penetration into the kingdom of darkness that had overtaken the world. Consequently, He bound Satan, the proverbial "strong man," entered his house and spoiled (robbed) his goods (Mark 3:27) by setting free those who were demon-possessed (Mark 5:1 ff); released those bound by deadly afflictions (Luke 8:2; 11:14; 13:16); and forgave those paralyzed by the guilt of sin (Mark 2:9-12; Luke 7:48, 49).[1]

In training His disciples, Christ taught them to do exactly as He did. Matthew wrote this concerning his Master: *Jesus was going throughout all Galilee, teaching in their synagogues and <u>proclaiming the gospel of the kingdom</u>, and <u>healing every kind of disease</u> and <u>every kind of sickness</u> among the people* (Matthew 4:23). When

Jesus, in turn, sent out His twelve disciples, He instructed them thus: "*And as you go, preach, saying: '<u>the kingdom of heaven is at hand</u>.' <u>Heal the sick, raise the dead, cleanse the lepers, cast out demons</u>. Freely you received, freely give*" (Matthew 10:7, 8). Christ did not only invite His disciples to partake in the fellowship of the kingdom, but He also gave them kingdom authority to extend its sovereign rule throughout the earth. When the seventy disciples returned from their kingdom assignment, they bore the glowing report, "*Lord, even the demons are subject to us in Your name*" (Luke 10:17) — to which Jesus replied:

> "*I was watching Satan fall from heaven like lightning. Behold, <u>I have given you authority</u> to tread on serpents and scorpions, and <u>over all the power of the enemy</u>, and nothing will injure you.*"
>
> Luke 10:18, 19

This legacy is the spiritual birthright of anyone who makes the life-changing decision to become a committed disciple of Jesus Christ. The King makes available to such a person the keys of the kingdom to open its storehouse of unimaginable abundance and authoritative power. Such access is possible only as the believer-disciple denies and submits himself to the daily crucifixion of his flesh — with all its hidden selfish desires — and makes room for the working of the Holy Spirit upon his spirit and mind.

Definition

There are more than one hundred references to the kingdom throughout the gospels alone. What appears rather interesting is that Matthew predominantly used the phrase "kingdom of heaven" in his reference to the kingdom — possibly to appeal to Jewish Christian piety which avoided the writing or pronunciation of the name of God.

On the other hand, Mark, Luke and John resorted to the phrase "kingdom of God." However, both usages are synonymous and would be regarded as such throughout this manuscript.

So what is this kingdom of God? How can humanity adequately define something that is infinitely bigger than our sphere of understanding? Such an attempt is feeble at best. Yet we must seek to grapple with its reality based upon the revealed Word of God. In my humble view, the kingdom of God is the unequivocal, eternal, sovereign rule of God over all His created works wherever they exist, and over creations yet unborn or unknown. Our heaven and earth are mere extensions of that kingdom, which, in the context of our redemption, speaks of God's divine intervention into our world to restore kingdom rule in the heart of fallen humanity and in an equally fallen, chaotic creation. The end result of this rule is the perfect fulfilment of his sovereign will on earth, just as it is performed in heaven above. It is important to realize that God's will is inextricably bound to His kingdom, whether that will is carried out in heaven or on earth; and to the extent that a person does His will, he is accorded his place and participation in that kingdom.

In His teaching, Jesus presented a three-dimensional view of the kingdom of God. He spoke of the kingdom with reference to the past when He said: "*In that place there will be weeping and gnashing of teeth when you see Abraham and Isaac and Jacob and all the prophets in the kingdom of God, but yourselves being thrown out*" (Luke 13:28; also Matthew 8:11). It is quite evident that the kingdom goes back in time to the patriarchs and the prophets of old.

Christ also made reference to the present reality of the kingdom of God when He told the Pharisees: "*The kingdom of God is not coming with signs to be observed; nor will they say, 'Look, here it is!' or, 'There it is!' For behold, <u>the kingdom of God is in your midst</u>*" (Luke 17:21). He further said, "*but if I cast out demons by the Spirit of God, then the kingdom of God has come upon you. Or how can anyone enter the strong man's house and carry off his property, unless he first binds the strong man? And then he will plunder his* *house*" (Matthew 12:28, 29). The obvious implication of Jesus' statement and question is that the kingdom of God is presently in operation because the "strong man" is rendered disabled and his captives are being set free. More pointedly, Christ declared that the kingdom of heaven was present from the time John the Baptist came out the wilderness preaching the gospel of repentance, in anticipation of the arrival of the King, his Messiah and Lord.

> <u>*From the days of John the Baptist until now*</u> *the kingdom of heaven suffers violence, and violent men take it by force.*
>
> Matthew 11:12

No doubt, Jesus also spoke of the kingdom in terms of the future, for He taught His disciples to pray: *"Thy kingdom come . . ."* (Matthew 6:10). He also gave several indications of the future kingdom when He portrayed Himself as the kingly Son of man returning in the clouds of heaven with power and great glory to reward every man according to his work (Matthew 16:27, 28; 24:30; 26:64). In Luke 21:31, He told His disciples that when they see the fulfillment of the signs that He said would precede His return, they must recognize that the kingdom of God is near.

> *"So you also, when you see these things happening, recognize that the kingdom of God is near."*
>
> Luke 21:31

Purpose

How is it ever possible for the kingdom to be past, present and future all at the same time? The answer is indeed very simple. The God who rules and reigns over the kingdom is the great I AM who inhabits eternity—past, present and future. His kingdom is an everlasting kingdom, and His throne is established forever and ever (Psalm 45:6). The goal of this book is to portray the connection of all three dimensions of the kingdom of God through the prophecy of Daniel 2—*the Mountain* (kingdom in the past), *the Stone* (kingdomin the present), and *the Glorious Mountain* (kingdom in the future)—and show God's eternal purpose through His church from the time of Christ to the end of the age.

Notes:

1. Glenn W. Barker, William L. Lame, and J. Ramsey Michaels, *The New Testament Speaks* (New York: Harper & Row Publishers, 1969), 83.

NOT JUST A STONE

1

And in the days of these kings shall the God of heaven set up a kingdom, which shall never be destroyed: and the kingdom shall not be left to other people, but it shall break in pieces and consume all these kingdoms, and it shall stand forever.

Daniel 2:44

One of the most vivid intimations of the coming kingdom of God was given by the prophet Daniel in the second chapter of the book named after him. This man of God stood before one of the greatest rulers that ever lived, declaring a divine secret that had mystified and troubled the fearless, heathen king. On heaven's timetable, God was ready to give a preview of future events that would have a direct impact on human history—from the reign of this great king, even to the end of the world. Using the vehicle of a dream, and imagery that was very familiar to Nebuchadnezzar, God revealed the future of Babylon and succeeding kingdoms; but He veiled the king's memory so that he could not remember his dream. In deep despair and desperation, Nebuchadnezzar turned to his most experienced heathen advisors, demanding of them not only to recall his dream but also to decode its meaning (Daniel 2:1-12). When these trusted soothsayers failed to provide the king the details and interpretation of his dream, his fear turned to anger. He gave the order to take the lives of his royal confidants and all the wise men in Babylon.

Daniel to the Rescue

When the news of the king's dilemma and decree of destruction reached Daniel, he paid a courtesy call on Nebuchadnezzar and told the king that he would reveal the dream and its interpretation if he were granted a little time. Daniel then approached his prayer-partners (Hananiah, Mishael and Azariah) and they asked favor from the One who sent the dream to Nebuchadnezzar (Daniel 2:16-18). It is very interesting to note that what God showed the king in a dream, He subsequently revealed to His servant Daniel in a night vision (Daniel 2:19). While both dreams and visions were often veiled representations of divine mysteries or messages, they were both characterized by different physical experiences. During a dream the recipient was in a state of unconscious sleep, while the panoramic episodes were played out on the walls of the subconscious mind. In a vision, however, the recipient was usually awake, in a conscious, but trancelike existence.

In loving response to the prayer request of Daniel and his companions, the God of heaven and earth revealed to His servant not only the detailed elements of Nebuchadnezzar's dream, but also the comprehensive interpretation of the same. Through the exile prophet, Providence had furnished a witness to declare to the king of Babylon, and all his future successors, a clear outline of the divine agenda pertaining to the political powers that would rule the world prior to the establishment of the kingdom of God in the earth. In one charismatic presentation, Daniel unfolded every iota of the king's dream, much to the surprise and relief of the miserable royal comforters, magicians, conjurers, diviners and Nebuchadnezzar himself. It is quite easy to imagine the king sitting wide-eyed, at the edge of his throne, anxiously listening to Daniel as he vividly painted the scenes from his dream. Daniel explained:

> *"You were looking, O king, and lo! There was a great statue. This statue was huge, its brilliance*

extraordinary; it was standing before you, and its appearance was frightening. <u>The head of that statue was of fine gold, its chest and arms of silver, its middle and thighs of bronze, its legs of iron, its feet partly of iron and partly of clay</u>. As you looked on, <u>a stone was cut out, not by human hands</u>, and it struck the statue on its feet of iron and clay and broke them to pieces. Then the iron, the clay, the bronze, the silver, and the gold, were all broken in pieces and came like the chaff of the summer threshing floors; and the wind carried them away, so that not a trace of them could be found. But the stone that struck the statue became a great mountain and filled the whole earth."

Daniel 2:31-35, NRSV

Nebuchadnezzar's relief from his anxiety spell was short-lived as Daniel moved right along into the interpretation of the king's dream. With quick, broad strokes of his prophetic brush, Daniel compressed hundreds of years of world history in one oratorical session, outlining the political demise of Babylon, its future global successors—Medo-Persia, Greece and Rome in that order—and the divided geo-political landscape of the world to the end of time.

"You, O king, the king of kings—to whom the God of heaven has given the kingdom, the power, the might, and the glory, into whose hands he has given human beings, wherever they live, the wild animals of the field, and the birds of the air, and whom he has established as ruler over them all—<u>you are the head of gold</u>. After you shall arise another kingdom inferior to yours, and yet a third kingdom of bronze, which shall rule over the whole earth. And there shall

> *be a fourth kingdom, strong as iron; just as iron crushes and smashes everything, it shall crush and shatter all these. As you saw the feet and toes partly of potter's clay and partly of iron, it shall be a divided kingdom . . . so the kingdom shall be partly strong and partly brittle. As you saw the iron mixed with clay, so will they mix with one another in marriage, but they will not hold together, just as iron does not mix with clay.*
>
> *And in the days of those kings the <u>God of heaven will set up a kingdom that shall never be destroyed</u>, nor shall this kind be left to another people. It shall crush all these kingdoms and bring them to an end, and it shall stand forever; just as you saw that <u>a stone was cut from the mountain not by human hands</u>, and that it crushed the iron, the bronze, the clay, the silver, and the gold. The great God has informed the king what shall be hereafter."*
>
> Daniel 2:37-45, NRSV

No doubt, Nebuchadnezzar was stunned by the accuracy of Daniel's portrayal of his dream, but this bold, unequivocal declaration of its interpretation filled the king with fear and trepidation. Daniel's closing words, *"the great God hath made known to the king what shall come to pass hereafter: and the dream is certain, and the interpretation thereof is sure"* (Daniel 2:45), were indelibly etched on the king's mind, leaving him with grim forebodings regarding the future of his glorious kingdom.

The third chapter of Daniel records Nebuchadnezzar's attempt to turn back the word of God regarding the interpretation of his dream. Whereas the head of gold on the great statue that towered over the king in his dream depicted Babylon, Nebuchadnezzar erected a counter-statue of all gold, symbolizing that he intended his kingdom to last forever.

Although the interpretation of the king's dream predicted the coming of an everlasting kingdom (Daniel 2: 35, 44, 45), that kingdom was neither going to be for his time; nor was it going to be his own. In the year 538 B.C., the kingdom of Babylon fell to the alliance of the Medes and Persians, under the leadership of king Darius, the Mede (Daniel 5:30), bringing to an end one of greatest empires the world has ever known. Indeed, Nebuchadnezzar's dream was certain, because it came from God, and Daniel's interpretation is sure, because God will fulfill His word.

A Sure Word of Prophecy

"We have also a more sure word of prophecy; whereunto ye do well that ye take heed, as unto a light that shineth in a dark place, until the day dawn, and the day star arise in your heart: Knowing this first, that no prophecy of scripture is of any private interpretation. For the prophecy came not in old time by the will of man: but holy men of God spake as they were moved by the Holy Ghost."

2 Peter 1: 19-21

When a Stone is Not Just a Stone

The fall of Babylon marked the beginning of the prophetic word that declared God's intention to establish the kingdom of Christ in the earth. Nebuchadnezzar rejected the interpretation regarding "the lowly stone", which was cut from a mountain without human hands (Daniel 2: 34, 35), and was destined to annihilate all earthly kingdoms as it grew into a worldwide mountain. Here is a "stone" of mysterious origin, untouched by human hands, without any sort of terrestrial interference. Its appearance, growth and establishment is solely the work of the great God of heaven.

This "stone" is not really a stone in the true sense of the word, but it is most certainly a symbolic representation of Christ and His kingdom. Isaiah makes this connection in two of his prophecies regarding the Messiah: *"Then He shall become a sanctuary; But to both the houses of Israel, <u>a stone to strike and a rock to stumble over</u>"* (Isaiah 8: 14). *"Therefore thus says the Lord God, 'Behold, I am laying in Zion <u>a stone, a tested stone, a costly cornerstone</u> for the foundation firmly placed. He who believes in it will not be disturbed'"* (Isaiah 28:16).

In Psalm 118:22, David also used the stone imagery to portray Israel's rejection of their Messiah, and to confirm God's appointment of Christ as the foundation stone for building the spiritual house of Israel—the kingdom of God (Ephesians 2: 11-22). Christ made reference to this passage (Psalm 118: 22) after using the vehicle of a parable to deliver a scathing rebuke to the leadership of Israel.

> *"Did ye never read in the scriptures, <u>the stone which the builders rejected, the same is become the head of the corner: this is the Lord's doing, and it is marvelous in our eyes</u>? Therefore say I unto you, <u>the kingdom of God</u> shall be taken from you, and given to a nation bringing forth the fruits thereof. And whosoever shall fall on the stone shall be broken: but on whomsoever is shall fall, it will grind him to powder"*
>
> Matthew 21: 42-44

In the above scripture, Christ clearly brings together the "stone" and the everlasting kingdom of heaven that are portrayed in the prophetic book of Daniel. It is very important to observe that this "stone" was cut from a mountain, and that this very stone, itself, became a great mountain. How amazing indeed! It is also true that this "stone" and the mountain from which it was taken are of one and the same element, and can only represent one and the same thing. The mountain in Nebuchadnezzar's dream is nothing less than the everlasting kingdom of heaven, and the stone is an extension of that kingdom.

This end-time prophecy of Daniel is a panoramic portrayal of God's great cosmic plan to restore the colony of earth to its rightful place in His kingdom. When God created man, He made him ruler of the earth, giving him complete *dominion over the fish of the sea, and over the fowl of the air, and over the cattle, and over ALL THE EARTH, and over every creeping thing that creepeth upon the earth* (Genesis 1:26, KJV). The earth was a reflection of the kingdom of heaven, ruled by heaven's governor (Adam), administering the kingdom's rule, principles and laws over all creation.

When the first family violated kingdom law, through disobedience, Adam lost his governorship and dominion, which were usurped by the archenemy of the King—the Prince of the kingdom of darkness. However, God did not leave man or His creation at the mercy of the despotic deceiver. He promised man a way out of his dilemma. The plan of redemption, made in the eternal council of heaven, made adequate provision for the tragedy of sin in the universe; for Christ, the vicarious Lamb, was considered slain for the sin of the world even before its foundation was laid.

Consequently, the moment man sinned, at that very instant he had a Savior, Jesus Christ, the Lamb of God. Man's dominion was not lost forever, for God spoke the promise of recovery directly to the enemy: "*I will put enmity between you and the woman, between your seed and her seed, He shall bruise you on the head, and you shall bruise Him on the heel*" (Genesis 3:15). It was through the Seed of the woman (Jesus Christ) that the kingdom of heaven on earth was going to be restored, and dominion was going to be returned to Adam's fallen race. This is the One of whom all of the patriarchs and prophets spoke—even Shiloh, the Star of Jacob, the righteous

Branch, the Deliverer, Root of Jesse, Comforter of Israel, Wonder, Counselor, that Prophet, the Messiah—to encourage the people of God through the annals of time.

Crumbling Kingdoms

Now the time had finally arrived for God to announce the appearance of Him, *whose goings forth have been from of old,*[even] *from everlasting* (Micah 5:2, KJV). Through the dream of a heathen king and the mouth of His chosen prophet, God revealed His hand as He declared His intention to change the course of human history by the coming of the Kingly Messiah. According to the interpretation He delivered to Daniel, the kingdom of Babylon (the head of gold) was to be followed by the kingdom of Medo-Persia (chest and arms of silver) in 538 B.C., and then by the kingdom of Greece (belly and thigh of brass).

Under the remarkable leadership of Alexander the Great, Greece came into power around the year 331 B.C. However, despite Alexander's military genius and swift, merciless conquest, his kingdom was destined to fall. History records that he died at the very young age of 33, after a drinking rampage that left him with a high fever that eventually claimed his life.[1] After Alexander's death, his kingdom was divided among his four leading generals, but that division made the empire an easy target for the growing threat from the west. By the year 168 B.C., this massive Grecian empire fell to the Republic of Rome, under the leadership of Julius Caesar. It was during the time of Rome that Daniel's prophecy regarding the lowly stone came into very sharp focus. The kingdom of iron held sway over the then-known world and the stage was set for the birth of the long-awaited Messiah of Israel. Rome would later fall apart because of political strife and moral corruption from within, and the invasion by the Germanic tribes (the ten toes on the feet of the great image of Daniel 2 and our modern European nations) from without.[2]

A very interesting feature in Daniel's prophecy regarding the statue in Nebuchadnezzar's dream is the components of the elements in its feet. Daniel said:

> *And whereas thou sawest the feet and toes, part of potters' clay, and part of iron, the kingdom shall be divided; but there shall be in it of the strength of the iron, forasmuch as thou sawest the iron mixed with miry clay. And as the toes of the feet were part of iron, and part of clay, so the kingdom shall be partly strong, and partly broken. And whereas thou sawest iron mixed with miry clay, they shall mingle themselves with the seed of men: but they shall not cleave one to another, even as iron is not mixed with clay.*
>
> Daniel 2:41-43

This strange mixture of iron and clay in the feet of the image does not only represent the strengths and weaknesses that characterize these last day nations, but also the religio-political influences of Rome that permeate their systems of operation. The Roman system of government and the structure and religious traditions that governed the Christian church during post-Apostolic era are very much present in the political and religious cultures of our post-Modern world. However, the world and all the machinery that drive this present age will soon give way to the advancing kingdom of heaven. The complete destruction of the image (by the "stone") is a progressive kingdom work that began with the demise of Babylon and will culminate in the establishment of the "mountain" of God that will fill the whole earth (Daniel 2:35).

The Return of Elijah

According to the gospel of Luke, Christ was born during the reign of Octavian Caesar, who was given the name Augustus (Luke

2:1) by the Roman senate in 27 B.C. It was during this period that the Holy One, who had given the dream to Nebuchadnezzar, and the vision and interpretation to Daniel, also commissioned angel Gabriel to initiate heaven's kingdom campaign with mysterious visitations to the land of Judea.

During his first visitation, the angel Gabriel appeared to a priest by the name of Zacharias, who was ministering before the altar of incense in the Holy Place (or first apartment) of the sacred temple (Luke 1:8-11ff). No doubt, Zacharias was terrified by the appearance, for he had no knowledge whether Gabriel's mission was one of mercy or judgment. Gabriel quickly put Zacharias at ease with the unexpected, but glorious news:

> *". . . your petition has been heard, and your wife Elizabeth will bear you a son, and you will give him the name John. And you will have joy and gladness, and many will rejoice at his birth. For he will be great in the sight of the Lord, and he will drink no wine or liquor; and he will be filled with the Holy Spirit, while yet in his mother's womb. And he will turn back the sons of Israel to the Lord their God. And it is he who will go as a forerunner before Him <u>in the spirit and power of Elijah</u> to turn the hearts of the fathers back to the children, and the disobedient to the attitude of the righteous; so as <u>to make ready a people prepared for the Lord</u>."*
>
> Luke 1:13-17

The content of Gabriel's message completely floored the aging priest, for God was not only prepared to give Zacharias a child, but a son, a very special son. This is just like God. He often gives us more than we ask for, because we do not really know what we need, or how to ask for what we desire (Romans 8:26). Moreover, God's gifts are never afterthoughts. They always meet a particular need, or serve a specific purpose. God was particular enough not only to name the son of Zacharias, John, but also gave detailed instructions regarding his birth, his diet and his mission. John was not just a product of human copulation, but the result of divine intervention. He was a Holy Ghost baby with a Spirit-directed agenda.

John the Baptist was a very key figure in heaven's kingdom initiative. He was appointed to be a reformer of Israel and the forerunner of the Messianic King. He was the returning Elijah, spoken of by the prophet Malachi (Malachi 4:6) and later endorsed by Christ, Himself (Matthew 11:12-14). Thus began the mysterious cutting of the stone, being cut without humans hands (Daniel 2:44)—the initial setting up of Christ's Kingdom through the ministry of John the Baptist.

Zacharias listened to Gabriel in utter disbelief, because the weakness of his human logic had eclipsed the power of his faith in God's ability to turn back the course of nature to produce fruitfulness out of barrenness. "I am an old man," said he, "and my wife is advanced in years," (Luke 1:18). What does it matter? "Is anything too difficult for the Lord?" (Genesis 18:14). Needless to say, Zacharias' doubt and confusion were met with Gabriel's presentation of his divine credentials, and his sentence of dumbness on the faltering man of God for his unbelief.

> *"I am Gabriel, who stands in the presence of God; and I have been sent to speak to you, and to bring you this good news. And behold, you shall be silent and unable to speak until the day when these things take place, because you did not believe my words, which shall be fulfilled in their proper time."*
>
> Luke 1:19-20

How instructive is this event for us today. Although Zacharias was praying for the gift of a son for a very long time (for he was now aging and still childless), when God's messenger showed up with the claim ticket for the gift, Zacharias was in complete disbelief. Indeed, the frailty of human flesh knows no bounds as *appearances,* wrapped in human reason, confront the *unseen*—that is, the things hoped for (Hebrews 6:1)—wrapped in dynamic faith. In the church and in the marketplace, in the pulpit and in the pews, we find perennial manifestations of the "Zacharias phenomenon." Zacharias ministered before the presence of God—the nearest place to heaven on earth, yet he failed to embrace the power of the One he was praying to because, in his estimate, fatherhood at his age was a human and medical impossibility.

We often succumb to the same weakness when we allow our judgment of our human situation to vanquish the miraculous possibilities associated with our faith. Therefore, we must be constantly reminded that the God of heaven cannot be measured or bound by human logic, empirical analysis, or the elements of space and time, for He is able to make ways where there is no way, and to call into being that which does not even exist (Romans 4:17).

About six months after his first visitation, the angel Gabriel was sent to the city of Nazareth to deliver another very important message to a young virgin named Mary, who was engaged to Joseph, a descendant from the house of David. While Gabriel's second appearance was not any different from the first, Mary's reaction was quite different from that of the aged, and more experienced, Zacharias. The young maiden expressed surprise, not so much at Gabriel's presence, but at his form of greeting; and as she pondered his salutation, Gabriel said:

> *"Do not be afraid, Mary; for you have found favor with God. And behold, you will conceive in your womb, and bear a son, and you shall name Him Jesus. He will be great, and will be called the Son of the Most High; and the Lord God will give the <u>throne</u>*

<u>*of His father David*</u>; *and He will <u>reign</u> over the house of Jacob forever; and <u>His Kingdom will have no end</u>.*"

Luke 1:30-33

In response to this most amazing declaration, young Mary said: "*Behold the bondslave of the Lord; be it done to me <u>according to your word</u>*," (Luke 1:38). This is a very remarkable statement of faith coming from a very young maiden and it reveals two important facts about Mary: (1) She trusted God, and was willing to surrender herself as a bond-servant to His divine purpose; and (2) she had faith in the power of God's word—"*let it be just as you say*" (my paraphrase). What a sterling example of faith and courage it was for this young woman to accept the stupendous responsibility of carrying the "Seed of God" in her womb for nine months when she never sexually knew a man. Undaunted by the possibility of her lover's (Joseph's) scorn and rejection, public shame and ridicule, young Mary embraced her faith, completely trusting in the word of her God.

It is very important to observe that Gabriel's message is full of kingdom language, and reflects the prophetic word spoken by Daniel, that "in the days of these kings—from the establishment of Rome to the end of time—the God of heaven will set up a kingdom which will never be destroyed . . . but <u>*it will itself endure forever*</u>" (Daniel 2:44). Gabriel's kingdom announcement also echoes God's message to David (the earthly forefather of the Messiah) through the prophet Nathan, and rightly so, since they both originated from the same Source.

> *When your days are complete and you lie down with your fathers, I will raise up your <u>descendant</u> after you, and I will establish his kingdom. He shall build a house for My name, and <u>I will establish the throne of his kingdom forever</u>. . . And your house and your kingdom shall endure before Me forever; your throne*

shall be established forever.

2 Samuel 7:12-16

While this passage has a typical application to David's son, Solomon—who was given the privilege building and dedicating the Temple of Jerusalem ("a house for My name" *v.* 13; also 1 Kings 5-9)—it clearly met its anti-typical fulfillment in the life and ministry of Jesus Christ, the true son of David. It was Christ who was going to build the true spiritual house unto God through His cross (Ephesians 2, pay particular attention to *vv.*16-22). It was Mary's Son, Jesus, who was going to sit on the throne of David and establish his kingdom forever (Luke 1:32, 33).

Interestingly, Gabriel's announcements regarding the births of John the Baptist and Jesus, the Messiah, bear marked similarities. These births were a part of the extraction process associated with the "stone" cut without hands, that grew into a mountain, which filled the whole earth (Daniel 2:34, 35 and 44, 45). They were both of divine origin—one, by divine intervention (God doing the unthinkable by miraculously turning back the course of nature in Zacharias and Elizabeth to bear a son in their old age), the other, by divine insemination (God implanting His Holy Seed in the womb of a young maiden, who never sexually knew a man—see Luke 1:34, 35). Humanity was only the willing, but passive, medium, but the omnipotent God was the active agent of the birthing process in each case.

Beside this birthing phenomenon, John and Jesus both got their names from the same divine Source (compare Luke 1:13 and 31). Gabriel also said that they were both going to be great in the sight of the Lord (Luke 1:15 and 32), and both of them were filled with the Holy Ghost from the time of conception (Luke 1:15 and 35). What an awesome and almighty God! These great and glorious acts of God were all linked together as preparatory steps towards the establishment of His everlasting kingdom.

In God's appointed time, the forerunner to the Messiah was born and the course of his life began to unfurl. At his circumcision, well-wishing relatives and friends tried to influence Elizabeth to change the name John to Zacharias (in honor of his father), but she graciously refused. When they brought the same suggestion to the child's mute father, Zacharias confirmed in writing that his only son should be called John. As simple as it may seem, this was an attempt of the enemy to use human hands to shape the course of the "stone." The name John came with the signet of heaven and was directly associated with his earthly mission as the forerunner of the Messiah. Consequently, as soon as the aged priest confirmed heaven's naming of his son, his tongue became loose, and, under the anointing of the Holy Ghost, he began to bless God and prophesied concerning John's mission.

> *"And you child, will be called the prophet of the Most High; for you will go on before the Lord to prepare His ways; To give to His people the knowledge of salvation by the forgiveness of sin, Because of the tender mercy of God, With which the Sunrise from on high shall visit us, To shine upon those who sit in darkness and the shadow of death, To guide our feet into the way of peace."*

> Luke 1:76-79

Mission Training

John's spiritual formation and training were not left to the fancies of his parents or the burdensome, self-righteous requirements of the religious elite of the community of Israel. The mission and kingdom that John was about to proclaim to Israel and the world were not only transcendental realities that ran contrary to the course of all human establishments, but they bore very grave import on the eternal future of all the inhabitants of the earth. Therefore, God did not allow John's development and education to be controlled or become tainted by the religious institutions of his day. Human hands were never permitted to shape or influence the ministry of John. This fact has a direct connection to "the stone that was cut without hands," Daniel 2:34, 45. Luke tells us that at a very early age, John was raised and educated in the secret place of the Most High—that is, the wilderness of Judea—under the watchful, caring tutelage of the Almighty. Further, John never appeared in public until he came forth from the wilderness preaching the kingdom of God, and the baptism of repentance and the forgiveness of sins (compare Luke 1:80; 3:3ff; Matthew 3:1, 2; Mark 1:4ff).

Announcing the Kingdom

It is very important to take careful note of the fact that John had a very specific evangelistic agenda. His divine mission assignment was to prepare the masses for the Lamb-King by proclaiming the imminence of His kingdom that was about to break in on the kingdoms of this world. Associated with this preparation were the calling of sinners to the baptism of repentance and the forgiveness of their sins. Most importantly, the center-piece of John's ministry was to identify publicly the Lamb-King to Israel and rest of the world—which was the true and only reason why John came baptizing by water (John 1:31-34).[3]

Nevertheless, John stuck to his heaven-born commission. Nothing else held top priority. He was forthright in acknowledging that he did not possess any earthly, or institutional, credentials. These were not mission requirements. John simply described himself only as a "voice" crying in the wilderness (John 1:19-23). Quite often that's all God needs to do His wonders—a voice that is willing to speak for Him. John's message was a reflection of his educational training. It was very simple, precise and uncompromisingly clear, just like that of his Master who was soon to replace him: *"Repent ye:*

for the Kingdom of heaven is at hand" (Matthew 3:2).

The Coming of the Lamb-King

John's unique introduction of Israel's long-awaited Messiah caught the masses and the Jewish ecclesiastical leadership by surprise. Even more amazing was the fact that John, himself, did not know the Messiah, because he never personally met Jesus before His presentation for baptism.[4] The meeting of these two kingdom initiators was clearly a Spirit-orchestrated encounter that gave legitimacy to the profound announcement John was about to make. As Jesus approached the Baptist, the Holy Ghost prompted John to announce His entrance as the long-awaited Messiah of Israel:

> *Here is the Lamb of God who takes away the sin of the world! This is he of whom I said, after me come a man who ranks ahead of me because he was before me.' <u>I myself did not know him; but came baptizing with water for this reason, that he might be revealed to Israel</u>.*

John 1:29-31, NRSV

This unusual presentation of the Messiah as the Lamb of God is the first and only such recorded reference of Christ in all of the gospels. Clearly, this was God's doing and not John's. The announcement represented God's unique way of serving early notice to the Jews, whose national pride and mental framework had no room for a dying Lamb or the Gentile world, that the kingdom of God was not of this world, and was not subject to the prejudices, boundaries, and categories formulated by puny, human minds. The Messiah was not destined to be the charismatic, freedom fighter for the Jewish nation, or any other religious organization. From the foundation of the world, the Lamb of God was covenanted to be heaven's

Ambassador and Liberator of the human race. Thus, while the chosen people of God wanted a kingly Messiah to deliver and preserve their Jewish world from the dominion of Rome, the God of heaven provided, instead, a Lamb-King to be the Savior of the whole world—Jews, Gentiles, and Romans included.

John was very much attuned to heaven's agenda, and, through this announcement, he was humbly preparing the way for his mission replacement. He knew that a whole new order was about to be established. Christ and His kingdom were about to replace the Jewish system of religion, as well as the kingdom of Rome and all her successors. Even more importantly, John was aware that he and his disciples were about to be superseded by Christ and His disciples. This was the reason for which he was born, and for which he became a witness for the gospel.

However, while John accepted his receding role as a dominant voice on the landscape of the Jewish world, the Jewish leaders were by no means prepared to accept the Messiah's role as the true leader of His people and Savior of the humanity. Instead, Israel and its leaders were consumed with their religio-political agenda, seeking to establish the kingdom of Israel rather than the kingdom of God. Following in the footsteps of their forefathers (See 1 Samuel 8), the Jews wanted their own private king, and a kingdom that would conquer Rome and rule the world. They wanted a king who was a conquering lion—not a dying lamb. In the days of Samuel, the Bible records:

> *"Then all the elders of Israel gathered themselves together, and came to Samuel unto Ramah, And said unto him, Behold, thou art old, and thy sons walk not in thy ways: now make us a king to judge us like all the nations. But the thing displeased Samuel, when they said, Give us a king to judge us. And Samuel prayed unto the Lord.*
>
> *And the Lord said unto Samuel, Hearken unto*

the voice of the people in all that they say unto thee: for they have not rejected thee, but they have rejected me, that I should not reign over them.
According to all the works which they have done since the day that I brought them up out of Egypt even unto this day, wherewith they have forsaken me, and served other gods, so do they also unto thee.
Now therefore hearken unto their voice: howbeit yet protest solemnly unto them, and show them the manner of the king that shall reign over them."

1 Samuel 8:4-9

Israel's earthly ambition drove the nation's leaders to trade the supernatural power that came through their alliance with, and dependence on, Jehovah, for political recognition through conceited nationalism and humanistic endeavors. As a result, the Jews presented themselves as the enemy of their surrounding neighbors and only made proselytes of those who would accept their terms of religion. Thus, through his artful maneuver, Satan had subtly prepared the way for the professed people of God to reject their Messiah, the Lamb-King.

Nationalistic pride, political ambition and human weakness had led the descendants of Abraham to make that major human error which led to the very painful history that has dogged the steps of this chosen people up to this present day. Accordingly, although Israel gained the sovereign statehood and the recognition she desired in the world, she virtually lost her sense of God's protection and peace. In the current political landscape, she has become the object of perpetual hatred and harassment to the nations that immediately surrounded her.

In the Wilderness

Immediately upon His baptism, Jesus was propelled by the Holy Spirit into the same wilderness from which John had only recently emerged (Mark 1:9-13), and with very good reason for doing so. On the divine timetable, this meeting at the Jordan represented the first crossing of the guards—one was leaving, the other was entering the wilderness. The wilderness was God's appointed place for kingdom preparation. For forty days and forty nights Christ was completely shut off from all human contact as He fasted and communed with His Father. Apart from Calvary, this was the most critical period of the Messiah's life—the acid test for His mission and ministry. The truth is, without the wilderness, there could not have been a Gethsemane or Calvary victory.

Christ's journey into the wilderness was a journey to crucifixion—the full and complete mortification of the encumbrance of His flesh, which He took on Himself after humanity was exposed to almost 6,000 years of sin and rebellion. The Son of Man had to go through the discipline of freeing Himself from the legacies of Adam in order to establish a new and living way in the spirit for Adam's fallen race. The Savior deliberately starved His flesh not only of food, but also of every imaginable lust and desire. By the time Satan got to Him, there was absolutely nothing in Christ to respond positively to the temptations of the Arch-deceiver. Christ would later confirm this by saying: ". . . for the prince of this world cometh, and hath nothing in me . . ." (John 14:30, KJV). The New International Version translation of this text appeals to me in a special way: ". . . *for the prince of this world is coming.* <u>*He has no hold on me*</u> . . ."

Just as in systems of law, cases are won in the lawyers' chambers and not so much in the courtrooms, and just as victories in team sports are won in locker rooms and not on the fields of play, so it was that Calvary was won, not on the cross, but in the secret chamber of the Most High—the wilderness of temptation, and by extension, the Garden of Gethsemane.

Yes, the Garden of Gethsemane was the wilderness the second time around. Again the Savior was stripped of every human support as, with intense agony, He battled with His recoiling flesh and the arch-enemy over the bitter cup (the cross of Calvary) He was about to drink. This death struggle with His humanity and the powers of darkness was so overwhelmingly fierce that His quivering, crumbling flesh released great drops of sweat, commingled with blood, through His gaping pores. The Savior trod the winepress alone, just as He did in the wilderness of temptation. In both of these episodes, the Father had to preserve the humanity of His Son from certain death by sending angels to minister to the Savior's dying flesh (see Matthew 4:11 and Luke 22:43). However, once these ordeals were over, victory over Satan and Calvary was a foregone reality.

Contrary to popular opinion which holds that Satan sought to gain an advantage by tempting Christ when He was at His weakest point (that is, almost starved to death), Jesus, though physically weak and emaciated, was really at the pinnacle of His mental and spiritual powers. Satan artfully tried to short-circuit the way to the throne by offering Christ the kingdom without sacrifice and the lucrative opportunity to be a king without becoming a lamb. However, the Savior's broken body and sovereign will were already surrendered completely to the eternal plan of the Father.

Through His forty days and forty nights of self-denial and self-abnegation, Jesus experienced a complete transformation that confirmed the Father and the Father's will as the dynamic center and controlling influence of His life. "I can of my own self do nothing," He would later say. "As I hear, I judge: and my judgment is just; because I seek not my own will but the will of the Father who hath sent me" (John 5:30, KJV). Operating from this impregnable platform, Christ was able to secure convincingly, the future of His kingdom and offer infinite hope to all humanity.

In the light of the foregoing truths, it becomes very evident that the wilderness experience of both John the Baptist and Christ were divine prerequisites for kingdom building. These watershed events represented God's refining process for the shaping of the "stone" for growth and development into the great mountain (the kingdom of God) that would fill the whole earth (Daniel 2:35). It was God's eternal initiative for preparing the Lamb to reign forever as King of kings and Lord of lords on the everlasting throne of David.

Wilderness and Kingdom Preparedness

The God of heaven and earth is the God of the wilderness. From this isolated command post, with its unpredictable, rugged, mountainous terrain, He calls His servants into His service. But why the wilderness? Because it is in the recluse of this spiritual boot camp that He teaches His servants the one eternal principle for successful service—that is, "man does not live by bread alone, but he lives by every word that proceeds out of the mouth of God" (Deuteronomy 8:3). In other words, a person does not live by his/her capacity to provide for himself/herself, but by his/her faith in God's ability to supply all his/her needs in copious abundance. Man's true life does not originate from the bread which only sustains his body, but from the Word (the Bread of Life) which sustains God's spirit that gave life to his body. Apart from this "breath of God" (that is, His spirit) and the Word from heaven, the form of clay (man) has no life within (Genesis 1:26; 2:7; John 6:53).[5]

It is in the wilderness that God transforms our earthly, human perspectives from self-reliance to reliance on God; from puffed up pride to graceful humility; from walking by sight (or human reason) to walking by faith and revelation (every Word of God, spoken or read); from operating in the weakness of the flesh, to moving in the power of the Spirit. The wilderness trains the spirit of man, exposes the true condition of the human heart, and predisposes the soul to resign itself to the will of the Almighty.

Speaking from His high and lofty mountain stronghold, God once instructed Moses to convey the following message to the children of Israel:

> *You <u>shall remember</u> all the way which the Lord your God has led you in the wilderness these forty years, that He might humble you, testing you, to know what was in your heart, whether you would keep His commandments or not. And he humbled you and let you be hungry, and fed you with manna which you did not know, nor did your fathers know, <u>that He might make you to understand that man does not live by bread alone, but man lives by everything that proceeds out of the mouth of the Lord</u>. Your clothing did not wear out on you, nor did your foot swell these forty years. Thus you are to know in your heart that the Lord your God was disciplining you as a man disciplines his son.*
>
> Deuteronomy 8:2-5

So how are we to relate to the wilderness of our "adverse" human experiences? We must know in our spirits and minds that the God of the wilderness is with us. He has called us to His holy mountain to teach us to rely on Him, and to change our myopic worldview to His divine perspective, and the foolishness of our logic (1 Corinthians 1:25-31) to the wisdom of faith in Him (1 Corinthians 2:1-5). We must possess the confidence—fueled by the Word of faith—that our call into the wilderness is a divine privilege to be personally mentored by the great "I Am," into a life of faith and submission through God-dependence.

Once we accept our wilderness call, our human perspective changes because God removes the scales from our eyes, and we begin to see life through the eyes of faith (in God), and not through the eyes of natural experience. We learn to trust less in our flesh, in our humanity, and in the systems of this world, and to lean more on the almighty power, goodness and faithfulness of Jehovah. We make the ultimate switch from a life dominated by human reason to the abundant life dominated by faith in God and divine revelation through our Lord, Jesus Christ. God often uses our wilderness experience to elevate us from the frustrations, disappointments, pain and loss associated with the kingdom of darkness, to the peace, power, joy and abundance associated with His kingdom of light and life.

One of my favorite authors has rightly said: "We are prone to look to our fellow men for sympathy and uplifting, instead of looking to Jesus. In His mercy and faithfulness God often permits those in whom we place our confidence to fail us, in order that we may learn the folly of trusting in man and making flesh our arm."[6] King David puts it this way: *"Do not put your trust in princes, nor in mortals, in whom there is no help. When their breath departs, they return to the earth; on that very day their plans perish. Happy are those whose help is the God of Jacob, whose hope is in the Lord their God, who made heaven and earth, the sea, and all that is in them; who keeps faith forever"* (Psalm 146:3-6, NRSV).

Essentially, this is what the wilderness experience is all about. It is about God training us in divine trust, teaching us to unhook from the unpredictable systems and ways of this world and to attach ourselves permanently *"to an inheritance that is incorruptible, and undefiled and that fadeth not away"* (1 Peter 1:4). Once this lesson is learnt and we submit to God's will and Word, we become linked to unlimited power, and, through the grace of God, we are able to perform the deeds of omnipotence.

Therefore, whenever our wilderness comes, we should not be surprised by it, "as though something strange were happening to us. But rejoice insofar as we are sharing Christ's sufferings, so that we may also be glad and shout for joy when His glory is revealed" (1 Peter 4:12, 13, NRSV). Always remember that God is in the wilderness with us, and when we are at our lowest point, thinking that all will be lost, He is ever near to minister to our fainting spirits. We must reach out in faith and claim His promises, transforming our wilderness into a fruitful oasis, filled with expectant hope and steadfast assurance, because God is preparing to take us to the next level in our walk with Him.

Christ's journey to the wilderness and His victorious encounter with the ruler of the kingdom of darkness opened a door of hope for all His kingdom citizens. Although His kingdom may suffer violence at the hands the Prince of darkness and his hosts; and although the children of the kingdom may become victims of the enemy; Christ's wilderness victory foreshadowed the ultimate triumph of the kingdom of God on the earth and in our lives. Therefore, every born again believer can joyfully live the kingdom lifestyle in the face of all adversity, and can pray with bold confidence: "Thy kingdom come, O Lord!"

Notes

1. Geoffrey Bruun and Wallace K. Ferguson, *A Survey of European Civilization* (Boston, MA: Houghton Mifflin Company, 1969), 41-42.
2. Ibid, 97-109.
3. For a more comprehensive understanding and a more extensive discourse on the mission of John the Baptist, see chapter 1 in Ruthven J. Roy's book, *The Explosive Power of Network Discipling* (Berrien Springs, MI: Rehoboth Publishing, 2010).
4. Ibid. 31, 32.
5. For a fuller understanding of this truth, see chapter 1, "In the Beginning," in Ruthven J. Roy's book, *Imitating God* (Berrien Springs, MI: Rehoboth Publishing, 2010).
6. Ellen G. White, *The Ministry of Healing* (Mountain View, CA: Pacific Press Publishing Association, 1942), 486.

LAUNCHING THE KINGDOM

2

Now when Jesus had heard that John was arrested, he withdrew to Galilee; . . . From that time Jesus began to proclaim, "Repent: for the kingdom of heaven has come near." As he walked by the sea of Galilee, he saw two brothers, Simon, who is called Peter, and Andrew his brother, casting a net into the sea–for they were fishermen. And he said to them, "Follow me, and I will make you fish for people." Immediately they left their nets and followed him.

Matthew 4:12, 17-20, NRSV

Once Christ entered the arena of Israel's salvation-history as the long-awaited Messiah, John the Baptist immediately acquiesced to the mission and ministry of his Master. Accordingly, he facilitated the transition of the rabbi-disciple relationship between his own followers and Christ by openly commending two of his disciples to Jesus (John 1:35-40). A little later, the Baptist fully endorsed the Messiah's ministry in the presence of his followers, the Jews, and even Christ's own disciples (John 3:22-36).

> "A man can receive nothing, unless it has been given him from heaven. You yourselves bear me witness that I said, I am not the Christ, but I have been sent before Him . . . He must increase, but I must decrease. He who comes from above is above all . . ."

John 3:27-28, 30-31

It was necessary for John to decrease so that Christ would increase, because the scope and effect of John's ministry were very limited, while the efficacy of Christ's ministry was limitless and universally significant. Shortly after commending his disciples to Jesus, John was imprisoned by Herod for his open condemnation of Herod's illicit relationship with his brother's wife, Herodias. That strong, fearless voice, which once cried aloud in the wilderness, was now muted by isolation in a sordid, solitary prison cell, *timely* terminating the short, prolific ministry of the Messiah's faithful forerunner. However, by providential design, the imprisonment of John became the initiating event to launch officially, the ministry of Jesus.

Kingdom Operative

Now after John had been taken into custody, Jesus came into Galilee, preaching the gospel of God, and saying, "<u>The time is fulfilled, and the kingdom of God is at hand</u>; repent and believe in the gospel."

Mark 1:14, 15

Christ wasted no time in carrying out the purpose for which He was sent, and for which He was anointed to fulfill. From the moment He found out that John the Baptist had been placed in prison, Jesus immediately left His wilderness retreat (Matthew 4:11, 12) and steadfastly began His kingdom campaign. By deliberately echoing John's proclamation (*"Repent ye: for the kingdom of heaven is at hand,"* Matthew 3:2) Christ was authenticating John's ministry as a part of God's overall plan for establishing the kingdom of heaven here on earth. He was affirming that both John's mission and His originated from the same divine source and pointed toward the same divine end—that is, the establishment of the God's kingdom on earth.

Significantly, it was the same angel Gabriel that announced

the birth and mission of both John the Baptist and Jesus (Luke 1:10-20; 26-38). They were both nurtured and nourished by the same God, in the same wilderness, from which they both emerged, declaring the same message: "Repent ye: for the kingdom of heaven is at hand" (Matthew 3:2, and 4:17). This, indeed, was divine operation at its best—God fulfilling His word that He had spoken through His prophet Daniel (Daniel 2:44).

However, unlike John, Christ did not only announce the arrival of God's kingdom, He was also its living representation, for without Him there was no kingdom. As the second Adam, He came to restore kingdom dominion and kingdom living (which were lost through the fall) to the earth. Christ, therefore, became the living extension and amplification of the voice of John the Baptist announcing the arrival of the kingdom of heaven on earth.

The Messiah left Nazareth for Capernaum with one purpose in mind—namely, to set the stage for launching His ministry and the kingdom of heaven. This ministry was driven by a singular, consuming passion, which Christ articulated in a very concise and pointed mission statement: ". . . the Son of Man came to seek and save the lost" (Luke 19:10, NRSV). Through the fall, mankind had lost his heavenly citizenship, and it was the mission of the King to rescue His citizens and return them to their rightful place in His kingdom. Thus, seeking and saving His lost citizenry was the only mission big enough, and important enough, to move the Son of God to become the Son of Man, and finally, to die as the Lamb of God who takes away the sin of the world. It was this driving force, catalyzed by the imprisonment of John, which drove Christ to leave the familiar environs of His upbringing for the city of Capernaum.

But Why Capernaum?

Christ's move to Capernaum was a part of His strategic initiative to reach the then-known world with the gospel of the kingdom. In fulfillment of Isaiah's prophetic declaration (Isaiah 9:1,

2), Christ began His ministry in the borders of Zebulun and Naphtali, by the way of the sea, in Galilee of the Gentiles. The 'way of the sea' was the Roman road connecting Damascus and Caesarea on the Mediterranean coast, a branch of which went along the west bank of the Sea of Galilee through Bethsaida and Capernaum, which became key towns in Jesus' mission operation.[1] Capernaum, was in a strategic location for spreading the good news about the kingdom of God around the circumference of the Sea of Galilee. It was a city with a population much larger than Nazareth, and its commercial centers attracted travelers from all over the then-known world.

Additionally, the Messiah chose Capernaum to launch His mission enterprise as a signal to the Jewish nation that the gospel of the kingdom was not restricted to the borders of Israel. Instead, this "Good News" was intended to penetrate the Gentile world, so that the people who sat in darkness would receive great light (Isaiah 9:2). It was Christ's way of saying that the Word of God must not be bound by the human elements of race, ethnicity, creed, color, or culture, but must have full and free access to the hearts of all people everywhere.

This historic launching of the kingdom of God begins with Christ walking along the shores of the Sea of Galilee (Matthew 4:18). However, this walk must not be misconstrued as some coincidental or casual event, pursued out of a desire to inhale some fresh air and admire the fishermen at their irksome task. Rather, it was an intentional step in the Savior's kingdom building initiative and mission strategy to seek and save the lost. Christ walked the shores of Galilee with the specific purpose of calling His first disciples into kingdom service. By that simple act, and without any fanfare, the Master Builder was laying the foundation for building and maintaining His kingdom. Make no mistake about this! The citizens of the kingdom of heaven are first and foremost disciples of the King.

However, that act of Christ ran against the grain of Jewish culture, which required the aspiring disciple to seek out a teacher (rabbi) of his choice and request the privilege of sitting at his feet as his student. Instead of the disciple seeking the teacher, Christ, the

Master Teacher, went in search of His disciples. In taking this approach, Jesus completely reversed the role of the "perceived" lesser (the disciple) seeking the higher (the rabbi), and, consequently, displayed a cardinal principle of His kingdom: "And whosoever will be chief among you let him be the servant" (Matthew 20:27, KJV). What an awesome example for would-be teachers and leaders of His people today! What an amazing contrast between Christ and His self-righteous, Jewish counterparts! He, the only righteous One, came seeking, serving, and saving the lost, while those who were self-righteously lost were serving themselves, while waiting on sinners to seek them.

Personal Invitation

"Follow me, and I will make you fish for people."

Matthew 4:19, NRSV

In this solitary sentence, Christ enunciates His simple strategy for saving lost humanity and reaching the whole world with the good news of the kingdom. At first glance "Follow Me" appears to be quite simplistic, rudimentary, and altogether non-strategic. However, on closer examination it would become very evident that in these two words reside the very potent seed for sustained , exponential growth of the kingdom of God. "Follow Me" implies more than just come after me. It is a call to imitate or duplicate the Master Discipler in word and life. It demands being what Jesus was in His private life, and doing as Jesus did in His public ministry and service. Every true disciple of Jesus has only two obligations— namely, (1) become like his Master, and (2) pass on the Master's teaching and way of life to others.

Through this very simple call, Christ establishes the explosive foundational principle of kingdom growth. It is called the principle of *self-duplication* (*self as pertaining to Jesus*). *Follow*

Me! Duplicate Me! Imitate Me!—as a true disciple would do with his own master in every aspect of his/her life. This is the essence of Christ's call to all would-be disciples. Over and over Christ repeated this principle in Scripture, and many Bible students just run over it like high-speed trains on unfamiliar tracks. See Matthew 8:22; 9:9; Mark 1:17; Luke 5:27; 9:59; John 1:43; 21:19.

The nature of Christ's call to discipleship and kingdom building are intently personal. (You) follow me! This call cannot be blocked, terminated, or cancelled by ecclesiastical or denominational mandate, or executive order. This is an authoritative command of the King and no born-again believer can escape its appeal. It is not transferable due to personal preference, or excusable due to some perceived "higher" obligation. In other words, the call of Christ is not only personal, but also primary and permanent. Jesus invites every disciple to follow, imitate, or duplicate His example. This involves being like the Master in mind, character, private disciplines, and public ministry. Discipleship calls for the full engagement of the believer's spirit, soul and body in obedience, submission and service to the Master. Just like the branch lives, grows, and produces fruit in full obedience to the inherent natural laws imbedded in the vine, so the disciple lives, grows, and produces fruit to the glory of God by the power of the indwelling Christ.

Powerful Transformation

The call to discipleship is not only personal, but it is also very powerful. Its potency lies in the fact that it is guaranteed and supported by Christ's promise: *I will make you!* Christ assures every disciple that He will not only qualify him for the task of reaching the lost, but will also endow him with His power to guarantee his success. The occupation or status of the individual at the time the call is received is inconsequential as a prerequisite for discipleship. All these human appendages and accomplishments, frailties and failures melt away in the presence and power of this encouraging promise; *I will make you!*

The Savior guarantees the profitable transformation of anyone who chooses to follow Him, regardless of what that person brings to the table in terms of personality, skills, and abilities. A. B. Bruce describes this truth in the following way: "Christ had no faith in any discipleship based on misapprehensions and by-ends; and, on the other hand, He had no fear of the drawbacks arising out of the external connections or past history of true believers, but was entirely indifferent to men's antecedents."[2]

What a pitiful group of men Christ chose to form the core members of His kingdom campaign! Their knowledge and experience did not extend to any degree beyond the requirements of their trades. Their backgrounds, characters and personalities were so diverse and discordant that they were a perfect recipe for utter failure and disaster. These men would not pass the test to qualify for fellowship in any Christian communion today. However, in the eyes of the Master, they held great promise, for Christ saw them not as they were, but as they would become through His personal instruction, example, and guidance.

How strikingly different are the ways of Christ and His kingdom to the ways of men and their earthly kingdoms. Human kingdom-building, be it personal, political, organizational, or religious, generally takes its departure by calling into question the ephemeral antecedents of race, culture, sex, color, creed, education, skill, physical appearance, and much more, before enlisting the service of a human agent. While these earth-bound elements are good to one degree or another, and may even be seen as necessary requirements for placement and advancement in the kingdoms of this world, they tend to be spiritually myopic since they generally fail to function in the realm of faith, and often make of non-effect the equipping, transforming power of Jehovah. Indeed the kingdom of Christ is not of this world (John 18:36); and God's thoughts are not like ours, and our ways are certainly not like His (Isaiah 55:8).

Obviously, Christ saw in His disciples only what the spirit-illumined eyes could behold in the worst of sinners. Bill Hull reiterates the fact that "Jesus sees His followers for what they will be, not for what they are in 'the spiritual raw.' Everyone is a candidate for something, and there are no exceptions. Regardless of what we might see in a person, pro or con, there is much more than meets the eye, things that only God understands."[3] The matchless grace and boundless love of our Savior are all sufficient to embrace any, and every, sinner who will heed His invitation. The only requirement and obligation the Master lays upon a would-be disciple is to follow Him, and nothing else! It is in following or duplicating the Master that the divine transformation begins to take effect in the life of the disciple.

Productive Occupation

Christ's call to His first disciples had an ultimate purpose in view—that is, to make them productive fishers-of-men. It is very significant to note that the driving force and emphasis of discipleship is not in the fishing, but it is in the following. Christ did not call His disciples to fish for people directly. He called them simply to follow Him. Fishing for people is always the unavoidable and inevitable result of following Jesus. It is of critical importance that this irreplaceable principle be understood and followed, for it is all too beguiling for one to engage in fishing for the lost while not really following the Master. One can become so caught up with the work of the Lord and forget the Lord of the work. There are many professed believers who would rather spend their time fishing, without following Jesus, since the former is, by far, much easier to do than the latter.

Christ did not ask His disciple to try to fish for people. Their sole responsibility was to follow the Master, and Christ promised to transform them into productive fishermen—in the true sense of the word. Christ holds Himself responsible for the fishing outcome, so there is no chance of the remotest failure here. This fact leads to one irrefutable conclusion. Since fishing is the unavoidable result of following Jesus, it becomes the acid test of one's true connection or relationship with Him. Simply put, if I am not fishing for unsaved people, I AM NOT A TRUE DISCIPLE OF JESUS! I may be following someone or something else—for example, religious leader, system, organization, or denomination—but I am certainly not following the King! Fishing for unsaved people is a primary kingdom activity, and one of the two irreplaceable hallmarks (the other, obedience) of discipleship.

Being a fisher-of-men means being like Jesus (the Master Fisher), and the only means by which this is made possibly is following or imitating the Master. Essentially, what Christ is saying to every believer is: "Follow Me, and I will make you what I am. You will be like Me—the Seeking, Saving, Son of Man!" By following Christ, we will learn to fish as He did. We will work for all types of people—regardless of their orientation, lifestyle, culture, or race—using different mediums, methods, and locations (baits, tackles, and fishing vehicles) to reach people where they are.

It is, therefore, very important to remember that it is not the work of the fish to adjust to the size and shape of our boat (building facilities), or to our attitudes and preferences as fishers. It is in our interest (and that of the kingdom) to make the strategic mental and tactical adjustments in order to land a catch. This is critically significant since all fish are not the same size or shape; neither do they share the same habitat or the same feeding or mating propensities.

Christ met sinners in their own arena, in their familiar environment, and gave to all unhindered, unfettered access to Himself. All His true disciples will do the same. He said: *"My sheep will hear My voice, and I know them, and they follow* Me" (John 10:27, KJV). We must cooperate with Christ in catching all kinds of fish, but He reserves the sole right to the fish-cleaning process. We will also do well to remember that no one can come to Christ unless the Father (not us), who sent Him, draws them (John 6:44). It is only

He who draws them that reserves the right to judge or clean them.

> *"For who are we to judge the servant of another. To his own master he stands or falls; and stand he will, for the Lord is able to make him stand."*
>
> Romans 14:4

Kingdom Concepts

> *"When Jesus saw the crowds, He went up on the mountain; and after He sat down, His disciples came to Him. He opened His mouth and began to teach them, saying, Blessed are the poor in spirit, for theirs is the kingdom of heaven. . ."*
>
> Matthew 5:1-3

Shortly after calling His first disciples into service, Jesus gave them a hands-on lesson on the nature of their new mission assignment and life work. The Bible says that He went about Galilee, teaching in their synagogues, preaching the gospel of the kingdom, and healing every kind of sickness and disease among the people—diverse ailments and pains, demoniacs, epileptics, paralytics (Matthew 4:23, 24). The impact of Christ's ministry (symbolic of kingdom entrance and supernatural dominance) was so powerful that it attracted great multitudes from across Galilee, Decapolis, Jerusalem, Judea and beyond the Jordan. This supernatural attraction of the masses set the stage for the Messiah's inaugural speech and "State of the Kingdom" address to His disciples—the ministers and preachers of the kingdom's gospel.

As the multitudes began to gather, Christ ascended the mountainside so that He could be seen and heard by all the people. The Word of God says that when He sat down, His disciples rallied around Him. By sitting down, Jesus assumed the official teaching position of a rabbi, and His disciples took the hint that their Master had something very important say. Therefore, they gathered around Him to receive instruction from His lips. When all were in place, Jesus opened His mouth and began to teach His disciples and the multitude the truth about the nature and principles of the kingdom of heaven. The Master was fully aware of the fact that in order for these men to preach the gospel of the kingdom effectively to a lost and dying world, it was necessary for them to understand firsthand, the character of that kingdom, the tenets that govern it, and the protocols by which it operates.

Christ begins His discourse by first describing the character traits of kingdom citizens who are living in exile from their heavenly home. These are the poor in spirit; those who mourn over the evil produced by their sins and the sins of others; the meek, patient and humble; those who hunger and thirst for righteousness; the merciful and compassionate; the pure in heart who possess clean hands; the peacemakers and reconcilers; and those who are persecuted because of their righteous deeds. He pronounced kingdom blessings upon all those who would possess these sterling moral qualities (Matthew 5:1-12).

The rest of the Master's message focused on teaching His disciples how to enter kingdom living while sojourning in a world that operates by principles diametrically opposed to kingdom rule and culture. He covered such areas as the disciple's relationship to the world (Matthew 5:13-20); the disciple's personal and social relationships (Matthew 5:21-48); the spiritual disciplines of prayer, giving of alms, fasting and stewardship of wealth (Matthew 6:1-24); life's primary priority (Matthew 6:25-33); the folly of seeking to judge others (Matthew 7:1-5); and life's alternatives and making the supreme choice for life's destiny (Matthew 5:13-27).

The Master used this Sermon on the Mount to establish these core principles of the kingdom among those who were called to be its ambassadors in a sinful and rebellious world. Thus, without any trumpet-blaring fanfare, loud hurrahs, elaborate organizational machinery, or protracted recruiting process, the King of the universe launched His kingdom—not from some towering, ivory, palatial structure, but from a lowly mountainside near the shores of a lake in Galilee. This He did with a most "insignificant," unpromising group of followers He called His disciples. From this humble, erstwhile beginning, the incarnate Son of God assumed His position as the Leader of a redemptive, people movement that was destined to become the next universal super power and the eternal kingdom of God.

Notes:

1. Donald A. Hagner, *Word Biblical Commentary* (Dallas, TX: Word Books Publisher, 1993), 73.
2. A. A. Bruce, *The Training of the Twelve*, (Grand Rapids: Kregel Publications, 1986), 19-20.
3. Bill Hull, *Jesus Christ Disciple-Maker* (Grand Rapids, MI: Fleming H. Revell, 1984), 20.

MISSING THE KINGDOM

3

Nicodemus said to Him, "<u>How can these things be</u>?" Jesus answered and said to him, "<u>Are you the teacher of Israel and do not understand these things</u>?"

John 3:9, 10

The above scripture forms a portion of a very interesting conversation between Jesus and Nicodemus, who was a religious teacher of the Jewish nation. It was apparent that this leader was struggling with issues pertaining to the identity and authority of Jesus. By this time the Lord had become a household figure for discussion among Jewish communities because of His powerful, authoritative healing, teaching and preaching ministry (Matthew 4:23; Mark 6:54-56; Luke 6:17-19). Nicodemus, therefore, sought for an audience with the Master to resolve the confusion of his soul.

The account says that he chose to meet Jesus at night. Perhaps Nicodemus came under the cover of darkness because he did not want the people under his tutelage to see him in the company of the One who was so openly denigrated and treated with disdain by the Jewish authorities. In addition, this Pharisee was afraid of the wrath of his mean-spirited, self-righteous colleagues, who might have bitterly criticized him, or might have altogether distanced themselves from him.

Nicodemus tipped his hand very early in the interview with the "tongue-in-cheek" pharisaical admission: *"Rabbi, <u>we know</u> that thou art a teacher come from God; for no man can do these things except God be with him"* (John 3:2, KJV). Who are these "we" Nicodemus was talking about? I believe that he was referring to his colleagues—the leaders of Israel's system of religion. They really knew who Jesus was but could not embrace Him because He did not represent what they stood for or what they wanted.

"Interestingly, "we know" represents an attitude that inwardly gives assent to the truth about Christ and His word, but outwardly follows the convenient path of popular opinion, tradition and group religion. This attitude is a fundamental characteristic of post-Modern Christianity that is driven by a form of godliness, but without any power (2 Timothy 3:5)—for example, *"we know* that the Bible is true, but . . ." *"we know* Jesus is the Son of God, but . . ." *"we know* that the Ten Commandments are still binding, but . . ." *"we know . . ." "we know . . ."*

"We know" reflects a very hollow religious profession, without any substance or intimate knowledge of Christ and His kingdom. This was, indeed, the case with Nicodemus and his elite, religious comrades. The kingdom of God was in their midst in the perfect person of the Messiah (Luke 17:20, 21), but these men had lost their connection with heaven, and their darkened eyes were blinded by the wickedness of their stubborn, selfish hearts. Their thirst for power, driven by their misinterpretation of Israel's political future, colored their thinking and behavior towards Jesus.

These leaders were characterized by a ravenous desire for material wealth and financial security through their self-righteous control of the resources of the masses. They saw Jesus not only as one standing in the way of their financial and political success, but they were also very fearful that His authoritative teachings and hard-to-deny miracles would draw away all the people, and undermine their pretentious support of their Roman masters. Consequently, they were constantly scheming to discredit and destroy Him. Their intentions became quite clear following the resurrection of Lazarus:

> *What are we doing? For this man is performing many signs. If we let Him go on like this all men will believe in Him, and the Romans will come and take away*

> *both our place and our nation. But a certain one of them, Caiaphas, who was high priest that year, said to them, "You know nothing at all, nor do you take into account that it is expedient for you that one man should die for the people, and that the whole nation should not perish."*
>
> John 11:47-50

While Nicodemus did not share the sentiments of his colleagues that sought the assassination of Jesus, and even tried to defend Him on one occasion (John 7:40-52), he certainly benefited from being in their company and was afraid of losing His place through any open association with Christ. Thus, he chose to be a secret disciple until after the death of Jesus (John 19:38-40). Insightfully (really intuitively) reading Nicodemus' hand, the Master completely sidesteps his pretentious compliment and discretely tells this religious leader that except he is born from above—that is, through Holy Ghost—he could not see the kingdom of God. Right away Nicodemus was thrown into mental confusion, for his institutionalized, priestly intellect could not grasp the things of the spirit realm. *"How can these things be,"* his carnal, logical mind inquired?

Although Nicodemus was actively involved in religious activities, he was only minding earthly things, and with such a world view, he was not able to see or operate in kingdom realities. Hence, he found it very puzzling in his attempt to understand what Jesus was saying to him. It is totally impossible for anyone to comprehend kingdom realities, enter kingdom living and ultimately the kingdom itself if that individual is not enlightened and controlled by the power from above. It is imperative that a person be able to perceive the kingdom of heaven first, before he is able to enter it. Such perception and understanding can come only through the grace of redemption and regeneration, effected by the Holy Spirit.

The Nicodemus Syndrome

Nicodemus was (and is) not alone in his pharisaical ignorance pertaining to the things of the kingdom of heaven. His priestly associates were just as ignorant and illiterate about the kingdom as he was, and so too are many professed believers today. These conscientious church people and their leaders are victims of the Nicodemus syndrome—the spiritual condition that reduces one's ability to see and operate effectively in the realm of the kingdom because of they are blinded by their "sacred," collegial ambitions, and preoccupied with their religious and earthly pursuits.

Although, like Nicodemus, they may be busily engaged in religious activities (managing institutions, programs, people, facilities, finances, and so forth), their sphere of operation is so earthly or institution oriented, that they are not cognizant of all God is doing in the kingdom that is growing all around them. Yet, quite often, those who may be somewhat kingdom conscious follow the path of convenience and least resistance, choosing to "preserve" and "protect" their coveted reputation or position, rather than openly aligning themselves with what they *know* Christ is calling them to do.

Like modern-day Nicodemuses, many continue to profess and confess, "*We know* . . . ," but their knowledge fail to reflect a true understanding of Christ and His kingdom. Driven by their private and organizational ambitions, they frustrate the grace of God in their attempt to use the systems and wisdom of the world to do kingdom work. Instead of adjusting their thinking and operations to fit kingdom principles, these seek to squeeze kingdom ideals and concepts into their organizational molds, in order to maximize their institutional goals and objectives. While professing to be born from above, their life and work testify of their earthliness and their terrestrial world-view. To such individuals, the words of Christ rings true—except a man be born from above, he cannot see the kingdom, or enter into its way of life.

Touching the Unseen

Now having been questioned by the Pharisees as to when the kingdom of God was coming, He answered them and said, "The kingdom of God is not coming with signs to be observed; nor will they say, 'Look, here it is!' or, 'There it is!' For behold, <u>the kingdom of God is in your midst</u>."

Luke 17:20, 21

These are very interesting Scriptural verses, for they most accurately portray the spiritual blindness of the religious leaders of Israel. These men represented the polluted religious fountain that fed the institutional tributaries of learning with their ignorance regarding the kingdom of God. They were standing in the midst of the kingdom stream and did not even have the slightest inclination that it was flowing all around them. They were in the very presence of the King of kings and did not know it, because their evil, self-righteous hearts were blinded by their bigoted, earthly ambition for a king like unto Caesar, who they hoped would establish and rule the kingdom of Israel. They had grown so accustomed to filling their Jewish pride with false dreams about an earthly kingdom, that when the mysterious stone (Daniel 2:34, 35) of Christ's spiritual kingdom broke upon the nation, they were completely oblivious of its presence, while, at the same time, denying its redemptive, liberating power.

On one occasion, these leaders saw Jesus demonstrating kingdom presence and authority by releasing a man who was bound by a blind and dumb demonic spirit, and they accused Him of operating under the influence of Beelzebul, the ruler of the demons. Jesus responded to their criticism with a most mocking rebuke:

"Any kingdom divided against itself is laid

> *waste; and any city or house divided against itself shall not stand. And if Satan casts out Satan, he is divided against himself; how then shall his kingdom stand? And if I by Beelzebul cast out demons, by whom do your sons cast them out? Consequently they shall be your judges. <u>But if I cast out demons by the Spirit of God, then the kingdom of God has come upon you</u>. Or how can anyone enter the strong man's house and carry off his property, unless he first binds the strong man? And then he will plunder his house."*
>
> Matthew 12:25-29

As it was then, so it is now. Many today stand in the flowing streams of the kingdom of grace and do not even know it. This lack of spiritual insight and sensitivity has contributed to their very critical stance against those who proclaim kingdom authority and demonstrate its power. As a result, they blaspheme against the Holy Spirit (Matthew 12:30-32) when they attribute to the powers of darkness what God is actually doing to bring redemption and release to many who are oppressed by the enemy.

These conscientious, but blinded, believers go about judging the works of others while entertaining the false, bigoted idea that the gifts of miraculous healing and deliverance can only flow through ministries belonging to their community of faith. Although they live and operate in the midst of the kingdom, they are unable to touch the unseen or unleash its power; and, as in the case of Nicodemus, it becomes very difficult, yeah impossible, for them to enter or gain access to a kingdom they cannot see (John 3:3, 5). Glenn W. Barker and others insightfully observed that:

> "Though for Jesus the Kingdom of God on earth remains a future Kingdom, its power is already at work in the present, impinging upon man's actual

situation. The Kingdom "exercises its force" (Matthew 11:12); it has "come upon" men (Matthew 12:28; Luke 11:20), and is "in their midst" (Luke 17:20). It can no longer be thought of in future terms alone, for the future belongs only to those who, in the present moment, welcome its redemptive power."[1]

Proclamation and Demonstration

And having summoned His twelve disciples, He gave them authority over unclean spirits, to cast them out, and to heal every kind of disease and every kind of sickness . . . These twelve Jesus sent out after instructing them, saying, "Do not go in the way of the Gentiles, and do not enter any city of the Samaritans; <u>But rather go to the lost sheep of the house of Israel</u>. <u>And as you go, preach saying, 'The kingdom of heaven is at hand</u>.' Heal the sick, raise the dead, cleanse the lepers, cast out demons; freely you received, freely give."

Matthew 10:1, 5-8

The Jews First

Initially, Christ instructed His disciples (the nucleus of His future church) to concentrate their ministry on the lost sheep of the house of Israel, and to announce to them that the kingdom of heaven had arrived. This move was very significant because God had originally appointed Israel to proclaim this same kingdom to the Gentile world, but the favored people allowed nationalistic pride to get in the way. Israel had exchanged the kingdom agenda for personal power and political advantage. The Jews had rejected God's global kingdom initiative and had organized a religious and political system that was geared to produce an earthly kingdom of Israel, which they presumed was ordained by God. Instead of making children of God (kingdom subjects) through faith in the promised Messiah, the Jews spent their days making Jewish proselytes through circumcision and religious traditions. Certainly, Satan had crafted an effective, devious scheme that rode on Jewish pride and prepared the way for the rejection of Jesus as God's Messiah, the true King of David.

Therefore, in His love and mercy, Christ wanted the kingdom message to first break on Israel to help salvage what little was left of the consciousness of God's true purpose among the people. It was a message to stimulate memory and restore hope in the God of their forefathers, who never failed to keep His promises. "The righteous (not political) scepter shall not depart from Judah, nor the ruler's staff from between his feet until Shiloh comes," were the prophetic words of dying Jacob (Genesis 49:10).

This prophecy met its fulfillment in Christ, the true Son of David (Luke 1:31-33), but the children of Jacob (Israel), consumed by the spirit of their uncle (Esau), were seeking to trade the righteous scepter (Numbers 24:17; Psalm 45:6, 7; Hebrews 1:8, 9) and the throne of David for a political scepter and the throne of Caesar. The leadership of Israel had become lost in the political malaise and morass of the Greco-Roman world, and the dominant message of the kingdom of heaven was God's wake up call to revive and rescue His wandering sheep from under their controlling tutelage.

Preaching the imminence of the kingdom of heaven was intended to renew vision and reestablish confidence in the glorious future that awaited the people of God. The Jewish masses were tired of the oppressive system of the Roman government, and had become disillusioned by the empty prophecies and promises of their religious leaders. They were longing for the light of hope and deliverance, and when it arrived through the announcement of John the Baptist and the arrival of the promised Messiah, their leaders sought to obscure their vision from the truth by denouncing the words and works of the Son of God. However, the kingdom message from the lips of John, Jesus, and the disciples remained uniquely consistent, refreshing and very forceful; and it became the hallmark and compass of the church that was birthed by its proclamation.

Kingdom Authority

> "*All authority has been given to Me in heaven and on earth*. *Go therefore and make disciples of all the nations, baptizing them in the name of the Father and the Son and the Holy Spirit, teaching them to observe all that I commanded you; and lo, I am with you always, even to the end of the age.*"
>
> Matthew 28:18-20

Christ did not only tell His disciples to preach the kingdom of God as they went to the lost sheep of the house of Israel; but He instructed them to "*heal the sick, raise the dead, cleanse the lepers, cast out demons . . .* (Matthew 10:8). In other words, He did not only assign His disciples their mission, He also gave them the authority to fulfill it successfully. He once told them: "*Behold, I have given you authority to tread on serpents and scorpions, and over all the power of the enemy, and nothing will injure you* (Luke 10:19). The disciples' mission, therefore, was not only one of proclamation but also one of powerful, supernatural demonstration.

Christ always anoints whom He appoints. These disciples were given authority over the works of the kingdom of darkness. These were not educated, articulate or perfect men, but Christ conferred on them executive power to cast out unclean spirits, to heal all manner of sickness and diseases, to raise the dead and to cleanse the lepers because they were willing and ready to obey Him. Luke said that these men went among the villages preaching the gospel and healing everywhere (Luke 9:6).

The mission and results were not different when Jesus appointed (and anointed) seventy other disciples and sent them out two by two to every city where He Himself was going to visit (Luke 10). When they returned, they delivered the most glorious report to their Master: "Lord, even the demons are subject to us in your name" (Luke 10:17). Jesus responded with ecstatic joy and jubilation: "*I was watching Satan fall from heaven like lightning*" (Luke 10:18). Jesus saw the foreshadowing of the demise of the kingdom of darkness in the victorious campaign of His disciples, and He began to celebrate in the Spirit. Luke reported that:

> *At that very time He (Jesus) <u>rejoiced greatly</u> in the Holy Ghost, and said, "I praise Thee, O Father, Lord of heaven and earth, that Thou didst hide these things from the wise and intelligent and didst reveal them to babes. Yes, Father, for thus it was well-pleasing in Thy sight."*
>
> Luke 10:21

Yes, Christ does not only have a sense of humor, but He is also capable of showing great emotion. Although the English translation tones down Christ victory celebration, the original Greek version does not. Luke uses the Greek "*agalliaō*" for the English "rejoiced greatly" in the text. However, this word is a compound verb consisting of two other Greek words—**agan** (very much), and **allomai** (to exult, to leap for joy, to show one's joy by leaping and skipping). Thus, Jesus was leaping and skipping around in the Spirit, giving praise to the Father for the victorious assault on the kingdom of darkness.

The future work of the body of Christ was mirrored by the work of His disciples in their aggressive assault on the kingdom of darkness. The preaching of the gospel of the kingdom must be accompanied by the demonstration of its power to change lives, and also life's situations. The real purpose of the kingdom is to destroy the works of the devil (1 John 3:8). Matthew said that Jesus went about all Galilee, teaching in the synagogues, proclaiming the gospel of the kingdom, and healing every kind of disease and every kind of sickness among the people (Matthew 4:23. See also Luke 4:43).

The preaching of the gospel of the kingdom is not without the visible evidence of its power. Open demonstration is heaven's confirmation that the kingdom of God *has come upon us.* Shortly before He ascended to heaven, Christ told His disciples:

> *"Go into all the world and preach the gospel to all creation. He who has believed and has been baptized shall be saved, but he who has disbelieved shall be condemned.*
>
> *<u>And these signs will accompany those who have believed</u>: in My name they will cast out demons, they will speak with new tongues; they will pick up serpents, and if they drink any deadly poison, it shall not hurt them; they will lay hands on the sick and they will recover."*
>
> *So then, when the Lord Jesus had spoken to them, He was received up into heaven, and sat down on the right hand of God. And they went out and preached everywhere, while the Lord worked with them, and <u>confirmed the word by the signs that followed</u>.*
>
> Mark 16:15-20

It is very important to notice a few pertinent points about this command that Jesus gave His disciples. This obviously is Mark's version of the gospel commission given in Matthew 28:18-20, which I will address a little later. Firstly, the disciples were to "go" (which involves movement away from and toward some given target) and "preach" (proclamation) "the gospel" (good news about God's free salvation through Jesus Christ) to "all creation" (every creature under the heavens). Secondly, the disciples were to baptize all those who had believed the gospel they preached. Thirdly, signs and wonders "in the name of Jesus" were to follow or accompany those who had believed that gospel. Fourthly, and most importantly, the risen Lord confirmed the proclaimed word by accompanying signs or miracles. The word of God cannot be clearer than this. The authentic preaching of the gospel of the kingdom must be accompanied (or confirmed) by the signs and miracles in the believing community of faith.

Legacy of the Early Church

This promise which Jesus made to His disciples in Mark 16:15-18 became a permanent legacy of the early church. It was heaven's token of the presence of the living Christ, in the person of the Holy Spirit (Matthew 28:20, *I will be with you always* . . . ; John 14:16-18)), within the believing community. From the day of Pentecost, this divine presence has been with the body of Christ until now. However, His ministry today is not as appreciated as it was during apostolic times, because the trappings of institutional religion has usurped His authority by rigid rules and bureaucracy, diminishing His dominant role and witness among the followers of Jesus. During the days of the apostles, the Holy Spirit was a living, active witness among the believers, bringing all the promised blessings of Jesus and His kingdom to the discipling community.

It was He (the Holy Spirit) who executed judgment against Ananias and Sapphira for conspiring to defraud the early believers by misrepresenting the amount of their offering (Acts 5:1-11). It was He who confirmed the proclamation of the word and work of the church with *many signs and* wonders (v. 12). Wherever the gospel of the kingdom was proclaimed, there was the corresponding demonstration of the kingdom's presence and power through the active witness of the Holy Spirit.

The deacon, Philip, went down to the city of Samaria and began proclaiming Christ unto its inhabitants, and God confirmed the Word with mighty demonstrations of His power. The Bible says that:

> *"For in the case of many who had unclean spirits, they were coming out of them shouting with a loud voice; and many who had been paralyzed and lame were healed. So there was much rejoicing in that city. . . But when they believed Philip preaching the good news about the kingdom of God and the name of Jesus Christ, they were being baptized, men and women alike."*
>
> Acts 8:7, 8, 12

Philip's witness of Christ and His kingdom was so overwhelmingly powerful that not only many men and women were baptized into that kingdom, but even Simon, the city's sorcerer, became a baptized believer as well. The Bible says that he followed Philip around and was constantly amazed as he observed the signs and great miracles taking place under Philip's ministry of the Word (Acts 8:13).

This twin legacy of proclamation and demonstration is the permanent witness to the fact that the kingdom of heaven has, indeed, invaded the kingdoms of this world, and is actively at work, breaking the dominion of Satan and *delivering those who all their lives were held in slavery by their fear of death* (Hebrews 2:15). It is the combined witness of proclamation and demonstration that the apostle Paul called the preaching of the "full gospel" of the kingdom.

> *"Therefore in Christ Jesus I have found reason for boasting in things pertaining to God. For I will not presume to speak of anything except what Christ has accomplished through me, resulting in the obedience of the Gentiles <u>by word and deed</u>, <u>in the power of</u>*

signs and wonders, in the power of the Spirit; so that from Jerusalem and round about as far as Illyricum I have fully preached the gospel of Christ."

Romans 15:15-19

In his dealing with immorality and rebellion in the church at Corinth, Paul made this very clear and concise statement as a warning to the proud and arrogant believers among them: *"The kingdom of God is not in word but in power"* (1 Corinthian 4:20). In other words, the kingdom is not just a matter of talk, but powerful evidence of its reality. The word Paul uses for power in this text is not ***exousia*** (meaning authority). He uses the word ***dunamis*** (the Greek word from which we get the word dynamite), signifying that the kingdom of God is not characterized by empty words, but powerful, supernatural demonstration. It is therefore quite evident that proclamation without demonstration or confirmation is foreign to the gospel of Jesus Christ.

The gospel of the kingdom is not fully preached until, and unless, there is a visible witness of the presence of the kingdom's power. Today, many professed Christian communities are satisfied to preach a gospel devoid of power, claiming that a verbal witness is all that Christ requires as a testimony against those who do not believe. They cite Matthew 24:14 in support of their position. Then there are others who suggest that the powerful demonstrations of kingdom authority are reserved for only special moments and selected, gifted believers. However, Paul tells us in 1 Corinthians 4:20 that the gospel of the kingdom is not simply a gospel of words, but of explosive power. Jesus told His disciples that signs (or miracles) will follow ALL those who have believed the kingdom's gospel (Mark 16:17).

The reason why there is so little active demonstration of the power of the kingdom's gospel in contemporary Christianity is that the majority of the professed believers have been taught not to believe in the signs (or miracles) that Jesus say would follow them. We have been served a gospel that has been imprisoned by human logic and religious tradition, instead of the good news of the kingdom that brings salvation and liberation because it is made alive through faith in every word that proceeds from the mouth of God. It is lamentably sad that while post-Modern Christians live and work in the midst of the invisible kingdom stream flowing with torrential blessings all around them, they are so bereft of the manifestations of its mighty power and dominion.

Now is not the time for us to be doing church work in spiritual blindness as did Nicodemus, who was woefully oblivious of the kingdom of heaven that was operating and growing all around him. Now is the time for us to yield to the holy influence from above so that our spiritual eyes could be fully open to see not only the glorious kingdom that surrounds us, but also to enter into the joys of kingdom living.

The prophetic word of Daniel 2:44 tells us that "in the days of these kings," the God of heaven will set up a kingdom that will never be destroyed, but will last forever. Clearly, "in the days of these kings" refer to during the time of the earthly kingdoms portrayed in Daniel's prophecy. This setting up process began with the ministry of John the Baptist and will culminate at the end of the age, when Christ, the King, returns, after officially receiving the kingdom from the Father (Luke 19:12-26). Christ, Himself, said that from the days of John until the time He (Christ) appears on the scene, the kingdom of heaven suffered violence, as violent men tried to enter it by force (Matthew 11:12). This is a very clear indication that the kingdom of heaven is here and now, and only those who are born-again from above have the potential to see and enter it now (John 3:3, 5). Right here, and now, individuals are either in or out of the kingdom.

Therefore, it behooves us now to give more earnest heed to the admonition of the King Jesus Christ:

"But <u>seek first</u> <u>His kingdom and His righteousness</u>,

and all these things will be added to you."

Matthew 6:33

Happy are we if we do these things, because the things of earth will not be able to eclipse our vision of the kingdom; but they will grow strangely dim[2] in the glorious light and grace of kingdom-living, right here and right now.

Notes:

1. Glenn W. Barker, William L. Lane and J. Ramsey Michaels, *The New Testament Speaks* (New York, N.Y.: Harper & Row, Publishers, 1969), 83.
2. Adopted from Helen H. Lemmel, *Turn Your Eyes Upon Jesus*, 1922.

THE CHURCH AND THE KINGDOM

4

*... Blessed are you, Simon son of Jonah! For flesh and blood has not revealed **this** to you but my Father in heaven. And I tell you, you are Peter, and on **this** rock I will build my church, and the gates of Hades will not prevail against it.*

Matthew 16:17-18, NRSV

Birthing His Church

The circumstances under which Jesus Christ chose to birth His church were uniquely interesting and certainly demand our attention. Matthew 15 presents a very informative backdrop leading up to this very important event. The leaders of Israel refused to acknowledge the Jewish carpenter from Nazareth, the "son of Joseph and Mary," as the prophesied Messiah of Israel, and they constantly sought to undermine His leadership and authority. On this particular occasion, they launched an indirect attack against Him by accusing His disciples of spiritual defilement (Matthew 15:1-20).

After capably unmasking their hypocrisy through the authoritative use of the Scriptures, Christ took His disciples into the Gentile coasts of Tyre and Sidon. There He met a Canaanite woman, who was seeking deliverance for her daughter from a demonic spirit. Christ seized the opportunity to teach the "would-be fathers" of His future church a very important lesson regarding their work and mission.

Church without Walls

In stark contrast to the leaders of His own people, who rejected His authority and Messiah-ship, this importunate seeker recognized Christ not only as Lord but also as the Son of David—this is indeed Messianic. *"Have mercy on me, O Lord, Son of David; my daughter is cruelly demon-possessed,"* was her woeful plea (Matthew 15:22). The Master pretended to ignore the plaintive cries of this troubled mother to the point that his disciples could not bear to hear them anymore. Their Jewish pride made them feel very uncomfortable and completely embarrassed by the public spectacle of this Gentile tail that was wagging behind them. So they came to Jesus and kept begging Him, saying: *"Send her away; for she crieth after us"* (Matthew 15:23). The disciples did not want to have anything to do with this "crazy" woman. They just wanted to get rid of her as quickly as possible.

Playing into their Jewish prejudice, Jesus addressed His disciples as though the woman were not even present: *"I am not sent but unto the lost sheep of the house of Israel"* (Matthew 15:24). But this desperate mother would not be ignored or denied. She had already given up on her sense of pride. She flung herself at the feet of Jesus and began to worship Him: *"Lord, help me!"* was her prayer (Matthew 15:25). At that point, it was absolutely impossible for Jesus to ignore this broken and contrite mother anymore. Sincere worship *always* moves the omnipotent arms of the Almighty. For the very first time since the encounter began, Christ chose to address the grieving mother directly, in the hearing of His disciples:

> *"It is not good to take the children's bread and throw it to the dogs."*
>
> Matthew 15:26

Obviously, the Master was still waiting to see how far His disciples' prejudice would allow Him to go before anyone of them would step in and intercede on behalf of this woman. On the other hand, the disciples may have been thinking that being called a "dog" would be insulting enough to turn the unwelcome spectacle of humanity away. However, this mother would neither wait for an intercessor, nor be deterred by Jewish bigotry. This was her moment of opportunity and she was determined not to allow it to pass her by without receiving her blessing. She knew she was in the presence of God and pressed her case to the limit of her humanity:

> *"Truth, Lord: yet the dogs eat of the crumbs which fall from their masters' table."*

Matthew 15:27

At once, the gates of heaven were opened by the key of faith in the heart of this humble, distraught mother, and the Bread of Life was given without measure to her and her daughter. The crumbs and the Bread are of one and the same element, and the power of the Bread is also the power in the crumbs. Anyone who, by faith, consumes this Bread or the crumbs from this Loaf will find life indeed, for Jesus said:

> *"I am the living bread which came down from heaven: if any man eat of this bread, he shall live forever: and the bread that I will give is my flesh, which I will give for the life of the world...Whoso eateth my flesh, and drinketh my blood, hath eternal life; and I will raise him up at the last day. For my flesh is meat indeed, and my blood is drink indeed. He that eateth my flesh and drinketh my blood dwelleth in me and I in him. As the living Father hath sent me, and I live by the Father, so he that eateth me, even he shall live by*

me...he that eateth this bread shall live forever."

John 6:48-58, KJV

Thus, when Jesus heard the response of this would-not-be-denied mother, the life that was in Him was instantly released to her and, through her, to her demon-possessed daughter. The Savior cried out: *"O woman, great is thy faith: be it unto thee even as thou wilt." And her daughter was made whole from that very hour* (Matthew 15: 28). What an amazing lesson this entire episode was for the disciples of Jesus, and is for us today! Their mission and the future of Christ's church depended on it. The gift of salvation, through the Bread of Life, was not to be confined by the prejudices of nationality, culture, ethnicity, color, religion, creed or any other human distinction. His community of faith was destined to be a church without walls, a house of prayer for all, embracing all and serving all.

As it was with the disciples in the time of Christ, so it is with us today. The socially disenfranchised and the religiously marginalized must become full beneficiary, not only of the scraps some may think they deserve, but also of the whole Bread of Life that heaven graciously provides for all mankind.

It is soberly thought-provoking that while the leaders and people of Israel were rejecting the Bread of Life, their Gentile neighbors were only too glad to have the crumbs that fell from the ungrateful children's table. Christ found more faith outside the borders of Israel than He did among His own people. Such was the case of the Roman centurion who requested healing for his paralyzed servant (Matthew 8:5-13). Of him Jesus said:

> *"Truly I say to you, I have not found such great faith with anyone in Israel. And I say to you that many shall come from the east and west, and recline at the table with Abraham, and Isaac, and Jacob, in the kingdom of heaven; but the sons of the kingdom shall*

> *be cast out into outer darkness; in that place there shall be weeping and gnashing of teeth." And Jesus said to the centurion, "Go your way; let it be done to you as you have believed." And the servant was healed that very hour.*

Matthew 8:10-13

Whatever little knowledge of God—*the crumbs*—that existed among Israel's neighbors, it was enough for them to express faith in a God they did not fully understand. However, they believed that through Him they would be able to reap the full blessings of heaven.

> *"Of a truth . . .God is no respecter of persons: But in every nation he that feareth him, and worketh righteousness, is accepted with him."*

Acts 10:34, 35

> *". . . for truly I say to you, if you have faith as a mustard seed, you shall say to this mountain, 'Move from here to there,' and it shall move; and nothing shall be impossible to you."*

Matthew 17:20

Signs and Wonders

The central truth that Christ wanted His disciples and us to understand and practice is that the blessings of salvation ought not to be limited by invented or prescribed human categories or boundaries. Instead, they must be freely given to all who are willing and ready to receive them. This, He further illustrated by the miracles He performed immediately following His ministry to the Canaanite woman. Matthew says:

> "*And Jesus departed from thence, and came nigh unto the Sea of Galilee; and went up into a mountain, and sat down there. And great multitudes came unto him, having with them those that were lame, blind, dumb, maimed, and many others, and cast them down at Jesus' feet; and he healed them: Insomuch that the multitude wondered, when they saw the dumb to speak, the maimed to be whole, the lame to walk, and the blind to see; and <u>they glorified the God of Israel</u>.*"

Matthew 15:29-31

This was the second major mountainside retreat for Jesus and His disciples—the first being on the mountainside from which he taught His disciples and the multitudes the principles of life in the kingdom of heaven (Matthew 5-7). Since both events occurred in "Galilee of the Gentiles," it is quite possible that this may have been the one and same mountainside. However, it is important to observe that there are some marked similarities between these two events. In the first instance, the healing of the multitudes occurred before Christ retreated to the mountainside, while the second event took place after Christ was seated on the mountainside. Both events were also very important teaching situations. In the first setting, Christ was teaching about His kingdom; now He was teaching His disciples, by example, about the unrestricted scope and magnitude of their mission and ministry. Therefore, it was very significant that Jesus chose to do these things outside the immediate borders of Israel. Isaiah prophesied concerning Christ's mission:

> "*But there shall be no more gloom for her who was in anguish; in earlier times He treated the land of Zebulun and the land of Naphtali with contempt, but*

later on he shall make it glorious, by the way of the sea, on the other side of Jordan, <u>Galilee of the Gentiles</u>. The people who walk in darkness will see a great light; those who live in a dark land, the light will shine on them. Thou shalt multiply the nation, thou shalt increase their gladness; they will be glad in your presence as with the gladness of harvest, as men rejoice when they divide the spoil."

Isaiah 9:1-3

In harmony with Isaiah's prophetic declaration, the mountainside multitudes glorified the *God of Israel* for the Light was shinning among them. Matthew said they wondered at the marvelous works of God through the Son of David, for Christ healed every person that was brought before Him—the lame, blind, dumb, crippled, and more (Matthew 15:30, 31). For three whole days this spiritually hungry crowd lingered on, without food, to receive as much as they possibly could from Jesus. For them, this was a day of opportunity. Light was dispelling their darkness and nothing else was more important to them—not even food—than reclining in the presence of the Messiah.

Moved by their souls' hunger, and encouraged by their faith, Jesus felt compassion for His attentive audience and made the executive decision to satisfy their physical hunger also. He said to His disciples:

"I have compassion on the multitude, because they continue with me now three days, and have nothing to eat: and I will not send them away fasting, lest they faint in the way."

Matthew 15:32

At the words of Jesus, the disciples were immediately placed in a state of panic and disarray. As their darkened eyes assessed the situation, they asked their Master: *"Whence should we have so much bread in the wilderness, as to fill so great a multitude?"* (Matthew 15:33) Up to that point, and even thereafter (See also Matthew 16:5-12), the disciples had absolutely no clue that they were in the presence of the Bread of Life, who led them to this wilderness to teach them the cardinal lesson of His kingdom: *"Man shall not live by bread alone but by <u>every word</u>* **(or crumb)** *that proceedeth out of the mouth of God"* (Matthew 4:4; Deuteronomy 8:1-3, parenthesis mine). They were consumed and completely put off by the facts of their situation, and were totally clueless about the Truth that was standing right in the midst of the facts that confronted them. They were altogether ignorant that the Word (John 1:1-3) who made the world was their Master, and that He was quite capable of taking care of this situation of need.

> *"By the <u>word of the Lord</u> [Word] the heavens were made and by the <u>breath of His mouth</u> all their host. He gathers the waters of the sea together as a heap; He lays up the deeps in storehouses. . . For <u>He spoke</u>, and <u>it was done</u>; <u>He commanded</u> and <u>it stood fast</u>."*
>
> Psalm 33:6-9

The disciples had yet to learn about the power that attended "every word" that fell—like crumbs—from the lips of the Bread of Life. So do we! *"For the word of God is <u>living</u> and <u>active</u>, and <u>sharper</u> than any two-edged sword..."* (Hebrews 4:12). Accordingly, Jesus requested His disciples to bring their ration to Him—seven loaves and a few little fishes. He ordered the multitude to sit down, gave thanks to His Father for providing more than enough food for feeding the people, and proceeded to break the bread and the fishes. As He did so, He passed the broken pieces to His disciples and then

His disciples passed them out to the people.

The order of distribution of the food was extremely important. Firstly, Jesus wanted His disciples to be a part of the miracle that was occurring before their very eyes and in their very hands. Secondly, He wanted to teach them that they could only give what they have received from Him, the Bread of Life. Only the Bread of Life can produce enough bread (all that sustains life) to feed the whole world, and with much to spare. Thirdly, the Bread of Life is satisfying. What Christ offers is guaranteed to fill the need of every hungry soul. Matthew said that the multitude of over four thousand men, beside women and children, ate their fill, and there were seven leftover baskets filled with food (Matthew 15:37).

Through these miraculous signs and wonders the Light was shining among the people who once sat in darkness. However, the people of Israel were rejecting this very Light, and Christ was hoping that His disciples, who were called from among them to be the foundation of His future church, did not share their blind, nationalistic sentiments. This dominant concern is what led Christ and His disciples to this truth-defining moment in the coasts of Caesarea Philippi.

God's Revelation

"Now when Jesus came into the district of Caesarea Philippi, He began asking His disciples, saying, Who do people say that the Son of man is?"

Matthew 16:13

The journey through Caesarea Philippi marked a major turning point in the mission and ministry of Jesus. Obviously, the Savior's thoughts were preoccupied with very pressing concerns of enormous proportions and eternal consequences. His days in the flesh were rapidly drawing to a climax and He needed all the time He could gain with His disciples, to prepare them for their mission assignment—that of replacing Him in proclaiming and growing the kingdom of heaven upon the earth. How could He ready His motley group of tetchy followers for the task of taking the good news of salvation and the kingdom to the whole world of sinners who would certainly perish without hearing both? How could these men successfully accomplish a mission which they knew precious little about? How could they truly understand their mission without first grasping the identity and authority of the One sending them?

It was quite clear to Jesus that His disciples were following Him by blind faith based on public opinion, and that they did not fully understand who He was or where He was taking them. The journey through Caesarea Philippi was to be a defining and very decisive experience. Even after witnessing all the miracles of healing, and being participants in the miracles of feeding more than nine thousand people with only seven loaves of bread and a couple of fishes, the disciples still did not fully grasp the truth about Jesus.

> *"You men of little faith, why do you discuss among yourselves that you have no bread? Do you not yet understand or remember the five loaves of the five thousand, and how many baskets you took up? Or the seven loaves of the four thousand, and how many large baskets you took up? How it is that you do not understand that I did not speak to you concerning bread? But beware of the leaven of the Pharisees and Sadducees?"*
>
> Matthew 16: 8-11

How often do we become consumed, distracted and distressed about the facts of our life-situation and miss the great truth that in EVERYTHING, God is ALWAYS (I mean always, even if we don't even understand) working for our good because we love Him who called us to His purpose (Romans 8:28)? We may not be able to wrap our reasoning around the facts of our situation; but that does not matter one bit. As long as we bring our puny thoughts under the authority of this truth (Romans 8:28), and hold on to it with the confession of our lips, the Truth will ALWAYS set us free. Some of us will have a very difficult time even believing this truth, but even that does not really matter. It is still the truth!

Life's Most Important Question

The disciples did not recognize Christ as the Bread of Life, who could supply without measure all their needs from absolutely nothing, save the very words of His mouth. So in the wake of the signs, wonders and miracles, and the disciples' obvious lack of understanding, Jesus decided to pose the very important question: *"Whom do men say that I the Son of Man am"* (Matthew 16:13)? Now this was a very important question, and the answer provided some interesting, good-to-know information. It ranked Jesus among the greatest of Israel's prophets.

> And they said, *"Some say John the Baptist; and others, Elijah; but still others, Jeremiah, or one of the prophets."*
>
> Matthew 16:14

There were many legends floating around in the Jewish communities about the prophets of Israel. Jesus called John the Baptist the greatest prophet that ever lived (Matthew 11:7-11), but King Herod was among the first to spread the rumor that Jesus was the resurrected spirit of John working miraculous deeds among the people (Matthew 14:1, 2). In delivering God's message to Zacharias, the angel Gabriel (Luke 1:17) declared that John the Baptist would go forth preaching in the spirit and power of Elijah as the forerunner to the Messiah—a connection that Jesus also later made (Matthew 11:14).

Therefore, it is quite easy to see why many among the Jews also associated Jesus with Elijah, because of Herod's idea about Jesus, and the Master's own testimony connecting John with Elijah. In Maccabaean tradition, Jeremiah was also portrayed as a forerunner to the Messiah, but not as the One. Finally, many Jews also believed that many of the prophets of old would return to be guiding lights to Israel (Luke 9:19), and that God was going to send them a prophet like Moses to teach His people about Him (Deuteronomy 18:15-18).

Now, was Jesus really interested in popular opinion polls about His identity and authority? Absolutely not! If Jesus were only a prophet like John the Baptist, Elijah, Jeremiah, Moses or any other, then He could not have qualified to be the Savior of the world. The Messiah had to be so much more in order to guarantee the victorious outcome of the eternal plan of salvation and the establishment of the everlasting kingdom of God.

"*Whom do men say that I the Son of Man am,*" was only the lead question to the real issue that was crowding the Savior's mind. Christ was about to turn His face toward Jerusalem and Calvary, and if He should go to the cross without the nucleus of His future church completely convinced about who He really was, then His entire mission as man's only hope would have failed. Therefore, Jesus was very determined to obtain the answer to the most important question of His life before His time ran out. He said unto His disciples: "*But who do you say that I am*" (Matthew 16:15)?

The word "but" is a very powerful and important literary connector that ties Jesus' second question to the first. The Master sets Himself up against all the prophets of Israel that ever lived, hoping that His disciples would see and know that He outclassed them all. Now that you have given Me the opinions of men, I want to hear your verdict regarding Me: "*And you, who do you say that I am?*"

Life's Most Important Confession

> *"And Simon Peter answered and said, Thou art the Christ, the son of the Living God."*
>
> Matthew 16:17

Jesus' question may have caught the disciples by surprise, because their opinion of Jesus had not gone to anything beyond the opinion poll of the general Jewish populace—that is, Jesus was just a prophet, may be the best they had ever seen. What higher place of honor can there be for a man than to be ranked with the best of God's prophets? Any place beyond that is to be regarded as God, Himself. For the devout Jew, the name of God is too sacred to be uttered by human lips, far more to ascribe that name to a carpenter from Nazareth, of all places.

Consequently, while these simple-minded, but conscientious, men were pondering the meaning of Christ's question, light from Heaven's throne room shone in Simon's soul. Instantaneously, Peter's mental picture of Christ's identity went through a miraculous shift from popular opinion to divine revelation of the Spirit. As he moved his lips to speak, the Holy Ghost filled his mouth with the seed of revelation that He had planted directly in Peter's spirit: *"You are the Christ (or Messiah) of God"* (Luke 9:20).

The Messiah

This confession of Peter was not just a statement of truth, but it was the revelation of a divine secret that was full of history, expectancy and meaning. The mysterious person of the Messiah held all the hopes and dreams of the future of Israel and the human race. Scattered throughout the writings of the Old Testament is a profusion of prophecies regarding His identity, His person and His work. His title is a transliteration of the Hebrew word meaning, "anointed one," and was later translated into Greek as ***Christos*** — the Christ. The Messiah was heaven's appointed Ambassador, consecrated by triple anointing to fulfill His triple ministry as Prophet, Priest and King of the people of God. In fulfillment of Isaiah's prophecy, Jesus entered the synagogue in Nazareth on the Sabbath day and read these words concerning Himself:

> *"The Spirit of the Lord is upon me, because he hath anointed me to preach the gospel to the poor; he hath sent me to heal the broken-hearted, to preach deliverance to the captives, and recovering of sight to the blind, to set at liberty them that are bruised, to preach the acceptable year of the Lord."*
>
> Luke 4:16-18

The acceptable year of the Lord is Christ's reference to the year of Jubilee which God instructed Israel to observe during their journey through the wilderness, and when they settled in the land of promise (Leviticus 25). Jubilee was the year of redemption, rest, release and restoration for every man and his property (whether he was an Israelite, stranger, slave or prisoner), every beast of the field, and all the land. God instituted it as a foreshadowing of the work of the Messiah — God's Jubilee for the eternal redemption, rest, release and restoration of everyone and everything in His lost creation.

Jesus Christ is our Jubilee who, by His sacrificial life, death and eternal intercession, dispenses grace and power, through the Holy Spirit to break every curse (sin, sickness, brokenness, depression, death, poverty, and bondage) of the enemy, and to release bountiful blessings (His righteousness, health, wholeness, joy, life, prosperity and freedom) to all who trust in Him. He invites all:

> *"Come to Me, all who are weary and heavy-laden, and I will give you rest. Take My yoke upon you, and*

learn from Me, for I am gentle and humble in heart; and YOU SHALL FIND REST FOR YOUR SOUL. For my yoke is easy and My load is light."

Matthew 11:28-30

As God's Prophet, He was the divine replacement of Moses (Deuteronomy 18:15, 18, 19; John 6:14, 48-58; 7:40; Acts 3:22, 23). As God's High Priest, He was pre-figured by Melchizedek, king of Salem and priest of the most high God (Genesis 14:18; Psalm 110:1-7; Hebrews 5:5-10; 10:10-14); and as heaven's King, He was the true Son of David (2 Samuel 7:12, 13, 16, 25, 26, 29; Psalm 132:11; Matthew 1:1; Luke 1:31-33). Through His life (as the Prophet), His sacrifice and intercession by His blood (as the Priest of the Most High God), and His eternal reign at the authoritative right hand of God the Father (as the King of kings and Lord of lords) Christ, by far, exceeds these earthly figures that foreshadowed Him. He was before all, and in all, and above all (Colossians 1:14-19; Hebrews 1).

The Messiah's Declaration

In response to Peter's profound confession, the Master pronounced a blessing upon Simon because he was the recipient of heaven's favor. *"Blessed are you, Simon Barjona, because flesh and blood did not reveal this to you, but my Father who is in heaven"* (Matthew 16:18). Jesus also wanted Simon and the other disciples to understand that what came out of Simon's mouth was not the result of the reasoning of his human intellect, but was the direct impact of divine impartation. For *"no one knows the Son except the Father; nor does anyone know the Father except the Son, and anyone to whom the Son wills to reveal Him"* (Matthew 11:27). God, the Father, honored His Son through the confirming witness of Simon Peter, very much like He did through the declaration of John the Baptist when he saw Jesus approaching him for baptism at the Jordan (John 1:29-34).

After pronouncing His blessing upon Peter, Jesus declared with unequivocal certainty:

> *"And I say also unto you that you are Peter, and upon <u>this rock</u> I will build My church; and the gates of Hades shall not overpower it. I will give you the keys of the kingdom of heaven; and whatever you shall bind on earth shall be bound in heaven: and whatever you shall loose on earth shall be loosed in heaven." Then He warned the disciples that they should tell no one that He was the Christ."*

Matthew 16:17-20

No doubt, the revelation given to Peter filled the Savior with joyous hope. It was a moment for which He lived and waited, because it held very high stakes for the future of His church and the kingdom. Moreover, the nature of Christ's response to Peter is equally profound as Peter's confession. "Just as I am the Christ (***Christos*** or Messiah) and not just another prophet, so it is that you are Peter (***Petros*** - the stone) and not just Simon, the son of Jonah— the flat-nosed (meaning of Simon), flaky character. "There is much more solid substance in you Simon, than that which meets the natural eye."

"You are Peter!" Clearly, Christ does not see people as they are, but as what they can become through His empowering grace. He sees potential and possibilities and not just flaws and failures. In declaring Simon's new name as Peter, Christ was prophesying a new future for this vacillating disciple. You will become the solid, cornerstone leader in My church, and I will give you the keys (*knowledge, wisdom and authority*) to operate in My kingdom.

This Rock (Petra)

There has been much theological debate as to the true meaning of the word "rock" upon which Christ declared that He would build His church. Four major views are predominantly discussed. (1) The Augustinian view is that the "rock" represented Jesus Himself. "You are Peter, and on myself I will found my Church." (2) The "rock" is the truth that Jesus Christ is the Son of the Living God. (3) The "rock" is Peter's faith. On the faith of Peter the Church is founded. (4) Peter, himself, is the rock in a special sense. He is not the rock upon which the whole church is founded; that rock is God. However, he is the first rock or stone of the whole Church since he was the first man to make this discovery concerning Jesus.[1]

The author of this volume believes that the scriptural context of Jesus' declaration concerning the "rock" favors the second view — that is, the "rock" is the divine revelation given to Peter by the Father, Himself, that Jesus is His (the Father's) Messiah. In other words, Jesus was saying: *"And you are Peter, and upon this rock of your confession—that I am the Messiah of God—I will build My Church, and the gates of hell shall not prevail against it."* Evidently, Jesus makes a very clear distinction between ***Petros*** (small stone referring to Peter) and ***Petra*** (a large rock referring to Peter's confession). He did not only switch genders, moving from the masculine (***Petros***) to the feminine (***Petra***); but He also switched person, moving from second person (***you***, meaning Peter) to the third person (***this***, meaning the rock).

Additionally, Christ's usage of the demonstrative adjective (***this***) clearly identifies the "something" (and not someone) upon which He intends to build His church—in this case, the rock (***Petra***) of Peter's confession. In verse 17, when Jesus said to Peter: *"Blessed are you, Simon Barjona, because flesh and blood did not reveal **this** to you, but My Father who is in heaven,"* it is quite clear that the *"**this**"* that is being referred to is nothing else than Peter's confession that He (Jesus) is the Messiah of God. This understanding unmistakably connects with, and identifies, the *"this rock"* in Jesus' declaration immediately following the blessing He conferred on Peter. Consequently, the *"this,"* of the revelation from the Father who is in heaven (Matthew 16:17), and the *"this rock"* upon which Christ says He will build His church (Matthew 16:18), refer to the one and the same thing—the confession that Jesus is the Christ (or Messiah), the Son of the Living God.

This confession that Jesus is the Messiah of God carries with it all that scripture teaches about the Son of God—the prophecies and their fulfillment regarding His origin, His eternal power and Godhead to deal effectively with all the issues of fallen man and his redemption, His incarnate birth, His sinless life, His compassionate ministry, His vicarious death, His glorious resurrection, His bodily ascension, His timeless intercession and His soon return as King of kings and Lord of lords. John, who was present with Peter when he (Peter) received God's revelation, could later declare that:

> *"Whoever believes that Jesus is the Christ is born of God; ... For whatever is born of God overcomes the world, and this is the victory that has overcome the world—our faith. And who is the one who overcomes the world, but he who believes that Jesus is the Son of God?"*
>
> 1 John 5:1, 3-4

Just as God gave the revelation to Peter, so He gives it to every believer through the person of the Holy Spirit. This is the reason why the gates of hell cannot prevail against the body of believers who is united by the common, supernatural conviction that Jesus is the Messiah of God and Savior of their souls. When, at conversion, the seed of this revelation is implanted by faith in the believer's spirit and mind, and that would-be disciple embraces Jesus as the Son of the Living God and Savior of his/her soul, he/she immediately becomes a part of the body of Christ.

The church of Christ is built upon the confession of faith in the immovable rock—Jesus is the Christ (or Messiah), the Son of the Living God. This supernatural revelation and conviction forms the only entrance into the body of Christ, of which Peter was the very first member. It is extremely important to recognize that this entrance into the body of Christ is entirely the work of God and not man. It is a supernatural transaction between God and the believer, with nothing and no one between. Entrance into the body of Christ is entirely by faith and not by the works or opinions of men. Upon *"this rock,"* Christ says, He will build His church and the gates of hell shall not prevail against it—the church and the rock upon which it is built.

Additionally, Christ specifically warned His disciples about revealing His identity to any man. This was not only a precautionary measure to avert premature hostility toward Himself and His embryonic Church, but He also knew that the revelation of His true identity was a supernatural gift of God and not a conclusion that can be drawn from presentation of facts about Him. Jesus said that "<u>no one</u> can come to Me, unless <u>the Father who sent Me draws him</u>..," (John 6:44). A few moments later He reiterated the fact: *"For this reason I have said unto you, that <u>no one</u> can come to Me, unless it has been granted him from the Father"* (John 6:65).

Therefore, conviction regarding the person of Jesus Christ is the work of the Father in heaven, and the same light that shone into Peter's soul must shine into the soul of everyone who hears the gospel, confirming that Jesus is indeed the Messiah, the Son of the Living God and Savior of the world. This is God's doing and it is marvelous in our eyes. The church and the kingdom are both instruments of God, and are symbolized by Daniel's mysterious stone that was cut from the great mountain, but without human hands.

Building His Church

Christ's declaration to Peter makes evident at least four very important facts about His church—namely: (1) The church was God's idea not man's, (2) Christ has "a" church, (3) Christ is the builder of His church, and (4) Christ has one building principle for His church. Although the church consists of human beings, it is not a human organization, even though at times we tend to relate to it as such. Christ is the One who first introduced the word "church" in the New Testament, and the only such usage in the gospels. The term came from the Greek *ekklēsia*, which means an assembly of called out ones. Christ made use of an Old Testament idea that identified Israel as the people of God (see Acts 2:38; Deuteronomy 5:22; Psalm 22:22; Joel 2:16; Micah 2:5) and assigned it to those who, by faith, embraced Him as God's Messiah and Savior of humanity.

The church, really, is not the building in which we assemble for worship, or the denomination to which one belongs. These are much too "small" to house the body of Christ. This sort of meaning was a later historical development that grew out of Roman institutionalism. These visible representations are only parts of the whole that vicariously transcend these human structures. Rather, the church is the assembly of Yahweh (God's new Israel of "called out" believers), which finds its unique identity in its relationship to Christ.

The *ekklēsia* is, in fact, the assembly or community of kingdom subjects, but never the kingdom itself. Jesus' disciples belong to the kingdom and the kingdom belongs to them; but they are not the kingdom. The kingdom is primarily the dynamic reign and kingly rule of God, and derivatively, the sphere in which that rule is experienced.[2] However, the *ekklēsia* (or church) is as mysterious as the kingdom to which it belongs. Just as the kingdom of heaven (*the stone cut without* "human" *hands* – Daniel 2:44, 45) emerged without human intervention and grows by the mysterious power of God, so does the church that Christ, Himself, is building (see Ephesians 2:14-22; 4:15, 16; 5:25-**32**).

Therefore, the church is simply not what men declare it to be. It is only what Christ declared it to be, and as such, it has a divine origin, with a divinely-appointed destiny—the kingdom of God. Additionally, Christ is the only one who can truly build His church, bringing into it men and women with different capacities and abilities, and from every imaginable ethnic group and station in life. It is very interesting to observe the grammatical transition in Christ's declaration (Matthew 16:18) that gave birth to His church. He moves from *"you are Peter"* (2nd person), to *"upon this rock"* (3rd person), and then to *"I WILL BUILD 'MY' CHURCH"* (1st person). Make no mistake about it; Christ is the Builder of His church. Hence the reason Paul said that all believers belong *to the general assembly and church of the firstborn who are enrolled in heaven* (Hebrews 12:23); for that's where our authentic citizenship (or legal right or entitlement to all the benefits of the kingdom) really is (Philippians 3:20).

In the light of the foregoing facts, it is impossible for humanity to own or control Christ's church. We can only embrace and participate in its building process, or reject it all together; but we can never lay claim to that process or the church itself. It must be acknowledged that some individuals and/or religious organizations may operate as though they do have ownership over Christ's church, or as though they could sway its growth and ultimate triumph. Christ once told a parable about some wicked vinedressers in the gospel of Matthew that clearly illustrates this point. He said:

> *"Listen to another parable. There was a landowner who PLANTED A VINEYARD AND PUT A WALL AROUND IT AND DUG A WINE PRESS IN IT, AND BUILT A TOWER, and rented it out to vine-growers and went on a journey. When the harvest time approached, he sent his slaves to the vine-growers to receive his produce.*
>
> *The vine-growers took his slaves and beat*

one, and killed another, and stoned a third. Again he sent another group of slaves larger than the first; and they did the same thing to them. But afterward he sent his son to them, saying, 'They will respect my son.'

But when the vine-growers saw the son, they said among themselves, '<u>This is the heir; come, let us kill him and seize his inheritance</u>.' <u>They took him, and threw him out of the vineyard and killed him</u>. Therefore when the owner of the vineyard comes, what will he do to those vine-growers?"

They said to Him, "He will bring those wretches to a wretched end, and will rent out the vineyard to other vine-growers who will pay him the proceeds at the proper seasons." Jesus said to them, "Did you never read in the Scriptures, 'THE STONE WHICH THE BUILDERS REJECTED, THIS BECAME THE CHIEF CORNER stone; THIS CAME ABOUT FROM THE LORD, AND IT IS MARVELOUS IN OUR EYES'?

Therefore I say to you, the kingdom of God will be taken away from you and given to a people producing the fruit of it. And he who falls on this stone will be broken to pieces; but on whomever it falls, it will scatter him like dust.

When the chief priests and the Pharisees heard His parables, they understood that He was speaking about them. When they sought to seize Him, they feared the people, because they considered Him to be a prophet."

Matthew 21:33-46

This parable had an immediate reference to the leadership of the people of Israel, and they recognized that application as soon as Jesus made his closing remarks regarding the wicked vine-dressers. When viewed in the given context, the landowner represented God the Father, for He owns everything. The Bible says that *the earth is the Lord's and the fullness thereof, the world and they that dwell therein. For He hath founded it upon the seas and established it upon the floods* (Psalm 24:1, 2). The vineyard that God planted and nurtured was the Jewish nation and the tenants were its religious leaders (Isaiah 5:1-4). The slaves referred to the prophets (including John the Baptist) that God sent to Israel with His messages of warning, reproof, counsel and repentance; but the leaders of His people rejected, abused and killed them.

When the Father finally sent His Son, the Messiah and our Savior, to reclaim His chosen heritage, the Jewish leaders saw Him as a threat to their political ambitions and livelihood, and they dogged His every step with their fiendish plots to get rid of Him. These wicked, self-opinionated men wanted the Heir out of the way so that they could have full control over His inheritance—that is, the people of God. When they finally succeeded in condemning Him to death, they threw Him out of the vineyard (Matthew 21:39) by crucifying Him outside the wall of the city of Jerusalem.

How accurately Jesus read the hearts of these evil men! It is also very interesting that Jesus tacitly allowed the chief priest and Pharisees the opportunity to pronounce their own judgment. They said to Him, *"He will bring those wretches to a wretched end, and will rent out the vineyard to other vine-growers who will pay him the proceeds at the proper seasons."* (Matthew 21:41)

This parable of the wicked vine-dressers is very pertinent to believers today, because it also has an eschatological (or end-time) application, as heaven gets ready to harvest the fruits of Christ's labor. Professed Christian leaders represent the new vine-dressers (renters or tenants) the Pharisees unwittingly referred to when they pronounced judgment on themselves. However, the parable takes on a new twist in the realm of the kingdom. Christ says that He is the true vine, His Father is the vine-dresser, more accurately, the Owner of the vineyard. Those of us who believe in Him are the branches, whom both He and the Father expect to bear fruit (John 15:1-11).

Although church leaders themselves are branches, since they cannot grow on their own apart from Christ, they are also appointed vine-dressers over Christ's inheritance (Ephesians 4:8-13). Therefore, church leaders are not owners of that heritage, even though some may act as though they are. They are only renters (or under-shepherds to use a more ecclesiastical term). What is said of church leaders can also be said about the organizations and denominations these leaders represent. These institutions are only stewards of Christ's heritage and must finally give an account to Him for the way in which they conduct His business and handle His precious vines and their fruits.

The body of Christ today must be instructed by His rebuke against the leaders of Israel for the way in which they exploited His chosen heritage in order to further their selfish ambitions. Many among the Jewish masses could not see or recognize Jesus as the Messiah, because their leaders and the religious system they orchestrated to perpetuate Judaism got in the way. I am afraid that this sad state of affairs is not just a relic of the past, but is also a major challenge for post-Modern Christians and non-Christians alike.

All too often, Christian believers and the unsaved cannot see the Savior, or come into the full blessings of His salvation, because the institutional church or system of religion to which they belong, gets in the way. Leaders and systems have control over the minds of God's children, distorting their view of the Scriptures and the precious promises of the Savior. Religious institutionalism creates a culture of church membership that gives preeminence to rendering loyalty towards a particular brand of denominationalism than to loyalty and obedience to Christ Himself. This produces believers who submissively choose to live by the creed and demands of their religious organization rather than *by every word from the mouth of God*.

Like the self-deceived vine-dressers, some church leaders and religious systems seek to usurp the authority of Christ in the lives of His precious children, burdening them with man-made traditions and requirements that nullify the finished work of Christ for their redemption. The precious promises and blessings of Christ are often not appropriated to these little ones (Matthew 18:6) because they have been nurtured to be dependent on men for what Christ has freely given to every believer through His sacrifice on Calvary.

Quite often such church leaders live in cyclical fear (the true catalyst for spiritual dictatorship) and avoid anyone or anything (including the gospel of Christ) that empowers these dependent believers to experience their full assurance of faith and freedom in Christ. However, the time is coming, and hastening apace, when the soon-coming King will break every human yoke that seeks to hold His children captive, and will prepare His universal church for its final assault on the kingdom of darkness, in preparation for His imminent return. This warning is mirrored in Christ's words to the house of Judah, through the prophet Jeremiah:

> *"Is My inheritance like a speckled bird of prey to Me? Are the birds of prey against her on every side? Go, gather all the beasts of the field, Bring them to devour!*
> <u>*Many shepherds have ruined My vineyard, They have trampled down My field; They have made My pleasant field A desolate wilderness. It has been made a desolation, Desolate, it mourns before Me; The whole land has been made desolate, Because no man lays it to heart*</u>*.*
> *On all the bare heights in the wilderness Destroyers have come, For a sword of the LORD is devouring From one end of the land even to the other; There is no peace for anyone.* <u>*They have sown wheat and have reaped thorns, They have strained*</u>

> *themselves to no profit. But be ashamed of your harvest Because of the fierce anger of the LORD."*
>
> Jeremiah 12:9-13

From the reading of the above scripture, one thing is most certain—that is, Christ will have the last say in this vineyard saga. He will dispense His final judgment on the work of every shepherd who serves in His vineyard, and will reward every person accordingly.

One Among the Many

William Barclay correctly stated that when Christ formed His church, "it was not a Church in the human sense, still less in a denominational sense . . . What began with Peter was the fellowship of all believers in Jesus Christ, not identified with any Church and limited to any Church, but embracing all who love the Lord."[3] Christ, indeed, has "a" church—one, not many. It is a discipling community without the walls and boundaries erected by religious institutionalism, denominationalism, social standing, color, creed, race, class or any other man-made distinction. It is a church united, not divided; a mysterious body of believers (like its kingdom birthmother) who has embraced, and who lives, by the truth about their Savior's identity. This identity points to the truth that He is certainly the Messiah of God and Redeemer of the world. It is this foundation stone that connects all Christian believers everywhere, and without it there could be no church. However, the growing multiplicity of religious institutions, organizations and churches pulling professed, confused believers in all directions, makes it painfully difficult for this singular, pivotal truth to be understood and received by the unbelieving world. Our Master prayed:

> *"I do not ask on behalf of these alone, but for those*

> *also who believe in Me through their word; that they may all be one; even as You, Father, are in Me and I in You, that they also may be in Us, <u>so that the world may believe that You sent Me</u>."*
>
> John 17:20, 21

When Christ said to Peter: **"Upon this rock I will build 'My' church**," did He have the present situation in mind? Absolutely not! When, in John 17, He prayed for all His disciples (past, present and future) to be one, was this His vision of that oneness? I do not believe so. It was the type of oneness that was the precursor to Pentecost. It was a singleness of spirit and mind for the reception of the promised Holy Spirit, for the salvation of the lost through the preaching of the resurrected Christ, and for the hastening of the establishment of the kingdom of God (Acts 1:6). George Eldon Ladd said that the oneness of the *ekklēsia*—the church or called out one—is illustrated by the two phenomena on the day of Pentecost. The appearance of something like tongues of fire dividing and resting on each one (Acts 2:3) suggests unity and diversity, . . . and the oneness of the *ekklēsia* and its universal scope . . . This new event in redemptive history is designed for the whole world and would unite men of diverse tongues in a new unity of the *ekklēsia*.[4]

The enemy of the gospel and the kingdom of God has certainly crafted a master strategy in his campaign against the church of Christ. He has subtly woven a very intricate situation that makes it appear extremely difficult for current denominational and institutional models of the church to return to the kingdom model of the church where the believers had all things in common and worked in concert for the common good of the kingdom. It is a situation that gives preeminence to the myopic view of institutional survival through member acquisition over the world-view of kingdom building through disciple multiplication.

The unwelcome, baneful truth is that parts of the body of

Christ have been institutionalized for so long that it is nearly impossible for many professed believers to visualize or realize, a functional Christian experience apart from the bricks and mortar of the religious institution or denomination which contain them. As a result of this spiritual and psychological phenomenon, denominational brand switching, religious proselyting and the multiplication of institutions and structures have become the order of the day for bewildered believers. Indeed, the Prince of the power of the air and darkness has diabolically designed religious institutionalism as an insidious, spiritual straitjacket to slow down the aggressive growth of the apostolic church, and skillfully used its multifaceted variations to immobilize the body of Christ down through the ages.[5]

Many churches and ministry leaders within the body of Christ are somewhat reluctant to address the spiritual and psychological inertia precipitated by religious institutionalism for fear of potential negative effects on their reputation and ministry. However, Christ, not men, is the Master Builder of His church, and He calls into it those who, by faith and the revelation of the Holy Spirit, receive Him as the Messiah of God and Savior of the world.

The religions of men may prescribe alternative ways for gaining entrance into their fellowship, and even seek to shut up the kingdom from sinners who are desperately seeking to go in (Matthew 23:13), but there is only one door of entry into the church that Jesus Christ is building—that is, confession of faith in Him as the Son of the Living God. To enter any other way is to be considered a thief or a robber (John 10:1, 2, 7, 9). This is the one principle upon which Christ builds His church and there is no other (Matthew 16:17, 18). He is the One who decides, in the end, who is really in or out of His church and His kingdom (Matthew 7:21-23).

The Mission of the Church

As the true Master Builder of His church, Christ is also the One who established its mission and operating agenda. That mission is an extension of His mission, and has as its singular objective and prophetic destiny the establishment of the eternal kingdom of God on earth (Daniel 2:44, 45). The true purpose of the church is not to privatize the kingdom but to proclaim its gospel—eternal salvation through the Messiah, Jesus Christ—to every creature under the heavens. The church is not called to be a center of performing arts with creative, charismatic performers, and an eclectic gathering of hard-to-please, self-serving spectators. It is called to be the visible, dynamic body of Christ—an equipping, empowering fellowship community of disciples—fully engaged in the singular task of building Christ's kingdom. The church comprises kingdom subjects, called disciples (not members), to whom Christ gave specific instructions regarding their mission and their relation to His kingdom.

The Great Commission[6]

> "And Jesus came up and spoke to them, saying, *All authority has been given to Me in heaven and on earth. Go therefore and make disciples of all the nations, baptizing them in the name of the Father and the Son and the Holy Spirit, teaching them to observe all that I commanded you; and lo, I am with you always, even to the end of the age.*"
>
> Matthew 28:18-20

Nowhere in scripture is the mission of the church, as it relates to the kingdom of God, more clearly outlined than it is in the above text found in Matthew's gospel. Jesus had paid the ultimate price for man's salvation and was getting ready to return to His Father in heaven. However, He had promised, through Mary Magdalene and Mary, His mother (Matthew 28:1, 10), to rendezvous with the disciples one last time before taking His departure. The appointed place for this final meeting was "the mountain" in Galilee—a place with which they were all very familiar, for Christ had taken them there many times (Matthew 5:1; 15:29-31; 28:16; Mark 3:13; Luke 6:12-13; 9:28; John 6:1-3, 15). For the very first time Luke identifies "the mountain" by name in the book of Acts (See Acts 1:9-**12**). Luke called "the mountain" Olivet.

This mountain was uniquely significant because it became a very powerful anchor point for important events in the ministry of Jesus and in the lives of His disciples. Great things happened on this mountain—Christ's first teachings on the kingdom and kingdom life (Matthew 5-7); miracles of healing and multiple feeding of thousands; the Master's transfiguration (Luke 9:28ff); and meetings for prayer and private instruction. As the eleven men (minus Judas) proceeded to "the mountain," they were not sure of what to expect, but they knew from past experience on that mountain that something very significant was about to take place. And it did.

While the four gospels focused on different scenes from Jesus' final hours with His disciples, only Matthew and Luke related those scenes as mountaintop experiences. However, I will reserve Luke's comments for the next chapter. Matthew said that the very first thing that happened on "the mountain" this last time around was worship. Although some of the disciples were a little apprehensive about the appearance of Jesus, they all bowed in worship before their risen Lord. This was (and is) a most appropriate response of the church, for the Lamb that was slain, who is our Savior and Lord, and is worthy of all worship and praise.

All Authority

Jesus responds to the worshipping disciples with the

declaration: "*All authority has been given to Me in heaven and on earth*" (Matthew 28:18). Although Christ was the long-awaited Messiah and Savior of the world, His supreme authority had to be preceded by His humiliation and His death. These efficacious experiences became His qualification to exercise complete authority over all creation in heaven and on earth. The apostle Paul wrote of Christ:

> *He humbled Himself by becoming obedient to the point of death, even death on a cross. For this reason also, <u>God highly exalted Him</u>, and bestowed on Him the name which is above every name, so that at the name of Jesus EVERY KNEE WILL BOW, of those who are in heaven and on earth and under the earth, and that every tongue will confess that Jesus Christ is Lord, to the glory of God the Father.*
>
> Philippians 2:8-11

> *... These are in accordance with the working of the strength of His might* [20]*which He brought about in Christ, when He raised Him from the dead and seated Him at His right hand in the heavenly places,* [21]<u>*far above all rule and authority and power and dominion, and every name that is named*</u>*, <u>not only in this age but also in the one to come</u>.* [22]*And He put all things in subjection under His feet, and gave Him as head over all things to the church,* [23]*which is His body, the fullness of Him who fills all in all.*
>
> Ephesians 1:19-23

How far did God highly exalt our resurrected Savior? The text says *far above all rule, [all] authority, [all] power, [all] dominion, and <u>every name</u> <u>that is named</u>*, not only in this world but also in the world to come. Furthermore, God put *all things* in subjection under the Savior's feet. No other Bible-writer has expressed Christ's supreme authority more fully than Paul. In his epistle to the Hebrews, he wrote:

> *And He is the radiance of His glory and the exact representation of His nature, and upholds all things by the word of His power.* <u>*When He had made purification of sins, He sat down at the right hand of the Majesty on high, having become as much better than the angels, as He has inherited a more excellent name than they*</u>.

Hebrews 1:3, 4

For Paul, Christ is God's superlative of everything that was done, and everyone whoever did it, in the heavens above and the earth beneath. Over and over again in this first chapter he compares the authority of Christ to that of the angels. Twice he confirms Christ's supreme majesty and authority over them by repeating the thought-provoking question, *"to which angel did God ever say . . .* [thus and so]" (Hebrews 1: 5, 13)? Once he expressed God's ultimate perspective:

> *And of the angels He says, "who makes His angels winds, and His ministers a flame of fire."* <u>*But of the Son He says*</u>, "<u>*thy throne O God, is forever and ever*</u>, *and* <u>*the righteous scepter is the scepter of His Kingdom*</u>*. . . Therefore God, thy God,* <u>*hath anointed Thee with oil of gladness above Thy companions*</u>. *And Thou, Lord, in the beginning didst lay the foundation of the earth, and the heavens are the works of Thy hands;"*

Hebrews 1: 7-10

Mission Priority

It is with reference to this surpassing authority and power that Christ gave the gospel commission to His disciples, who were the foundation believers of His church (Matthew 28:18-20). This is the surpassing authority (for there is no other) that He delivers to all disciples who faithfully honor His mandate for building His kingdom. No higher authority, also means no higher priority or calling on the lives of Christ's disciples. The "all authority" is both given and received only in the context of the "great commission," and in no other way—that is, to make, baptize and teach disciples, not members. When leaders and believers understand and live the commission as though there is no higher priority on their lives, the "all authority" would be given, and a powerful witness for the kingdom of God will be the result.

Go! Make! Baptize! Teach!

Understanding and living the "great commission" is the paramount calling of every Christian. This commission represents a dynamic fourfold command, which contains four action-packed verbs—of doing, not just being. The first two-letter verb is "Go." Jesus uses the adverb "therefore" to link His command ("Go") to His authority. The "all authority" is experienced as the disciples follow through with going among all the nations. This authority is not received by passively sitting in a church, or before a television, listening to a sermon, although these activities may be good and necessary for the nurturing of the believer's faith and experience. Rather, Christ's authority is graciously dispensed as one actively engages the lost—through word or deed—with a positive witness for the kingdom of God.

However, if disciples of Christ could experientially internalize this "all authority" that is freely given to all who believe and obey His command, the world would experience the most compelling witness of the kingdom of God it has ever seen. Sin and sinners, sickness and sadness, devils and demons, principalities and powers will all recant and recoil before the authoritative power of Christ, resident in, and on, His believing disciples. This is extremely powerful stuff, and it is available to all who are willing and ready to receive it. Christ and all heaven are still waiting to honor this unfulfilled promise.

In fulfilling the "Go" command, the unsaved person is not expected to come to the church, on the church's terms or turf, but the church is expected to go and find lost men and women wherever they reside. Today, many believing communities refer to lost people as "seekers," when, the members who comprise these congregations, should be the ones doing the seeking. Believing communities create, what they refer to as, "seeker services" to which they hope the wandering and lost would come, instead of training their members to be faithful disciples who will go in search of the wandering and the lost. Seeker services, of themselves, are good, but they also reinforce the paradigm that places the center of the believer's experience in the church than in the world of lost humanity. The disciple, like His Master, should be a seeker and a facilitator of the salvation for all unsaved people.

The other three action verbs follow the word "go" in orderly succession—that is, "make" disciples, "baptize" them, and "teach" them all that Christ commanded. It is very interesting that all these action verbs are expressed in the Greek present participle, which indicates continuous, repetitive action. Simply put, what Jesus said was: "Keep on going, keep on making, keep on baptizing and keep on teaching disciples among all the nations of the earth, until you make the last disciple for the kingdom of God." Notice that the authority is given to make disciples of Christ and not converts to a particular brand of Christianity. Therefore, in the context of the "great commission," making converts or members to anyone or anything else would be highly superfluous. Christ has only one body (Ephesians 2:14-16; 4:4; 1 Corinthians 12:12-14), and doing so would stand in clear violation of His command and purpose, which calls for building His kingdom through the process of disciple duplication.

In Matthew 10:24, 25, Christ says that *"it is enough for a disciple to be like his teacher."* Clearly, Christlikeness is the goal of discipleship—that is, to make a disciple become like Jesus, the Chief Discipler. It is Christ who invites all would-be disciples with the call: "Follow Me!" (Matthew 4:19)—that is, "Be like Me!" "Duplicate Me!" "Do as I did!" This is not the work of a moment, or a day, but the work that extends far beyond one's lifetime.

Thus, making a disciple is not a one and done act as in the making of a "convert" to a particular denominational preference, but a continuous process of growing and developing a believer into the *stature of the fullness of Christ* (Ephesians 4:13). As His ambassadors (2 Corinthians 5:20), believers are commissioned to extend heaven's invitation to the unsaved to receive Jesus as Savior and Lord. They must make the commitment to spend the rest of their lives pursuing Christlikeness, while, at the same time, sharing Christ's love and life with those who do not know Him.

According to Christ's command, baptism is the official entrance into His school of discipleship. He said that His disciples must make disciples and baptize "them" in the name of the Trinity (Matthew 28:19). It is quite obvious that the word "them" refers to the disciples who were made from among all the nations and tribes of the earth. The word Christ uses for "baptizing" is the Greek present participle *baptízontes* (from *baptízō*, which means to dip or immerse, as in water). Such usage suggests continuous or repetitive action in relation to the main verb (in this case, **make disciples**). In other words, what Christ is saying is that whenever we make disciples among the nations, we must also baptize those disciples in the name of Father, and of the Son and of the Holy Spirit.

As it is with the baptizing, so it is with the teaching. We are to teach the same ones that we baptize—that is, disciples. Again, Christ uses the present participle of the Greek *didaskō* (to teach), which indicates that the teaching of disciples must occur whenever the making and the baptizing of disciples happen. Thus, teaching (all that Christ commands) is an extension of the discipling process. However, it is very important that the order of these three activities be preserved for the process of discipling to be effective.

Although some measure of teaching must occur in order for a person to arrive at an intelligent decision to become a disciple of Jesus Christ, the process of teaching continues long after the person has been baptized in the name of the Trinity. In discipleship, one enters a school from which one can never graduate in this life. Graduation is only possible when the disciple becomes like his Master—Jesus Christ. Therefore, as one grows and matures in Christ, so does the level of teaching, of knowing, and of becoming like Christ.

Teaching believers "to observe" all that Christ commands involves more than teaching them about Christ. It involves teaching His disciples to be like Him. The word "observe" (present infinitive of the Greek *tēréō*), means more than merely taking notice of something. It means observe with the intent to emulate or practice, as you would do with an ordinance. Correctly translated then, "observe all that I command you" means practice everything I have said to you. Furthermore, all that Christ commanded included more than just all that Christ said. It also embraced all that Christ did. His life was a constant lesson-book for His disciples, for it gave power and clarity to all the lessons He spoke and taught. Christ's invitation to His disciples, "Follow Me," encompasses both His life and His words.

Interestingly, Christ spent more time teaching about and demonstrating the presence of His kingdom than any other subject in the gospels. *"The Kingdom of heaven is like . . ."* was the favored opening line of most of His parables. There are at least 12 such openings in the gospel of Matthew, with six of them occurring in chapter 13 alone. It is rather obvious that Jesus was thoroughly aware of the fact that every disciple would face the major challenge of living the life of the kingdom in a world at war with that kingdom, and in one that operates by principles and standards contrary to the nature of that kingdom. Therefore, the great thesis of His teaching was about the kingdom of God and life in that kingdom, of which there are more than 100 references in the gospels alone. The Savior, who called us, invites us to follow Him in building His kingdom, and He promises to be with us, even unto the end of the age (Matthew 28:20).

Hasten the End

The purpose and mission of the church is to proclaim the gospel of the kingdom and to strengthen the kingdom people by keeping before them their life's priority—*"seek first the kingdom of God and His righteousness. . ."* (Matthew 6:33). It is very wholesome and helpful to remember that it was not the church that created the kingdom, but rather the kingdom that gave birth to the church, and designated its global kingdom assignment. Consequently, the kingdom, through the sovereign rule of its omnipotent King, Jesus Christ, has endowed the church with an abundant, inexhaustible supply of all the necessary resources—gifts, talents, and material and financial wealth too—for the nourishing, edifying, sustaining, strengthening and maturing of its disciples as it engages in Christ's mission of universal kingdom expansion (Ephesians 4:7-13).

Jesus said that *this <u>gospel of the kingdom</u> shall be preached in the whole world for a witness to all the nations; and then the end shall come* (Matthew 24:14). Notice, that this gospel is not called the gospel of the church or denomination or anything else; but the gospel of the kingdom. The major problem of modern Christianity is that many professed systems of religion have substituted the preaching of the gospel of Christ and of His kingdom with the preaching of many other gospels—gospel of denominationalism, institutionalism, traditionalism, materialism, proselytism, elitism, asceticism, to name a few—creating division and confusion within the body of Christ. However, it is only when institutional, man-made agendas become subject to the authority of the only true Head of the church, that the body of Christ would unite in proclaiming the full gospel of the kingdom as a witness to all the nations of the earth and the end would come, hastening the glorious return of our conquering Lord and King.

Notes:

1. William Barclay, *The Daily Study Bible: The Gospel of Matthew* (Edinburgh: Saint Andrews Press, 1986), 140-141.
2. George Eldon Ladd, *A Theology of the New Testament* (Grand Rapids: William B. Eerdmans Publishing Company, 1974), 111.
3. William Barclay, 142.
4. George Eldon Ladd, 348.
5. See Chapter 7 and also Ruthven J. Roy, *The Explosive Power of Network Discipling* (Berrien Springs, MI: Rehoboth Publishing, 2010), 18-21, for details on Satan's two-prong strategy.
6. For a more comprehensive discussion of this gospel mandate, see the 4th chapter of *The Explosive Power of Network Discipling* (Berrien Springs, MI: Rehoboth Publishing, 2010).

PENTECOST AND KINGDOM EXPANSION

5

But you shall receive power when the Holy Spirit has come upon you; and you shall be My witnesses both in Jerusalem, and in all Judea and Samaria, and even to the remotest part of the earth.

Acts 1:8

The Kingdom Priority

Restoring the kingdom of heaven on earth was Christ's primary mission agenda. Kingdom consciousness and kingdom imminence formed the cornerstone of the first message He announced to Israel and the world when He began His earthly ministry (*"Repent for the kingdom of heaven is at hand,"* Matthew 4:19). The same theme was the centerpiece of the last instruction He gave to His disciples before His ascension to the right hand of His Father in heaven. In his treatise to Theophilus concerning the validity of Jesus being God's Messiah, Luke wrote:

> [1]*The first account I composed, Theophilus, about all that Jesus began to do and teach,* [2]*until the day when He was taken up to heaven, after He had by the Holy Spirit given orders to the apostles whom He had chosen.* [3]*To these He also presented Himself alive after His suffering, by many convincing proofs, appearing to them over a period of forty days and <u>speaking of the things concerning the kingdom of God</u>.*

Acts 1:1-3

In this particular scripture, Luke was actually connecting with where he left off (Luke 24:36-49) in his first report to Theophilus, validating all that he (Theophilus) had heard concerning Jesus, the Messiah of God (Luke 1:1-4). Luke confirms that after Christ's death, burial and resurrection, the Savior made several appearances to His disciples over a period of forty days. During that time He opened their understanding of the Scriptures concerning the Law of Moses and the Prophets, the Psalms, His life and passion (Luke 24:13-48), and *things concerning the kingdom of God* (Acts 1:3). However, on this particular occasion recorded in Acts, Luke reveals that the resurrected Savior had gathered His disciples together for their last rendezvous on the mount of Olive (Acts 1:12), to give them His final instruction before His departure.

This was a most momentous occasion because it was going to be Christ's last face-to-face conversation with His disciples, the number of whom had grown to about one hundred and twenty (Acts 1:15). One can only imagine the thoughts that were running through the Savior's mind, and, even more, the emotional conflict of His waiting audience. What are we supposed to do now? What will He tell us? Is He going to restore the kingdom of Israel at this time? In spite of all the questions that may have been crowding the disciples' thoughts, one thing was very certain—that is, whatever the Master was about to say was going to be of supreme importance and they were all very eager to hear it.

Wait For the Promise

> *"You are my witnesses of these things. And behold, I am sending forth the promise of My Father upon you; but you are to stay in the city until you are clothed with power from on high."*

Luke 24:48, 49

In this gospel account, Luke reveals that Christ's final words to His followers were statements of confirmation regarding their role as His disciples and the *promise of the Father.* Christ reminded the group: *"You are witnesses of these things"* (Luke 24:48). The disciples were the only viable containers of all that Christ taught and the living witnesses of all that He did, and He was staking the future of the church and the kingdom on their testimony regarding Him to the world. What a daunting task this must have seemed to these simple-minded men and women, who, only a few days ago, did not even have the courage enough to acknowledge their tormented Master. Yet, He, who knows *what is in man* and understands the thoughts of men, saw in them a most promising future under the enabling power of the "Promise" from on high. What a glorious hope this offers to all believers who, though beset with all manner of human encumbrances, can find a productive future in the kingdom of God through the transforming, empowering grace of the divine Helper. This promised "Gift" was supposed to clothe them with supernatural power.

It is quite obvious that Christ was here referring to His Successor, the Holy Spirit, for in the gospel of John, He told His disciples:

> *"I will ask the Father, and He will give you another Helper, that He may be with you forever; <u>that is the Spirit of truth</u>, whom the world cannot receive, because it does not see Him or know Him, but you know Him because He abides with you and will be in you. "I will not leave you as orphans; I will come to you . . . But the Helper, the Holy Spirit, <u>whom the Father will send in My name</u>, He will teach you all things, and bring to your remembrance all that I said to you."*
>
> John 14:16-18, 26

Now the time was drawing near for the fulfillment of the promise concerning the divine Helper, and Christ instructed His disciples to wait in the city of Jerusalem until He, the Holy Spirit of truth, should arrive. This specific instruction was very significant for at least three reasons—namely, (1) there could be no kingdom expansion without supernatural induction—humanity was woefully inadequate and insufficient for the kingdom assignment; (2) the disciples (the eye-witnesses) were not ready to be clothed with, nor were they able to handle, the power that the Holy Spirit was designated to bring to them; and (3) kingdom restoration had to begin first in Jerusalem, but it certainly was not to stop there. The disciples asked: *"Lord, is it at this time You are restoring the kingdom to Israel?"* Jesus replied and said to them:

> *"It is not for you to know times or epoch which the Father has fixed by His own authority; <u>but you shall receive **power** when the Holy Spirit has come upon you; and you shall be My witnesses both in Jerusalem, and in all Judea and Samaria, and even to the remotest part of the earth</u>."*

Acts 1:7, 8

Up to that time, the disciples still held the nationalistic view of kingdom privatization, but Christ did not allow Himself to be drawn into Jewish political ambitions. Instead, He was very straightforward in pointing His disciples' attention to the promised "Blessing" and the kingdom mission. *"You shall receive* power," He said. The kingdom of God is never without power and dominion. When John the Baptist and Christ came preaching the *"kingdom of heaven is at hand,"* they were both clothed with power from the womb (Luke 1:15, 35). Unlike John, Christ did not only proclaim the kingdom of heaven; He was its living representative. When Christ arrived, the kingdom of heaven arrived, for He is the totality of the kingdom of heaven, and without Him there is no kingdom. The kingdom came in power and dominion and cannot advance without the same, and everyone who is called to proclaim its tenets must be clothed with that same power from on high. Hence, the disciples had to wait to receive that supernatural endowment.

These important truths need to be fully understood and incorporated into the experience of all who profess to be followers of Christ. Firstly, the instruction and the power are given to *witnesses*—those who experience the reality of the Messiah and the power of His ministry. If you consider yourself to be a witness of Christ, then this instruction, along with the power, is pertinent to you. Secondly, this power does not exist in isolation in any believer. Only God possesses power in isolation. He is power all by Himself, for all power resides in Him. However, whenever He dispenses His power or shares it with an inferior (be it angel or humankind), it is always with a purpose.

Notice again Jesus' parting words to His disciples: "*You shall receive* power . . . and *you shall be* My witnesses . . . (Acts 1:8). In other words, the power is given for the specific purpose of bearing witness to the Life (Acts 5:20) and ministry of Jesus, God's Messiah. Thirdly, the promise of power is given to the *witnesses* who wait for it. In our secular age of high speed electronics, convenient drive-through, à la carte service menus, and instantaneous self-gratification, all who are called to proclaim the gospel of the kingdom must discipline themselves to wait before the Majesty of heaven to be clothed with the power from on high.

Although we live in a post-Pentecost era, the Holy Spirit does not clothe every "willy-nilly" who runs about professing to proclaim the kingdom he/she knows precious little about. How often our humanity gets in the way of the mission of Christ, making of non-effect the gospel that is equipped to transform the lives of sinners. How many are running in the "power" of their humanity—academic achievements, material wealth, religious and institutional endorsements, generational legacies, and so forth—because waiting is not a line item of their ambitious agenda or list of to-do's? Paul characterizes this phenomenon as *a form of godliness without power* (2 Timothy 3:1-5), and as a sign to be avoided (along with many others) in the perilous times of these last days.

However, in the kingdom of God and the plan of heaven, the reception of power must be preceded by the discipline of patience — waiting for the Holy Spirit instead of running before Him. Additionally, the instruction to wait was not a request to just sit idly by, hoping for something to happen. Power is given to those disciples who are waiting with a purpose. There are so many professed believers who just sit in churches week after week, just waiting and hoping for that "big" miracle, or spiritual break-through to happen. Christ's call to wait is a call to prayer, deep soul-searching, heart-felt confession of sin and repentance. It is a call to mend brokenness and broken relationships; to cultivate the fellowship of praise and the Christ-centered consciousness for saving lost humanity.

Ready for *"THIS"*

Luke reported that after the disciples received their last instruction from Jesus, *they returned to Jerusalem with great joy and were continually in the temple praising God* (Luke 24:52, 53). These transformed men and women were no longer characterized by fear and apprehension, but they were filled with faith and anticipation as they looked forward to the reception of the precious Gift from heaven. Greatly encouraged by their Master's last words and this promise, they all returned to Jerusalem with ecstatic joy and great rejoicing. Their protracted strife for supremacy, driven by their selfish ambitions for positions of power in the "kingdom of Israel," was already shattered by the arrest, suffering and crucifixion of the One they had hoped would be their king. However, their resurrected Lord gave them a renewed perspective on the true nature of His kingdom and the role they were expected to play in its advancement.

In full assurance of faith and obedience to their Master's

command, these impassioned disciples gathered in the upper room where they once huddled together in fear and abandonment (John 20:19). This time they gathered with one mind and heart, and devoted themselves continually to prayer and praise in the Spirit. Luke said:

> *"These all with one mind were continually devoting themselves to prayer, along with the women, and Mary the mother of Jesus, and with His brothers."*
>
> Acts 1:14

Through this experience, the disciples became a fully united group, drawn together by their common love for, and devotion to Christ, weighted by a common burden for lost humanity, and driven by the common desire to advance the kingdom of heaven. Thus, by the time the day of Pentecost came, *they were all with one accord and in one place* (Acts 2:1, KJV). Then it happened! Suddenly! From out of nowhere in the heavens, there was a powerful explosion, as a mighty rush of air engulfed the house, and the appearance of tongues of fire rested on every disciple in the room.

In full recognition of the disciples' readiness, and in fulfillment of the promise, the Holy Spirit took possession of all the disciples and gave them the ability to speak in other dialects, foreign to their mother tongue. Clothed with new power from above and brimming with excitement from the revelations of their risen Lord, these energized men and women poured into the streets of Jerusalem and headed towards the temple, praising God in the dialects of the countless pilgrims that converged upon the city to celebrate the religious festivals.

In wonder and amazement, people from all quarters of the Roman Empire and beyond, heard the wonderful news of the risen Christ in their native tongue, and were in great perplexity as to the meaning of this mysterious event. They turned to one another and asked the million-dollar question: *What meaneth "THIS"* (Acts 2:12,

KJV)? In response to their inquiry, Peter stood up and seized the opportunity to preach the gospel with unmistakable clarity and convincing power. He began by saying:

> *"Fellow Jews and all of you who live in Jerusalem, let me explain THIS to you; listen carefully to what I say. These men are not drunk, as you suppose. It's only nine in the morning! No, THIS is what was spoken by the prophet Joel: 'In the last days, God says, I will pour out my spirit on all people. Your sons and daughters will prophesy, your young men will see visions, your old men will dream dreams. Even on my servants, both men and women, I will pour out my Spirit in those days, and they will prophesy.'"*

Acts 2:14-18, NIV

Obviously, the Jewish leaders and the visiting masses that gathered in the temple were not ready for the *"THIS"* that Peter was about to explain, for they were not attuned to the divine frequency and completely misinterpreted the meaning of the supernatural visitation. Although Joel's prophecy was a well-known vignette in Israel's historical rehearsals, and Pentecost was a yearly ritual celebration, both priests and people were completely unaware of heaven's agenda.

Had the chosen people of God not rejected and crucified the Holy One who was the total embodiment of all their feasts and ceremonies, they would have known the time and meaning of *"THIS"* visitation. Now the crucified One, through His promised Spirit, was establishing a whole new order of operation for accomplishing God's eternal plan of redemption for humanity. By empowering His disciples, Christ was making null and void Israel's system of religion that had shut up the kingdom of heaven against men and women, and He was opening up a new and living way (faith in Him alone) to give all sinners unfettered access to the merits of His sacrifice. What a wise and loving God!

Unmistakably, Pentecost was a landmark experience for the church. It did not only represent the beginning of a new evangelistic era through the omnipotent ministry of the Holy Spirit, but, more so, it symbolized the divine endorsement of the kingdom movement that was about to change the course of human history. It was the inauguration of a free, radical, discipling community (John 8:31-36), unleashed by its Founder, to revolutionize the world through the foolishness of preaching and its dynamic, persuasive, Christ-centered witness.

Peter's powerful preaching on the day of Pentecost added over three thousand precious souls to the community of believers, and these converts adopted the same "upper-room" spirit of praise, prayer, fellowship, and one-mindedness that characterized the disciples prior to their heavenly anointing. Moreover, the spirit of genuine discipleship was transferred from believer to believer as the Lord daily added to the church and the kingdom those who were being saved (Acts 2:41-47).

David's Kingdom Legacy

It was necessary for the kingdom witness to begin first in Jerusalem in order for the promise that God made to His servant David to be fulfilled:

> *"For the sake of David Your servant, do not turn away the face of Your anointed. <u>The LORD has sworn to David a truth from which He will not turn back</u>: <u>Of the fruit of your body I will set upon our throne</u>. If your sons will keep My covenant And My testimony which I will teach them, their sons also shall sit upon your throne forever. <u>For the LORD has chosen Zion; He has desired it for His habitation</u>. This is My*

> *resting place forever; Here I will dwell, for I have desired it. . . There I will cause the horn of David to spring forth; I have prepared a lamp for Mine anointed. His enemies I will clothe with shame, but upon himself <u>his crown shall shine</u>."*
>
> Psalm 132:11-18

As the "fruit" of David's body and God's Anointed King, Christ came to Zion (another name for Jerusalem, as is also the City of David), to establish forever the kingdom of David among the chosen people of God. But they rejected the Holy One of Israel and chose the throne of Caesar (John 19:15) in His place. What the Jewish people did not fully understand was that through the eternal covenant made in the council of heaven before the foundation of the world, the kingdom of heaven and the kingdom of David were one and the same kingdom.

The kingdom of heaven was extended through the God-man alliance initiated in Eden, but got infiltrated by the enemy through the fall. Now that same kingdom was being restored through the coming of the Son of David, even Jesus Christ. Jerusalem (the City of David) was intended to be the "type" (or figure) to the "New Jerusalem" that the apostle John saw coming down from God out of the heavens (Revelation 21:1, 2)—the very center of God's redemptive operations for the salvation of all mankind. Moreover, the son of David (Jesus) was not only a "Man-King," but He was also the "God-King"—fully man, yet fully God all at the same time. Israel's failure to recognize the time of her visitation prevented the nation from fulfilling her God-given assignment and from achieving the kingdom dominance and glory that God had promised His servant David. Paul reminded the early believers, just as he reminds us today, of the following truth:

> *"For you have not come to a mountain that can be*

touched and to a blazing fire, and to darkness and gloom and whirlwind, and to the blast of a trumpet and the sound of words which sound was such that those who heard begged that no further word be spoken to them. For they could not bear the command, 'IF EVEN A BEAST TOUCHES THE MOUNTAIN, IT WILL BE STONED.' And so terrible was the sight, that Moses said, 'I AM FULL OF FEAR and trembling.' <u>But you have come to Mount Zion and to the city of the living God, the heavenly Jerusalem</u>, and to myriads of angels, <u>to the general assembly and church of the firstborn who are enrolled in heaven</u>, and to God, the Judge of all, and to the spirits of the righteous made perfect, and to Jesus, the mediator of a new covenant, and to the sprinkled blood, which speaks better than the blood of Abel."

Hebrews 12:18-24

A few points of interest need to be noted here. First of all, Paul compares two mountains: Mount Sinai, the abode of the old covenant, and Mount Zion, the "stone" that grew into the mountain of God—even the New Jerusalem that houses the new and better covenant. He also compares the approaches of two people—Israel, under Moses approaching Sinai with great fear and trembling, and the church of the firstborn, under Christ, coming with joy and boldness before God and the heavenly assembly through the redemptive blood of Jesus, our Mediator. The focus of the citizens of the kingdom should no longer be on the "old" Israel and Jerusalem of the Middle East, but on the "new" Israel (called the general assembly and church of the firstborn) and the heavenly Jerusalem.

This church of the firstborn (Colossians 1:18) is a unique expression that has it roots in Christ, its Head and elder Brother of the Father's new creation of born-again children (Hebrews 2:8-18).

These precious ones, Paul says, are enrolled, not in the books of men upon the earth (even though some names may be there), but in heaven itself, where the records are not subject to the erroneous, self-righteous standards and scrutiny of fallen humanity. Praise the name of Jesus!

> *"For our citizenship is in heaven, from which also we eagerly wait for a Savior, the Lord Jesus Christ; who will transform the body of our humble state into conformity with the body of His glory, by the exertion of the power that He has even to subject all things to Himself."*
>
> Philippians 3:20

Now, we who live after the cross and Pentecost, have been made partakers of David's kingdom legacy through the blood of Christ (Acts 2:39). Paul admonishes us to remember that at one time we were:

> *"separated from the Christ, excluded from the commonwealth (citizenry) of Israel and strangers to the covenant of promise, having no hope and without God in the world. But now in Christ Jesus you who formerly were far off have been brought near by the blood of Christ. . . So then you are no longer strangers and aliens, but you are fellow citizens with the saints, and are of God's household."*
>
> Ephesians 2:12-19

All glory to God! What we have lost in Adam, we have now gained in Christ our Lord. Just as Adam was created a king to have dominion and rule over the whole earth and all it contained, so it was that Christ, through His virgin birth, was born a King in the City of David to rule over the house of Jacob forever (see Luke 1:31-33; 2:11; Matthew 2:1-3). Christ was born to reign and rule! When Pilate asked Jesus if He were a king, Jesus answered and said: *"You are right in saying I am a king. In fact, <u>for this reason I was born</u>, and for this I came into the world, to testify to the truth. Everyone on the side of truth listens to me"* (John 18:37). Jesus came into this world not only to die as the Lamb of God for our sins but also, through sacrifice and death, to live, reign and rule over the everlasting kingdom of David.

It is very important for all to understand at this point that "kingship" is not a "vote-right" but a "birthright." It is not acquired through the ballots of an electorate, an act of parliament, or the consensus of public opinion. Rather "kingship" is the transferred right of a royal lineage. Only a king can give birth to a king. Christ, as the second Adam, was born a king, only because David, His father (speaking only in the earthly sense, because Christ literally pre-existed David—Matthew 22:42-45) was a king. And David became a king only because God appointed him king. Only God has the divine right to appoint someone else as king, because He alone is the Creator and Ruler of all things visible and invisible (Psalm 24:1, 2).

David was not born to royalty. Not one drop of royal blood flowed through his veins; but God made him king because he shared God's heart. When God removed David's predecessor for his selfish disobedience, he declared through the prophet Samuel: *"I have found David son of Jesse <u>a man after my own heart</u>; he will do everything I want him to do"* (Acts 13:22; 1 Samuel 13:14). Although He did not inherit a royal lineage, David possessed a king's spirit. A king, in the divine sense, was a spiritual leader, compassionate benefactor, provider, protector and defender (Psalm 89:18) of all his citizens. David was all that and more. Thus, this son of Jesse was the only king in human history who truly received his kingship through divine right. All other historical kings who claimed this superior title did so by ambitious, earthly assumption and rule of power. Through the incomprehensible mercy of God, David became the possessor of royal seed, and from the loins of this man after God's own heart came Jesus, the Anointed One.

As the second Adam and Son of David, Christ, through His cross, completely nullified the curse of sin, and all its deadly derivations against the Adamic family. He now lives as God's *firstborn from the dead* (Colossians 1:18) and Father of a new Adamic race that will reign in life with Him forever (see 1 Corinthians 15:20-26). Paul further testifies to this fact in his letter to the church at Rome:

> *"Nevertheless <u>death reigned</u> from Adam until Moses, even over those who had not sinned in the likeness of the offense of <u>Adam, who is a type of Him who was to come</u>. But the free gift is not like the transgression. For if by the transgression of the one the many died, much more did the grace of God and the gift by the grace of the one Man, Jesus Christ, abound to the many. The gift is not like that which came through the one who sinned; for on the one hand the judgment arose from one transgression resulting in condemnation, but on the other hand the free gift arose from many transgressions resulting in justification.*
>
> *For if by the transgression of the one, <u>death reigned</u> through the one, much more those who receive the abundance of grace and of the gift of righteousness <u>will reign in life</u> through the One, Jesus Christ. So then as through one transgression there resulted condemnation to all men, even so through one act of righteousness there resulted justification of life to all men.*
>
> *For as through the one man's disobedience the many were made sinners, even so through the*

obedience of the One the many will be made righteous. The Law came in so that the transgression would increase; but where sin increased, grace abounded all the more, so that, as <u>sin reigned in death</u>, even so <u>grace would reign through righteousness to eternal life</u> through Jesus Christ our Lord."

Romans 5:14-19

Throughout this passage Paul makes use of kingdom language. On account of the fall of the first Adam, death "reigned" over the human race, placing all under the dominion of its power. We were once the children of darkness (Ephesians 5:8), shut up in a kingdom of slavery and death; but through the grace of Christ and the efficacy of His cross, we, who were sometimes darkness are translated, by faith, in the kingdom of light. Now we "reign" in life through Jesus Christ our Lord. Paul says in Hebrews:

"Therefore, since the children share in flesh and blood, He Himself likewise also partook of the same, that through death He might render powerless him who had the power of death, that is, the devil, and <u>might free those who through fear of death were subject to slavery all their lives</u>."

Hebrews 2:14, 15

Therefore, we no longer live in slavery to sin or death, but reign in dominion and victory over sin and the grave (Romans 6:12, 14), for God has *delivered us from the domain of darkness, and transferred us to the kingdom of His beloved Son* (Colossians 1:13). The unmistakable truth is that on His cross, Christ did not only die for us; Christ died as us. *I was crucified with Christ: nevertheless I live, yet not I, but Christ liveth in me: and the life which I now live in the flesh I live by the faith of the Son of God, who loved me, and gave Himself for me* (Galatians 2:20, KJV). When Christ was buried, we were buried, and when He rose from the dead, so did we; and our water baptism bears testimony of these truths (Roman 6:4-7).

Paul, in his letter to the Ephesians, said that when we were dead in our trespasses and sins God had made us alive <u>together with</u> Christ, and raised us up <u>with Him</u>, and seated us <u>with Him</u> in the heavenly places in Christ Jesus (Ephesians 2:4-7). Now, because He lives, we live. Because He reigns, we also reign, for we are a kingdom of royal priesthood, a chosen race, a holy nation and a people for God's own possession (1 Peter 2:9). This is the gospel of the kingdom and Pentecost came to give power to the witness of the same.

Consequently, the kingdom explosion and the proclamation of the life-changing gospel of the risen Christ had to begin in Jerusalem, for it was heaven's purpose to restore true kingdom consciousness to the City of David. The people of Israel had to recognize and come to grips with the truth that the One they had crucified between two malefactors was, indeed, their King, the Son of David, even God's Messiah. Shiloh had come to Israel and she knew it not. God needed a witness to these happenings and He, most certainly, had one. Peter declared at Pentecost:

> *"Men of Israel, listen to these words: Jesus the Nazarene, a man attested to you by God with miracles and wonders and signs which God performed through Him in your midst, just as you yourselves know—this Man, delivered over by the predetermined plan and foreknowledge of God, you nailed to a cross by the hands of godless men and put Him to death. But God raised Him up again, putting an end to the agony of death, since it was impossible for Him to be held in its power."*
>
> *"For David says of Him, 'I SAW THE LORD ALWAYS IN MY PRESENCE; FOR HE IS AT MY*

RIGHT HAND, SO THAT I WILL NOT BE SHAKEN. 'THEREFORE MY HEART WAS GLAD AND MY TONGUE EXULTED; MOREOVER MY FLESH ALSO WILL LIVE IN HOPE; BECAUSE YOU WILL NOT ABANDON MY SOUL TO HADES, NOR ALLOW YOUR HOLY ONE TO UNDERGO DECAY. ..' "This Jesus God raised up again, <u>to which we are all witnesses</u>. Therefore having been exalted to the right hand of God, and having received from the Father the promise of the Holy Spirit, He has poured forth THIS which you both see and hear.

"For it was not David who ascended into heaven, but he himself says: 'THE LORD SAID TO MY LORD, SIT AT MY RIGHT HAND, UNTIL I MAKE YOUR ENEMIES A FOOTSTOOL FOR YOUR FEET.' Therefore let all the house of Israel <u>know for certain</u> that God has made Him both Lord and Christ—this Jesus whom you crucified."

Acts 2:22-36

After Pentecost, the disciples and the church were never the same. Neither was Jerusalem! What happened in the city was not done in a little corner, for the Holy Spirit announced His presence in a dramatic, undeniable way. The Pentecostal wave was sweeping through the house of Israel with signs and wonders, and many of the dwellers of Jerusalem were captured in its wake. Luke explains: *And at the hand of the apostles many signs and wonders were taking place among the people; and they were all with <u>one accord</u> in Solomon's portico. . . and all the more believers in the Lord, multitudes of men and women were constantly added to their* number (Acts 5:12, 14).

After Peter preached his second sermon, an additional five thousand men (not counting women and children) believed the gospel. Certainly, the kingdom of heaven had come to Jerusalem, and leaders and rulers were powerless in their attempts to contain its explosive growth. In absolute frustration and complete derision, Annas, the high priest, uttered the ultimate truth in his attempt to silence the authoritative witness of Peter and John: "*. . . you have filled Jerusalem with your teaching, and intend to bring this man's blood upon us*" (Acts 5:28). *And the word of God kept on spreading; and the number of the disciples continued to increase greatly in Jerusalem, and a great many of the priests were becoming obedient to the faith* (Acts 6:7).

Kingdom Beyond Israel and Judaism

. . . and you shall be My witnesses both in Jerusalem, and in all Judea and Samaria, and even to the remotest part of the earth.

Acts 1:8

Indeed, God had found Himself living witnesses in the City of David, through the life-changing testimonies of the disciples of Jesus. The gospel of the kingdom had shaken the very foundations of the Jewish economy as the victorious name of Jesus became the battle cry and rallying point for deliverance and salvation, miraculous signs and wonders, and for the explosive growth of new communities of believers throughout Jerusalem. However, what started in Jerusalem was not intended to end in Jerusalem. Jesus told His disciples that their witness of His life and the kingdom must start at Jerusalem and expand to Judea, Samaria and to the ends of the earth. This command is a clear fulfillment of Daniel's prophetic word regarding the "growing stone" that was cut out ("without hands") of the side of the mountain, and mushroomed to fill whole earth (Daniel 2:.34, 35, 44, 45).

Prior to Pentecost, the disciples shared the dream that was a source of pride of every Israelite—the City of David, even Jerusalem, would rise to political dominance over Rome and the entire world. Consequently, they had posed the loaded question to Jesus: *"Lord is it at this time You are restoring the kingdom of Israel"* (Acts 1:6)? What the disciples had failed to understand, and what we must be constantly placed in remembrance of, is that the kingdom of heaven cannot be contained by the systems of man's religions. Judaism was infinitely too small, in every imaginable way, to place any boundaries or limitations on the kingdom of God.

In the very same way, all the post-modern "isms" are miserably inadequate to contain the "mysterious" church that Christ is building. The religions of men are too constricted and narrow to embrace all the possibilities and diversities that heaven sees in lost humanity. Hence, the reason Christ, and Him alone, can truly build His church and His kingdom, for should this eternally significant process be left to the fickle, self-righteous judgments of men and their systems, the plan of salvation would be placed in calamitous jeopardy.

We do not have to look very far to see the perennial tensions that developed in the early church between Jewish and Gentile Christians as each group jostled for its rightful place in the body of Christ and the kingdom of God. The Jewish Christians were still trying to claim sacred rights to the gospel of the kingdom through the imposition of religious customs upon their Gentile brethren, but God was already doing a new thing in Gentile communities beyond the Jewish world.

The gospel of the kingdom was not going to be defined by Jewish norms and standards of the "old" Israel, for Christ, through His cross, had liberated His church (the "new" Israel) from the bondage of the Jewish world and from the religious caricatures of our age. *"For all of you who have been baptized into Christ have clothed yourselves with Christ. There is neither Jew nor Greek, there is neither slave nor freeman, there is neither male nor female; for you are all one in Christ Jesus* (Galatians 3:27, 28; See also Colossians 3:10, 11). The church and the kingdom of heaven have room enough to embrace all, without any distinction.

Accordingly, the gospel we are called to preach must move us beyond the narrow confines of our traditions and practices, our cultural world view and ethnocentric expectations, our "precious" prejudices and religious biases. This gospel of the kingdom that Christ has called us to proclaim requires much more than preaching and teaching the fundamental doctrines of our Christian religions, much more than making converts to a particular brand of Christianity, and much more than building elaborate structures and multiplying our facilities. While the preaching of the kingdom's gospel may embrace all these things, there is yet a much higher purpose.

This gospel, which we are called to preach, must bear witness to kingdom imminence, dominion and authority in the earth; to the rulership, lordship and kingship of the exalted person and name of Jesus Christ; and to the power of God to liberate His estranged children from the kingdom of darkness and death, and to transfer them into the kingdom of light and life in Jesus Christ. These verities form the great themes of the gospel proclaimed by the apostolic church as it expanded rapidly beyond Jerusalem and throughout the Roman world. They bore testimonies to truths that now make us free—namely, the kingdom is here; Jesus is alive and well; we are delivered from sin through your faith in Him, and have authority over all the powers of the devil.

Persecution: A Tool for Expansion

The explosive growth of the early church and the kingdom of God was seen as a serious threat to the power structures of the Greco-Roman world, stirring up unwelcome and unfounded fears among the religious and political authorities. Moreover, this mounting phenomenon was making significant, hard-to-deny inroads into the kingdom of darkness as demons and devils recanted before the powerful, spirit-directed witness of the disciples. As a direct reaction to this Pentecostal wave that was sweeping everything in its path, the deadly alliance forged by the religio-political and underworld forces, unleashed systematic persecution upon the young, but mushrooming church. However, what the forces of evil designed to eradicate the body of Christ (called the "Way"), the Spirit of God used to facilitate and propel its growth and expansion. After the death of Stephen, open, barefaced persecution, spearheaded by Saul of Tarsus, broke out upon the church in Jerusalem.

> *"Saul was in hearty agreement with putting him to death. And on that day a great persecution began against the church in Jerusalem, and they were all scattered <u>throughout the regions of Judea and Samaria</u>, except the apostles.*
>
> *Some devout men buried Stephen, and made loud lamentation over him. But Saul began <u>ravaging the church, entering house after house</u>, and dragging off men and women, he would put them in prison.*
>
> *Therefore, those who had been scattered went about preaching the word. Philip went down to the city of Samaria and began proclaiming Christ to them. The crowds with one accord were giving attention to what was said by Philip, as they heard and saw the signs which he was performing. <u>For in the case of many who had unclean spirits, they were coming out of them shouting with a loud voice; and many who had been paralyzed and lame were healed</u>. So there was much rejoicing in that city."*

Acts 8:1-8

In His parting instructions, Christ specifically told His disciples that their witness to the gospel of the kingdom was to extend far beyond the borders of Jerusalem (Acts 1:8). However, the disciples did not envision that this expansion would be accelerated through the fires of persecution. The death of Stephen was not only a very powerful testimony for the gospel, but this open attack on this dynamic church leader ignited an inferno of hatred against the growing community. Saul, the silent supporter to Stephen's martyrdom, used this incident to fuel his self-righteous hostility towards the Way. He *began ravaging the church, entering house after house, and dragging off men and women* to put them in prison (Acts 8:5).

Providentially, the early church was not encumbered by the structures or bureaucracies that characterize the religious institutions of our day. The body of Christ was not housed in a particular edifice in some central location, making it a very vulnerable target for the enemy of the faith. Rather, the church was a growing network of dynamic house-fellowship communities, scattered through the city of Jerusalem. Thus, Saul was compelled to go from house to house in order to dislodge believers and carry them off to prison. Consequently, at a moment's notice, the church was poised to move from one place to the next, without breaking the rhythm of communal fellowship or vibrant proclamation of the gospel of the risen Christ. The Bible says that *those who were scattered went about preaching the word*, and *Philip went down to the city of Samaria and began proclaiming Christ to them* (Acts 8:4, 5). What a marvelous testimony and example for the body of Christ today!

The parting words of Jesus were fulfilled with pinpointed accuracy, for Samaria's time for hearing the gospel had come, through the arms of persecution, in the ministry of Philip. That city was never going to be the same again, for *when they believed Philip preaching the good news about the kingdom of God and the name of Jesus Christ, they were being baptized, men and women alike* (Acts 8:12). It is very interesting that the Samaritans, who were once separated from the commonwealth of Israel and isolated from the covenant of promise, were now beneficiaries and partakers of the new covenant, given to God's new Israel (the church) through the blood of Jesus Christ, its living Head. *And so, when they* (Philip,

Peter and John) *had solemnly testified and spoken the word of the Lord, they started back to Jerusalem, and were preaching the gospel to many villages of the Samaritans* (Acts 8:14, 25). Thus, *the church throughout all Judea and Galilee and Samaria enjoyed peace, being built up; and going on in the fear of the Lord and in the comfort of the Holy Spirit, it continued to increase* (Acts 9:31). All glory to God!

Breaking Barriers

Now, it was time to take the good news of the kingdom to the ends of the earth and the God of the kingdom was already paving the way for this to occur. While Philip, Peter and John were preaching the gospel to the Samaritans (en route to Jerusalem), an angel of the Lord spoke directly to Philip: *"Arise and go south to the road that descends from Jerusalem to Gaza"* (Acts 8:26). Kingdom expansion is God's business, and He will personally intervene, whenever necessary, to activate or accelerate the process. God was placing Philip in the path of an Ethiopian eunuch (a court official of Candace, queen of the Ethiopians) to show him that the gospel treasure in his possession, transcended all racial and ethnic distinctions he may encounter in his witness for the kingdom. The Almighty was initiating the crossing of all racial, religious and political divides, for He hath made of one blood (Adam) all nations of the earth (Acts 17:26), and through the blood of one man—even Jesus Christ, the last Adam—He intended to save all mankind (Romans 5:14-21; 1 Corinthians 15:22).

Thus, the Holy Spirit instructed Philip: *"Go up and join this chariot"* (Acts 8:29). As Philip followed through with the command, he heard the eunuch reading the prophecy of Isaiah concerning the suffering and death of the Messiah, and asked the eunuch if he understood what he was reading. This court official confessed his ignorance and invited Philip to sit beside him and teach him about the suffering Lamb of God. As Philip unfolded the Scriptures to the eunuch, the light of God began to shine in the soul of this seeker of truth. Then, along the way, God provided a spring in the heart of the desert and the eunuch, seizing the opportunity, immediately requested to be baptized in the name of Jesus. Philip replied: *"If you believe with all your heart, you may."* And he answered and said, *"I believe that Jesus Christ is the Son of God"* (Acts 8:37).

This confession was the very one made by Peter (Matthew 16:16) and came to the eunuch only through the revelation of the Holy Spirit. At that very moment, the eunuch was born into the kingdom of God and the body of Christ. He commanded his charioteer to stop the carriage, descended into the pool with Philip, and was baptized. The eunuch then went on his way rejoicing, taking with him the precious seed of the gospel to plant it among the people of his nation. Meanwhile, the Spirit whisked Philip away to continue preaching the gospel to all the cities from Azotus to Caesarea, Philippi (Acts 8:38-40).

The Gentile Apostle

While the Holy Spirit was extending the kingdom of God to regions way beyond Jerusalem, Saul was busy preparing for what was to be his last persecution run against the disciples of the Lord. He went to the high priest in Jerusalem to receive official warrants to arrest anyone in Damascus belonging to the Way, to bring them in bonds to Jerusalem (Acts 9:1, 2). As he journeyed toward his intended target, he was suddenly struck to the ground by a light which shone from heaven, and he heard a voice asking: *"Saul, Saul, why are you persecuting Me?"*

When Saul asked the "Me" to identify himself, the "Me" said: *"I am Jesus whom you are persecuting"* (verses 4, 5). Now this is very interesting. The first verse of Acts 9 says that Saul was persecuting the disciples of the Lord; the second verse says that he was in pursuit of those belonging to the Way. However, in the fourth and fifth verses Jesus clearly identified Himself as the one was being persecuted by Saul.

Therefore, it is most certainly evident that the disciples, the Way, and Jesus are all one and the same, and any attack on the disciples (the church) or the Way (the original name of Christ's followers) is a direct assault on the person of Jesus. Christ takes it very personal when anyone makes himself/herself an enemy of His body and seeks to bring harm to it in any way. He will show Himself strong whenever it suits His pleasure and purpose to do so. Saul had to learn by experience that it was painfully hard to kick against the pricks.

Undoubtedly, Saul was a rising opponent to the spread of the gospel of Jesus in the regions around Jerusalem, and many in the young church feared him. However, no weapon formed against the body of Christ will prosper, for the gates of hell cannot prevail against the church of the living God. Christ is both a barrier-breaker and a bridge-builder for the redemption of all mankind.

> *"For it was the Father's good pleasure for all the fullness to dwell in Him, and through Him to reconcile all things to Himself, having made peace through the blood of His cross; through Him, I say, whether things on earth or things in heaven. And although you were formerly alienated and hostile in mind, engaged in evil deeds, yet He has now reconciled you in His fleshly body through death, in order to present you before Him holy and blameless and beyond reproach."*
>
> Colossians 1:19-22

Through His infinite mercy and grace, Christ was able to break and transform Saul—the tool of fear and destruction in the hand of the devil—into an instrument of righteousness and a "slave" of the Lord, Jesus Christ. He became a fearless bridge-builder for the kingdom of God and an apostle to the Gentiles. In the process, Jesus gave Saul instructions regarding His servant Ananias, while at the same time, He was preparing Ananias to receive and minister to this former enemy of the church (Acts 9:6-12). The Lord said to Ananias: *"Go, for he is a chosen instrument of Mine, to bear My name before the Gentiles and kings and the sons of Israel; for I will show him how much he must suffer for My name's sake"* (Acts 9:15, 16). How marvelous indeed are the ways of God!

However, there was still a barrier of fear between the disciples at Jerusalem and the newly converted apostle to the Gentiles; but God took care of this inhibition through the ministry and endorsement of Barnabas, the son of consolation (Acts 9:26-28). Subsequently, the Holy Spirit forged such a strong bond between Barnabas and Saul that He personally confirmed their apostleship before the church at Antioch and separated them for ministry among the Gentiles, in regions far beyond Jerusalem and its environs (Acts 13:1, 2). It was after receiving this public divine endorsement that Saul of Tarsus became known as Paul, the Gentile apostle (v. 9).

Needless to say, he who was a slave for the kingdom of darkness, became the prisoner and bond-slave of his Lord Jesus Christ (Ephesians 4:1; Romans 1:1). Paul transferred his former zeal as a persecutor of Jesus (the Way) to his ordained apostleship (1 Corinthians 1:1). He even took his passion up many notches, to the point of death. Moreover, his ambitious mission was to proclaim the name of Jesus where it was never before heard. In his letter to the disciples in Rome, Paul wrote:

> *"But I have written very boldly to you on some points so as to remind you again, because of the grace that was given me from God, <u>to be a minister of Christ Jesus to the Gentiles</u>, ministering as a priest the gospel of God, so that my offering of the Gentiles may become acceptable, sanctified by the Holy Spirit.*
>
> *Therefore in Christ Jesus I have found reason*

for boasting in things pertaining to God. For I will not presume to speak of anything except what Christ has accomplished through me, resulting in the obedience of the Gentiles by word and deed, in the power of signs and wonders, in the power of the Spirit; so that from Jerusalem and round about as far as Illyricum I have fully preached the gospel of Christ.

And thus I aspired to preach the gospel, <u>not where Christ was already named</u>, so that I would not build on another man's foundation; but as it is written, "THEY WHO HAD NO NEWS OF HIM SHALL SEE, AND THEY WHO HAVE NOT HEARD SHALL UNDERSTAND."

Romans 15:15-21

Religion and Prejudice

Although open persecution of the church spread the gospel of the kingdom beyond Jerusalem, the early believers were not ready for all that Jesus, through the ministry of the Holy Spirit, was about to do in the Gentile world. These disciples of Jesus were still very much Jewish in their orientation and lifestyle. They were not spiritually mature enough to conceive or accept that the gospel they were called to proclaim would place the Gentiles on equal footing with them as co-beneficiaries of all the blessings of the new covenant they had received through the blood of Jesus Christ.

To the Jew, the Gentiles were an inferior race, and receiving the gospel of Jesus did not cancel their inferiority. Gentiles could only become second class citizens (or spiritually naturalized aliens, for the use more modern language) in the kingdom of God and could never be elevated to be called a seed of Abraham. Thus, religious pride and cultural prejudice were formidable barriers that posed a continuous threat to the mission assignment of the early church. While the disciples did not openly oppose the preaching of the gospel to the Gentiles, it would appear that the normal expectation was for the Gentiles to come to them. They did not think that they should keep company with, or go to, the homes of such foreigners (Acts 10:28, 29).

This prevailing, bigoted, Jewish mindset was the target of the Holy Spirit when He gave the first member and leader of Christ's church a very clear vision and reality check regarding the true purpose of Christ for His church and His kingdom. In his vision, Peter saw the sky open and a great sheet, supported from its four corners, lowered to the ground. In this sheet there were all manner of four-legged animals, crawling creatures and all types of birds, and Peter heard a voice inviting him to rise up and eat for he was really very hungry. However, Peter protested: *"By no means, Lord, for I have never eaten anything unholy or unclean"* (Acts 10:14).

Now, this is a very interesting comment by Peter. It suggests that Peter was very familiar with God's command regarding clean and unclean meats, given to the children of Israel through God's servant, Moses (See Leviticus 11 and Deuteronomy 14). God was using something with which Peter was very familiar to teach him a lesson about an important truth with which he was very much unfamiliar—taking His disciple from the known to the unknown. Therefore, the voice replied to Peter's refusal: *"What God has cleansed no longer consider unholy"* (Acts 10: 15). This was done three times and the sheet returned to heaven from whence it came.

Was Christ trying to teach Peter a lesson about clean and unclean meats? Absolutely not! Peter already knew the dietary code delivered through Moses, and that is why he was greatly perplexed as to the meaning of the vision. While Peter was still searching for understanding on the matter, the Holy Spirit had already provided the interpretation the day prior to his encounter. God is the prime Mover. He is the One who gives dreams and visions regarding His mysterious purposes in His great plan of redemption. He is the One who breaks down barriers of resistance to the gospel and builds bridges of peace and reconciliation among people who are estranged from one another. Thus, while Peter was pondering his vision, three Spirit-directed men from Cornelius' house were already standing at the door requesting an audience with him (Acts 10:17-19).

It is quite possible that the Roman centurion, Cornelius, was influenced in some way by Philip's evangelistic exploits in the region of Caesarea, Philippi (Acts 8:40). Nonetheless, this Gentile soldier was a God-fearing man with a prayerful attitude and a compassionate, benevolent spirit. God honored his earnest quest for righteousness by bringing him in contact with Peter. The angel of the Lord instructed Cornelius to send men to Joppa to invite Peter to bring the gospel of the risen Christ to his house. So, while the three men stood at the gate to Simon's house, the Spirit of God said to Peter: "*Behold, three men are looking for you. But arise, go downstairs, and accompany them without misgivings; for I have sent them Myself*" (Acts 10:19, 20). The Holy Spirit had to neutralize Peter's Jewish mind-set in preparation for the ministry he was to perform among Gentiles in the home of Cornelius.

When Peter got to Cornelius' house, he found a large number of people eagerly waiting to hear him, and he began his discourse with the open confession:

> "*You yourselves know how unlawful it is for a man who is a Jew to associate with a foreigner or to visit him; and yet God has shown me that I should not call any man unholy or unclean. That is why I came without even raising any objection when I was sent for. . . . I most certainly understand now that God is not one to show partiality, but in every nation the man who fears Him and does what is right is welcome to Him.*"
>
> Acts 10:28, 29, 34, 35

However, long before Peter arrived, God was already there, preparing Cornelius' household for the new revelation of Jesus Christ. God was already making preparations for kingdom expansion among the Gentiles. Therefore, as Peter was addressing the assembly, *the Holy Spirit fell upon all those who were listening to the message, and all the Jewish believers who accompanied Peter were amazed, because the gift of the Holy Spirit had been poured out upon the Gentiles also; for they were hearing them speaking in tongues and glorifying God* (Acts 10:44-46).

Through this repetition of the Pentecostal outpouring, God was making a very clear statement to the Jewish believers then, and to all succeeding generations who might choose to adopt their bigoted, nationalistic or ethno-centric mind-set. While He (God) might choose to work through humanity to accomplish His purposes, He would not allow the human elements of race, religion, culture, wealth, or any other earth-bound influence to cut, shape, or control the "mysterious stone" of His kingdom. Building His church and growing His kingdom is Christ's work, not man's, and it is marvelous in the sight of men.

It is very interesting, yet disconcerting, that when Peter returned from his visit to Cornelius, the believers in Jerusalem who were of the circumcision took serious issues with Peter for visiting the "uncircumcised" and eating with them (Acts 11:1-3). These men were still trying to mold, or more accurately, smother the new kingdom movement, the Way, with their Jewish traditions. They were not rejoicing over the fact that Gentile sinners were on par with them in coming to salvation the very way they did, through Jesus Christ. Rather, they were annoyed by the fact that Peter kept company and fellowship with them.

This selfish, arrogant attitude was the sad reflection of the influence of the leaven of the Scribes and Pharisees that had permeated the very psyche of the Jewish people, for these believers echoed the very words of their "former" self-righteous teachers: *"This man (Jesus) receives sinners and eats with them"* (Luke 15:1,

2). How insidious the baggage of religious and cultural prejudice can be, even among professed Christians! It was not until Peter ended his testimony of God's grace among the Gentiles with the following very cogent question that the believers of the circumcision conceded their position and pretended to give glory to God.

> "_Therefore if God gave to them the same gift as He gave to us also after believing in the Lord Jesus Christ, who was I that I could stand in God's way?_" When they heard this, they quieted down and glorified God, saying, "Well then, God has granted to the Gentiles also the repentance that leads to life."
>
> Acts 11:17, 18

The Kingdom of the FREE!

Although Peter's powerful testimony about God's confirming the Gentiles in the faith of Jesus Christ had quelled the poison of prejudice for a moment, many of the believers who went to Phoenicia, Cyprus and Antioch because of persecution, were proclaiming the word only to Jews and Jews alone (Acts 11:19). However, the Spirit of God was working mightily with those who chose to take the gospel to Gentile communities, so much so that the rapid growth of the church among the Gentiles sparked great jealousy among the Jews. As a result, many Jewish believers took it upon themselves to subvert the teachings of Paul and Barnabas, following them from place to place, stirring up the minds of the Gentiles against these servants of God, and inciting rebellion in the churches and cities (Acts 13:44-46; 14:1-19).

On one occasion, brethren from the Jerusalem circumcision tried to impose, through their teachings, this Jewish rite upon Gentile believers in Galatia (now southern Turkey), which was a Roman province stretching from Lycaonia, Iconium, and parts of Phrygia and Pisidia. That incident precipitated such great dissension and unending debate among the disciples that the situation had to be settled by the most authoritative body of the early church—the first apostles and elders of the Jerusalem council (Acts 15:1-35).

Without a doubt, the gospel of the risen Christ and the rapidly growing kingdom of the free were creating mental distress and frustration among those who held sacred the passing traditions of a religion of works and restrictions. However, the enemy of Christ had planted a pernicious seed of resistance among the kingdom citizenry (see Matthew 13:24-30, 36-43). That seed became rooted within the believing community, sprouting diverse blossoms of teachings and traditions that have yielded the fruit of religious confusion that we still see among professed Christians today. Jesus said that the children of the kingdom and the children of the evil one will coexist until the time of harvest, at the end of the age (Matthew 13:30). This will be addressed more fully in chapter seven.

Nevertheless, during the days of his ministry, the apostle Paul continually and consistently addressed the Jewish religious imprints that frustrated the faith of early Gentile believers. These religious imprints are still dogging the body of Christ today. Paul's letter to the church in Galatia was a strong reaction to the influence of "Christian" Judaizers who were unsettling the fragile faith of new converts. In the fourth chapter of this letter, especially verses 21 through 31, he clinches his argument by making use of powerful symbolism to portray the legacy of the two covenants in the figures of Hagar, who represented Mt. Sinai and present Jerusalem, and Sarah, who represented Mt. Zion and the New Jerusalem. Through this literary device, Paul makes the incontrovertible point that just as the enemy of Christ planted the seed of the bond woman (Hagar) within Abraham's house to contend with the seed of faith through the free woman (Sarah), so he has also planted the tares of slave disciples within the kingdom field to choke the freedom of its citizens. All this in his continuous attempt to keep God's blood-bought children in absolute bondage and hopeless fear.

> *"Now this Hagar is Mount Sinai in Arabia and corresponds to the present Jerusalem, for she is in slavery with her children. But the Jerusalem above is free; she is our mother. For it is written, "REJOICE, BARREN WOMAN WHO DOES NOT BEAR; BREAK FORTH AND SHOUT, YOU WHO ARE NOT IN LABOR; FOR MORE NUMEROUS ARE THE CHILDREN OF THE DESOLATE THAN OF THE ONE WHO HAS A HUSBAND."*
>
> *And you brethren, like Isaac, are children of promise. <u>But as at that time he who was born according to the flesh persecuted him who was born according to the Spirit, so it is now also</u>."*
>
> Galatians 4:25-29

Today, some two thousand years later, many are still trying to frustrate the spiritual experience of the free citizens of the kingdom of heaven—the New Jerusalem. They spy out their liberties which they have in Christ Jesus, in order to bring them under a yoke of bondage, through the vain philosophies of men and their systems of religion (Galatians 2:5). The children of works (slavery) are still striving with the children of promise in post-Modern Christianity, trying to impose the requirements and traditions of men upon those who embrace the finished work of Christ as the means for their salvation. They repeatedly use external rules as control mechanisms to regulate behavior and to bring conformity to a particular religious culture.

By doing this, they fail to trust in God's grace, operating through the power of Christ's incorruptible seed-life, to teach believers to deny ungodliness and worldly lusts, and to live soberly, righteously and godly in this present world (Titus 2:11, 12). In this regard, Paul's warning to the church at Colossae to be on guard for those who seek to propagate a system of bondage and slavery within the body of Christ is also very pertinent to us today.

> *"See to it that no one takes you captive through philosophy and empty deception, <u>according to the tradition of men</u>, according to the elementary principles of the world, <u>rather than according to Christ</u>. For <u>in Him all the fullness of Deity dwells in bodily form</u>, and <u>in Him you have been made complete</u>, and <u>He is the head over all rule and authority</u>."*
>
> Colossians 2:8-10

Therefore, as far as salvation and the entire Christian experience are concerned, the "buck" begins and ends with Christ, for He is the embodiment of God's total mystery, the Reservoir of all the treasures of wisdom and knowledge (vv. 2, 3), and the Head over all rule and authority (v. 10). As we, therefore, have received the Lord, Jesus Christ, so we are to continue walking (really living) in (and with) Him (v. 6), for the incorruptible seed of Christ's life in us is the complete personification of all that the Law or the Word of God demands. It is the principle of the Spirit of righteousness operating in this life (Christ's seed life in us) that has set us free from the law of sin and death resident in our Adamic nature (Romans 8:2).

The Bible says that *it was for freedom that Christ set us free; therefore keep standing firm and do not be subject again to a yoke of slavery* (Galatians 5:1). In other words, do not allow anyone or any system of religion to impose any man-made traditions or requirements upon you as a prerequisite for salvation or for membership into their religious communities. In the same measure that the Word of God is not bound (2 Timothy 2:9), so also are the citizens of the kingdom who are reproduced by that Word. So what does the Word of God say?

"CAST OUT THE BONDWOMAN AND HER SON, FOR THE SON OF THE BONDWOMAN SHALL NOT BE AN HEIR WITH THE SON OF THE FREE WOMAN. So then, brethren, we are not children of a bondwoman, but of the free woman."

Verses 30, 31

Without any doubt, the kingdom of heaven is the kingdom of the free, for whosoever the Son makes free shall be free indeed (John 8:36)!

ATTACKS ON THE KINGDOM

6

"If the world hates you, you know that it has hated Me before it hated you. If you were of the world, the world would love its own; but because you are not of the world, but I chose you out of the world, because of this the world hates you. Remember the word that I said to you, 'A slave is not greater than his master.' If they persecuted Me, they will also persecute you; if they kept My word, they will keep yours also. But all these things they will do to you for My name's sake, because they do not know the One who sent Me."

John 15:18-21

Christ Confronts Caesar

Through the Spirit-led (Acts 13:2), expanding ministry of Paul and his associates (like Silas and Barnabas) the gospel of the kingdom was carried to Europe and Asia Minor (Acts 16-20) in rapid pace, but not without many trials and hardships. In his farewell message to the leaders of the churches in the region, this faithful apostle of the Gentiles reminded them:

"You yourselves know, from the first day that I set foot in Asia, how I was with you the whole time, serving the Lord with all humility and <u>with tears and with trials which came upon me through the plots of the Jews</u>; how I did not shrink from declaring to you anything that was profitable, and teaching you

publicly and from house to house, solemnly testifying to both Jews and Greeks of repentance toward God and faith in our Lord Jesus Christ. . . And now, behold, I know that all of you, among whom I went about <u>preaching the kingdom</u>, will see my face no more. Therefore I testify to you this day that I am innocent of the blood of all men."

Acts 20:18-26

Paul also forewarned the leaders to be on the alert for external and internal threats, from malicious wolves and false brethren who would seek to attack the flock and draw away weak disciples among them (vv. 29-30). These warnings were not far-fetched or unnecessary, because evil forces were already at work seeking to undermine the faith of believers and restrain the growth of the young church. Christian Judaizers were a present threat, attempting to undo the work of the apostle. However, the church was growing so rapidly that it quickly moved beyond Jewish communities and became prevailingly non-Jewish as it expanded its network of believers throughout the Greco-Roman world.

As believers began multiplying, and as the church became a notable presence in the public domain, its surprising growth and influence began to spark jealousy and hatred among Jews and pagans alike. Very soon the body of Christ became the center of public criticism, the target of false accusations, and a magnet for indiscriminate persecution. All these negative reactions were grounded in the fear that a strangely powerful, dynamic force had entered the public domain that was characterized by a very unstable economic and political order. Consequently, the growing networks of these "foreign" communities were viewed as a threat to the existing social structures.

A most dominant fear was that Christians did not only abstain from social customs that many believed held the fabric of the society together, but they also denounced the pagan practices as demonic and sinful. Many saw Christianity as an evil force of disequilibrium operating within the society and began to blame Christians as the primary cause for any adverse event that affected the normal course of community life. Bruce L. Shelley shed some light on this situation in his quote from Tertullian's *Apology*: "If the Tiber floods the city, or if the Nile refuses to rise, or if the sky withholds its rain, if there is an earthquake, a famine, a pestilence, at once the cry is raised: 'Christians to the lions.'"[1] Christians were thrown wholesale to wild beasts in blind judgment as the single cause for societal ills.

Indeed, the kingdom of light had entered the kingdom of darkness, and the witness of its powerful rays was creating major discomfort among the masses, for *men love darkness more than light because their deeds are evil* (John 3:19). How poignantly accurate are the words of Jesus: "*If you were of the world, the world would love its own; but because you are not of the world, but I chose you out of the world, because of this the world hates you*" (John 15:19). Tertullian wrote: "We have this reputation of living aloof from the crowds."[2] A difference in life-style at any level of society has a tendency to attract envy, jealousy, discrimination and hatred. As it was then, so it is even today; but Jesus encourages all His would-be disciples:

> "*Blessed are you when people insult you and persecute you, and falsely say all kinds of evil against you because of Me. Rejoice and be glad, for your reward in heaven is great; for in the same way they persecuted the prophets who were before you.*"
>
> Matthew 5:11, 12

Nero (A.D. 54-68)

The first wave of major persecution that broke upon Christ's unshakeable kingdom occurred in A.D. 64, during the reign of Emperor Nero. A huge fire raged through the city of Rome for six days and nights, devouring large sectors of its thoroughfares. Rumors rapidly circulated that the city was set ablaze by Nero himself, and the tide of public opinion quickly turned against him. In an effort to diffuse public hatred, Nero pinned the blame of the terrible conflagration on Christians and opened the floodgate of persecution against them. It is reported that Christians were wrapped in the skin of wild beasts and then torn to pieces by big brutal dogs. Others were nailed to crosses, set ablaze and planted as human torches to light up the night sky of Nero's personal garden, which became the stage for his fiendish circus of human torture and destruction. Tradition holds that both Peter and Paul were put to death during Nero's reign of terror, and that Peter's remains lie buried beneath the high altar in the cathedral that bears his name, erected in what was once Nero's garden.[3]

Domitian (A.D. 81-96)

After Nero, there was another brief period of persecution under Emperor Domitian, during which time the Apostle John was exiled to the isle of Patmos. It was from this isle that John wrote the book of Revelation to encourage the believers in the seven churches of Asia Minor to hold firm to their faith in the soon-coming Savior (See Revelation 1:4, 9). These horrendous scourges against the body of Christ had both positive and negative effects upon the believing community. Many Christians went into hiding, others renounced the faith; and not too few embraced martyrdom as worthy yoke-fellow, in order to be identified with their Master's suffering and death. Others saw it as the entrance to the open door into everlasting life in Christ's glorious kingdom. The Master had warned His disciples:

> *"But beware of men, for they will hand you over to the courts and scourge you in their synagogues; and*

> *you will even be brought before governors and kings for My sake, as a testimony to them and to the Gentiles. <u>But when they hand you over, do not worry about how or what you are to say; for it will be given you in that hour what you are to say. For it is not you who speak, but it is the Spirit of your Father who speaks in you</u>. Brother will betray brother to death, and a father his child; and children will rise up against parents and cause them to be put to death. <u>You will be hated by all because of My name, but it is the one who has endured to the end who will be saved</u>."*
>
> Matthew 10:17-22

These words of Jesus were a source of encouragement to church fathers like Ignatius, bishop of Antioch, whose inspiring letters and sacrificial life not only guided the early church through a very difficult period, but also bolstered the courage of those who would be called to suffer for their faith. In one such letter, which Ignatius wrote while on the road to martyrdom, this resolute, renowned bishop penned the following testimony:

> "May I have the pleasure of the wild beasts that have been prepared for me; and I pray that they prove to be prompt with me. I will even coax them to devour me properly, not as they have done with some, whom they were too timid to touch. And if when I am willing and ready they are not, I will force them. Bear with me—I know what is best for me. Now at last I am beginning to be a disciple. May nothing visible or invisible envy me, so that I may reach Jesus Christ. Fire and cross and battles with wild beasts, mutilation, mangling, wrenching of bones, the

hacking of limbs, the crushing of my whole body, cruel tortures of the devil—let these come upon me, only let me reach Jesus Christ!"[4]

This very courageous disciple of Jesus followed in the footsteps of his Master as he was given to the wild beasts in the Roman amphitheater around A.D. 110. However, his martyrdom was an inspiration to many others who followed him. Not very long after his execution, his old friend and bishop of Smyrna, disciple Polycarp, would be called to the same fate for his refusal to renounce his allegiance to Christ. It is believed that Polycarp was a disciple of Apostle John at Ephesus[5] and probably the last of those who actually talked with eyewitnesses of Jesus. Tradition reports that when this aged bishop of Smyrna stood before Antoninus Pius and the pagan masses that filled the amphitheatre to witness his execution, he boldly and forthrightly challenged every suggestion made by the governor. When he was asked to swear by Caesar and repudiate the Christ whom he served throughout his entire life, Polycarp replied:

"Eighty-six years have I served him, and he has done me no wrong; how then can I blaspheme my King who saved me... I am a Christian. If you would learn the doctrine of Christianity, assign me a day and give me a hearing."

The proconsul said: "Persuade the people,"
Polycarp said, "As for you, I hold you worthy of a discourse... but as for these, I do not hold them worthy."

Whereupon the proconsul said: "I have wild beasts here and I'll throw you to them, except you repent."
Polycarp replied: "Call for them."
To which the proconsul replied: "If you scorn the beasts, I'll have you burned, except you repent."

"You threaten me with the fire which burn for a season and is quenched, and you are ignorant of the fire of the future judgment and eternal punishment, which is reserved for the ungodly. But why do you delay? "Come now and bring it on."[6]

What a powerful witness to the gospel of Jesus Christ! This amazing testimony[7] became the touchstone for a large genre of martyr literature that developed after Polycarp's martyrdom about the middle of the second century. Following that period, martyrdom became a celebrated event among Christians, leading to the erection of shrines and churches, and the veneration of martyrs and their artifacts. Names of martyrs were carefully kept in the records of churches and their "birthdays" into eternal life were remembered by annual celebrations at their tombs.[8]

Marcus Aurelius (A.D. 161-180)

Not long after Polycarp, another notable figure and defender of the faith, whose witness earned him the name "Justin Martyr," was put to death under the hand of Marcus Aurelius. Justin was a Christian teacher in Rome who protested against the unjust policies of the Roman government towards Christians, and wrote two Apologies that challenged the pagan criticisms of Christianity.[9] These were written during a time of great political and economic difficulty, when it became increasingly convenient to blame Christians for all the social and political ills of the day.

Nevertheless, during the first half of the third century, persecution of Christians was sporadic at best, and believing communities were growing at a rapid pace as many people were seeking comfort and security in religion. However, this space of relative calm was going to be short-lived, for new storms, which were calculated to bring the surging growth of the Christianity to an abrupt and disastrous halt, were gathering quickly.

Decius (A.D. 249-251)

The most severe persecution against the faith swept through the Empire at the imperial command of Emperor Decius in A.D. 249. No one knew for sure what his motives were, but his attack on the kingdom was very short, aggressive and deadly. The persecution was so severe that many believers denied their faith. Others bought certificates of compliance, and great numbers were imprisoned or executed—among them Origen, bishop of Rome, and the bishops of Antioch and Jerusalem. The scourge under Decius came to an abrupt halt, just as it began, when he perished in battle in A.D. 251.

Valerian (A.D. 253-260)

After the demise of Decius, another storm, with double the fury, broke upon the church, which, by this time, had taken to the catacombs of Rome. During this catastrophe in A.D. 257, Emperor Valerian directed his attack on the leaders of the church, demanding that they pay homage to the Roman gods under the pain of exile or even death. Christians were threatened with the death penalty if they so much as attend any of the meetings or services of the Church, whether public or secret; or even visited a Christian cemetery to pay respect to slain martyrs. During this scourge, the bishop of Rome was taken while teaching. He was seated in his chair in one of the catacombs, while four of his seven deacons were slain.

Another faithful leader, by the name of Lawrence, was roasted to death on a gridiron; Cyprian, the bishop of Carthage was beheaded; and the bishop of Spain, along with two of his deacons, was burnt at the stake in an amphitheatre. However, this spate of persecutions ended abruptly when Valerian was captured while at war with the Persians in A.D. 260. Nothing more was heard about him after his seizure and he just disappeared from history.[9]

Emerging from these dark and horrible days, the church sprouted like a bud bursting into full bloom, with a fresh addition of martyrs to reinforce hope and courage among the scattered believers and new converts to the faith. The ensuing years were relatively peaceful, and the reenergized believers took full advantage of this time of lull to push the frontiers of the kingdom well beyond the Roman Empire and into the Mediterranean region. Estimates put the number of Christians during this period anywhere between five in every hundred, and about half the population of the known world.[10]

Diocletian (A.D. 284-305)

Nonetheless, the enemy's campaign of destruction against the rapidly growing church was not even nearly over; for the last and most vicious storm was about to break upon Christians throughout the Roman Empire, from Arabia in the east to Britain in the west. When Emperor Diocletian rose to power in A.D. 284, he consolidated his control of the Empire by sharing his authority with a very close friend, Maximian, whom he gave charge over the western provinces. Because of escalating socioeconomic and military turmoil that placed enormous strain upon the administration of the limited resources of the sprawling Empire, both Diocleatian and Maximian appointed deputies (Galerius by Diocletian, and Constantius by Maximian) to help stabilize the government. This they were able to do successfully for a period, a little short of two decades.

Then in A.D. 303, for reasons unknown to historians, the aging Emperor ordered his army to be purged of all Christians. Imperial edicts followed, commanding officials to destroy church property, ban Christian worship, and burn the Scriptures. Bishops were rounded up wholesale, imprisoned, tortured, and many put to death, while the power of the imperial throne was turned loose to wipe out the rest of Christianity in blood.[11]

This Empire-wide open attack on Christians and their sympathizers became known as "the Great Persecution." However, just as suddenly as this persecution began, Diocletian suddenly abdicated the throne in A.D. 305, and forced his fellow Augustus,

Maximian, to do the same. Nevertheless, what was started and, for the most part, ended in the west did not come to an end in the east. Galerius, the Augustus of the Eastern Empire, of whom, many believers were convinced was the instigator of the scourge, continued in his ambitious campaign to exterminate completely all Christians from the Empire.

Although Galerius unleashed persistent, calculated attacks on Christianity, leaving rivers of blood in his trail, Roman citizens were growing weary and disgusted of what had become a campaign of senseless bloodletting. What the enemy of the cross of Christ tried to do to destroy the saints of the Most High God and suppress the growth of His kingdom, only served to publicize the Christian faith and demonstrate the kingdom's power as many pagans openly embraced what they once hated.

The martyrdom of the saints rained like fertilizer on the seed of the gospel, sprouting more conversions and witnessing communities than the Roman authorities were prepared for, or capable to handle. The continuous, exponential replacement of the fallen faithful ultimately revealed that the diabolical strategy of extermination through persecution was powerless against the forces of the invincible Galilean who confidently vowed: *"Upon this rock I will build My church and the gates of hell shall not prevail against it"* (Matthew 16:18).

Upon his deathbed, in A.D. 311, Galerius regretfully conceded that his hateful policy of open persecution against the followers of Jesus was an utter failure, for the throne could no longer afford the risk of continuing the torturing, maiming and killing of innocent, defenseless people. Thus, in his last official act, he reluctantly and grudgingly issued an edict of toleration towards Christianity, which, for all practical purposes, brought an end to the worst Roman persecution against the disciples of Christ.[12]

A Change in Policy

With the death of Galerius in the Eastern Empire, his successor, Maximin, completely ignored his deathbed edict, which he probably interpreted to be a sign of weakness on the part of the crown. Thus, he continued a policy of vicious persecution against the faith, with ignominious brutality especially to Christians in Egypt. However, Constantius Chlorus, the contemporary of Galerius and the Augustus of the West, never openly endorsed any anti-Christian measures, but followed a policy of toleration toward the Christian faith. Upon his death in A.D. 306, his son, Constantine, was proclaimed Emperor by his troops, much to the displeasure of his many rivals. In A.D. 313, Constantine and Licinius, who was then Augustus of the East, endorsed the edict of Milan which granted religious freedom to all Christians. This edict mainly affected the eastern half of the Empire since Constantine had already given this liberty to Christians in the West. Nevertheless, after a long, protracted struggle with his opponents, and after many political maneuvers, Constantine finally emerged as the sole Emperor of the Roman Empire in A.D. 323.

A Christian Emperor?

There has been continuous debate regarding the integrity of the alleged spiritual conversion of Emperor Constantine. Many historians attribute the title Christian to Emperor Constantine because of the report of Eusebius regarding Constantine's testimony of his victory over Maxentius at the Milvian Bridge, and his policy of toleration towards the Christian faith. Notably, Eusebius was the most eminent church historian of his day and his endorsement of the Emperor's account of his "miraculous" victory over Maxentius influenced the thinking of church leaders and fellow-historians alike.

According to Eusebius, Constantine reported that while he was praying for victory over his enemy, he had a vision of a cross of light in the heavens bearing the inscription, "Conquer by this." Constantine also indicated that confirmation came to him in a dream in which God appeared to him with the same sign and commanded him to make a likeness of it and use it as a safeguard in all encounters with his enemies.[13] From that point on Constantine used the symbol of the cross encircled by a golden wreath as his military standard.

However, it is very important to note that although Constantine extended religious courtesies to Christianity—namely, giving the same tax exemptions to Christian ministers as he did to pagan priests; encouraging and facilitating the erection of churches and religious institutions; and abolishing execution by crucifixion. In A.D. 321, he declared Sunday as a holy day of rest and worship, but he did not make Christianity the sole religion of the Empire. Much of paganism remained.

Constantine retained the pagan title *Pontifex Maximus* (chief priest of the pagan state religious cult) to the end of his days and did very little, if anything at all, to curtail the ceremonies associated with the imperial religion. The coins he minted in his early years bore the image of *Sol Invictus* (the Unconquered Sun), which was also inscribed with the triumphal arch he erected in Rome to celebrate his victory over Maxentius. Ironically, when Constantine gave Sunday to the Christian Church as a day of rest and worship in A.D. 321, he did so in honor and respect of "the venerable day of the Sun"[14] and not the resurrection of the Son of God. This association was a later adoption of the Church in order to distance itself from the imperial cult, but Sunday sacredness has its roots in paganism, not in Christianity, as many profess to believe.

To say the least, Constantine portrayed a faith that was, in whole or in part, very syncretistic and accommodating, endeavoring to press Christianity into a pagan mold. While he professed to embrace Christianity on the one hand, he never denied the imperial cult on the other. Constantine never declared his faith through the rite of baptism until upon his death bed in A.D. 337, when he was baptized by Eusebius of Nicomedia. As the leading public figure of the State, Constantine's example of religious syncretism (the marrying of Christianity and paganism), set the stage for major spiritual fallouts that the then favorable and rapidly expanding church was unprepared to handle.

By thrusting the church into public life as a privileged institution endorsed by the State, re-born "Christianity" became the religion of choice. Whereas, before Constantine, conversions to the faith came through spiritual conviction, now many who came to the church were politically ambitious, religiously disinterested, and still half-rooted in paganism.[15] Thus, while the church was gaining adherents, it was losing its distinctiveness and powerful witness. While believers found a new measure of comfort in the protection of the State, they also discovered a new source of discomfort in their spiritual faith and practice.

The Mystery of Iniquity

No wonder, for even Satan disguises himself as an angel of light. Therefore it is not surprising if his servants also disguise themselves as servants of righteousness, whose end will be according to their deeds.

2 Corinthians 11:14, 15

It is not very difficult for anyone, who is somewhat familiar with the great controversy between the kingdom of light and the kingdom of darkness, to see or understand that the mastermind behind the policy of destruction against Christianity is the Prince of darkness. Force, deception and subtlety have always been hallmarks of the kingdom of darkness, and Satan will use any of these with the help of anyone, to accomplish his purpose. After almost three centuries of vicious attacks on the disciples of Christ, Satan saw that the kingdom campaign of Jesus did not become any weaker. Rather, it grew stronger as the believers embraced torture and martyrdom with mystifying courage, and onlooking pagans yielded to the powerful witness of the faith. What force could not accomplish because it was transparently unjustified and wicked, and engendered too much sympathy for the Christian faith, subtle deception would achieve because it was more convenient.

Consequently, Emperor Constantine became a very expedient tool to accomplish the enemy's purpose. He came at a time when the church was reeling to and fro from the repeated assaults of terrible persecutions, and his olive branch of religious tolerance was dipped in the sea of his public favor. This was a much welcomed relief for the church, enticing her to be more conciliatory towards the cultic overtures of the State. Granted, Constantine did what any observant, crafty Emperor would do to consolidate his control of such a vast, unstable Empire that faced the external threat of impending invasion, and the internal menace of moral decadence and political corruption.

Even when the Arian controversy over the Deity of Christ threatened to split the church, Constantine called the first general church council of Nicea in A.D. 325 to settle the issues, because it was in the interest of the stability of the Empire to keep the church as a united front. In spite of Constantine's efforts, and the endeavors of many others that followed him, a major split in the church occurred in 1054. The Eastern half of the Empire, dominated by the Greek Christians, established its headquarters in Constantinople, while the Latin Church in the west, kept its headquarters in Rome.

However, the church (predominantly in the West) flirted with the State and traded her dependence on faith and the power of God for the social, financial and political endorsements of her devious lover. Ironically, the situation is not much different today. Although many religionists profess to favor a separation of powers between Church and State, the real situation appears to be one of only economic and political expediency. Nonetheless, during the reign of Constantine, the enemy of Christ used this time of peace to infiltrate the kingdom field, sowing his tares of corruption through his policy of patronization, spiritual compromise, institutionalization and indoctrination.

It was during this period that the seductive spirit of syncretism infiltrated the church, tainting its cardinal beliefs with pagan philosophies and ideas. This gave birth to teachings and traditions aimed at bridging the great gulf "fixed" between Christianity and paganism, replacing the worship of the Romans cultic gods with "Christian" surrogates. Paramount among these were the doctrines of Mariology,[16] Sainthood,[17] and traditions like Easter and Christmas—which remain the two most celebrated "Christian" holidays (really holy days) of our times. There is absolutely no biblical foundation for the association of the resurrection of Jesus Christ with the celebration of Easter, which was a ritual to the goddess of fertility—hence the abundance of Easter bunnies and Easter eggs. Neither is there any scriptural association for the birth of Christ and the celebration of Christmas, with its perennial tales of an over-indulgent Santa Claus, feasting on the milk and cookies left behind by little children in exchange for precious toys.

Moreover, the church did not only modify its teachings, practices and liturgical style in order to accommodate the influx of pagans who were seeking "membership" within its ranks; but it also began exhibiting the coercive characteristics of the State that supported it, through its systematic policies of power and control over the "faith" (and fate) of the "faithful." Now elevated as the revered State institution, the fear of the Church replaced the fear of God in the heart of the worshipper, and the Church, not Christ, became the dominant figure influencing the lifestyle and practice of all believers. Those who chose to denounce or separate themselves from its grasp and influence were forced to face the wrath of its self-righteous dogmas.

Deadly Alliance

By the year 380, the residual effects of the Constantinian

legacy became quite evident during the administration of Emperor Theodosius, who transformed Christianity into a religion of force, not of faith, implicitly linking God's will with his. How true was Jesus' warning to His disciples when He said:

> "All this I have told you so that you will not go astray. They will put you out of the synagogue; in fact, a time is coming when anyone who kills you will think he is offering a service to God. <u>They will do such things because they have not known the Father or me. I have told you this, so that when the time comes you will remember that I warned you.</u> I did not tell you this at first because I was with you."
>
> John 16:1-4, NIV

Through his imperial command, Theodosius thought he was carrying out the divine will of God when he issued the follow statement:

> It is Our Will that all the peoples we rule shall practice that religion which the divine Peter the Apostle transmitted to the Romans. We shall believe in the single Deity of the Father, the Son, and the Holy Spirit, under the concept of equal majesty and of the Holy Trinity. We command that those persons who follow this rule shall embrace the name of Catholic Christians.The rest, however, whom we adjudge demented and insane, shall sustain the infamy of heretical dogmas, their meeting places shall not receive the name of churches, and they shall be smitten first by divine vengeance and secondly by the retribution of Our own initiative, which We shall assume in accordance with divine judgment.[18]

Thus, this marriage between the Church and the State was consummated in the blood of the saints of the Most High. The Church did not only mirror the character of the State through its religious policies, dogmas and retributive judgments, but it also reflected the spirit of deception and coercion inherent in the Evil one who gave power to the throne. John, the beloved disciple, prophesied of this corrupt union between the Church and the State of Rome while in exile on the Isle of Patmos for his faith in the Word of God and the testimony of Jesus Christ (Revelation 1:9).

John skillfully masked the union in symbolism to hide the true content of his message from this axis of evil that sought to destroy the true followers of Christ who separated themselves from the corrupt religious system. He portrayed the union between the Church and the Roman state as a beast of many deceptive and destructive characteristics (those of a leopard, bear and lion combined), empowered by the dragon, who is none other than Satan himself (See Revelation 12:9). Here is John's description:

> *"And the beast which I saw was like a leopard, and his feet were like those of a bear, and his mouth like the mouth of a lion. <u>And the dragon gave him his power and his throne and great authority</u> . . . and they worshiped the dragon because he gave his authority to the beast; and they worshiped the beast, saying, 'Who is like the beast, and who is able to wage war with him?' . . . <u>It was also given to him to make war with the saints and to overcome them</u>, and authority over every tribe and people and tongue and nation was given to him."*

Revelation 13:2, 4, 7

While this volume does not allow me the space and time to attend to all the details of this prophetic word, suffice it to say that the annals of church history are replete with references of the systematic persecutions meted out by the State church upon all those who rejected her policies and dogmas. This deadly alliance between the Church and the State of Rome to wage war against the saints of the most High God was really a microcosm of the larger supernatural warfare between the kingdom of light and the kingdom of darkness.

In Revelation 12 and 13, which are really mirror images of each other, the apostle John portrays this great controversy between these kingdoms. Chapter 12 describes the war which started in heaven between Michael, the warrior title of Christ (Daniel 12:1) and the dragon, one of the aliases of Satan (Revelation 12:9), and later transferred to earth after Satan and his angels were cast out from their celestial domain.

> *"And there was war in heaven, <u>Michael</u> and his angels waging war with the dragon. The <u>dragon</u> and his angels waged war, and they were not strong enough, and there was no longer a place found for them in heaven. And the <u>great dragon was thrown down, the serpent of old who is called the devil and Satan, who deceives the whole world</u>; he was thrown down to the earth, and his angels were thrown down with him.*
>
> *Then I heard a loud voice in heaven, saying, 'Now the salvation, and the power, and the kingdom of our God and the authority of His Christ have come, for the accuser of our brethren has been thrown down, he who accuses them before our God day and night. And they overcame him because of the blood of the Lamb and because of the word of their testimony, and they did not love their life even when faced with death.*
>
> *For this reason, rejoice, O heavens and you who dwell in them. <u>Woe to the earth and the sea,</u>*

<u>*because the devil has come down to you, having great wrath, knowing that he has only a short time.*</u>"

Revelation 12:7-12

This same warfare which started in heaven is currently being fought on earth. When the dragon, called the devil and Satan (v. 9), saw that his place was no longer found in heaven, he began to persecute the woman who gave birth to a son (Revelation 12:13). This woman and her seed were first prophesied in Eden, when God addressed the demonized serpent: "*And I will put enmity between thee and the woman, and between thy seed and her seed; it shall bruise thy head, and thou shalt bruise his heel*" (Genesis 3:15).

This prophetic word found its fulfillment in the Virgin Mary, who is a type of the true Israel of God, and the "Holy Thing" (Seed) planted in her by the Holy Ghost. This "Holy Seed," Gabriel said, was the Son of God, who was born as a descendant of David. Following this prophetic scenario, Jeremiah likened the people of God to *a comely and delicate* woman (Jeremiah 6:2). John, the exiled apostle on the Isle of Patmos, also gave a very clear end-time description of this woman in Revelation 12.

> "*A great sign appeared in heaven: a woman clothed with the sun, and the moon under her feet, and on her head a crown of twelve stars; ²and she was with child; and she cried out, being in labor and in pain to give birth . . . ⁵And she gave birth to a son, a male child, who is to rule all the nations with a rod of iron; and her child was caught up to God and to His throne.*"

Revelation 12:1, 2, 5

Note that the crown with twelve stars on the head of the woman is a symbolic representation of the twelve tribes of Israel and the twelve apostles of Christ. The moon is a symbol of Israel under the old covenant, and the sun signifies God's new Israel under the glory of the new covenant with its better sacrifice and life-giving promises.

When Satan, the dragon, saw that he was defeated at Calvary and Christ ascended victoriously to His throne in the heavens, the arch-deceiver turned his anger on God's new Israel, which was the church birthed by Christ through His apostles. Satan persecuted her for 1260 prophetic days (Revelation 12:6). In Bible prophecy, a prophetic day is equivalent to a literal year (Numbers 14:34; Ezekiel 4:6). Thus, the 1260 days really represent 1260 literal years. John mirrors the dragon's wanton attack against the woman and her man-child in Revelation 12 with the fiendish rule of the beast power, seen in the alliance of the apostate church and State of Rome in Revelation 13.

It is very important to notice that although the instrument of persecution in Revelation 13 is different, this beast power receives its seat and great authority from the great red dragon of chapter 12 (Revelation 12:3, 4; 13:2). Through this evil confederacy, Satan continued his campaign of destruction against the kingdom of heaven by persecuting those who stood firm for the truth of the gospel which was greatly compromised by the fallen State church.

Two very notable sects among the victims of this persecution were the Albigenses (also called the Cathari) and the Waldenses (named after their founder Peter Waldo). The Albigenses were very out-spoken against the sacraments, crosses, relics and images that inundated the life and liturgy of the State church. They saw these as evil compromises with Roman cult worship and completely separated themselves from the body that upheld them. This sect met the fierce wrath of the Church and the State, especially in southern France where they were slaughtered mercilessly by the thousands. Those who escaped wandered across Europe to places like Germany, Bohemia, Hungary, and even to orthodox Spain.

Although the Waldenses were not as extreme in their teachings as the Albigenses, their efforts to call men back to the simple teachings of Christ, and away from the politics, wealth and worldliness of the Roman Catholic clergy, were also met with great clerical displeasure. Forbidden to preach the gospel, they were forced to separate themselves from the Church of Rome, in order to further justify their position that any good Christian had an obligation to share his faith and take the gospel of Jesus Christ to the world. Moreover, the Waldenses repudiated the Church's claim that the sacraments were necessary for salvation, and strongly protested the ecclesiastical monopoly over Christ's blood-bought heritage and the salvation He so freely offers to all men. How much influence the lifestyle and teachings of the Waldenses had in preparing the way for reformers like Wycliff, Huss, Jerome, and Luther is somewhat uncertain, but the reality of the connection appears rather undeniable.[19]

Supernatural Warfare

"For our struggle is not against flesh and blood, but against the rulers, against the powers, against the world forces of this darkness, against the spiritual forces of wickedness in the heavenly places."

Ephesians 6:12

What we have seen in this chapter is a very clear outworking of Satan's enmity against God, and his purposeful, systematic and relentless attack against the kingdom of heaven. Although his methodology may change with the passing of time, his motive and goal is still the same—that is, to forestall Christ's kingdom expansion (since he cannot destroy it) through inhumane torture and persecution, sinister misrepresentation and distortion of the truth of God's word, and creeping compromise and confusion. Through all these avenues, Satan has been successful in securing the cooperation of zealous, influential human beings—Jews, Gentiles and even professed followers of Christ—to carry out and perpetuate his hateful campaign against God and humanity.

This is not at all surprising, for it has always been the enemy's standing trademark to mask his evil devastations against God's creation through inappropriate use of the elements of nature and more directly, through humanity itself. Then he artfully deceives those afflicted by his wanton destruction to blame the God of heaven for their misfortunes. However, the Word of God reminds us that our true enemy is not our heavenly Father and those who offend us. Our real warfare is not against humanity, but against the demons and evil spirits of the underworld, who perform spiritual wickedness in high places. Jesus warned his disciples:

> *"For false Christs and false prophets will arise and will show great signs and wonders, so as to mislead, if possible, even the elect. Behold, I have told you in advance."*
>
> Matthew 24:24

Paul told the Thessalonian believers that the "mystery of lawlessness" was already at work among them, and that one was coming who, through the influence of Satan, will exhibit all power and signs and wonders, with all the deception of wickedness. Paul also said that this "man of sin" will lead away those who did not receive the love of the truth (2 Thessalonians 2:9, 10). Such manifestations of the kingdom of darkness will continue to increase as we approach the end of this age, and the children of the kingdom of light must stand alert and ready to meet these spiritual counterfeits with a clear and decisive "thus said the Lord." In this supernatural warfare, every disciple is called to *test every spirit to see whether they are from God; because many false prophets have gone out into the world* (1 John 4:1).

Our unshakable faith in the infallible Word of God is our only line of defense and offense, and unless our minds are daily renewed through the study of its revelations and principles we stand in great danger of falling to Satan's artful deceptions. Every miracle-working spirit is not necessarily evidence of the presence of God's power, and our natural senses are wholly insufficient to test the authenticity of the supernatural signs and wonders that will be manifested in these last days. While in exile, John said he saw:

> *"coming out of the mouth of the dragon and out of the mouth of the beast and out of the mouth of the false prophet, three unclean spirits like frogs; for they are spirits of demons, performing signs, which go out to the kings of the whole world, to gather them together for the war of the great day of God, the Almighty."*
>
> Revelation 16:13, 14

Although the enemy of our souls has not relinquished his strategy of open frontal attacks on the kingdom of heaven, he has incorporated false prophets among the believers (so-called preachers and spiritual leaders) and opportunistic disciples very much like Judas, to lead souls away from the truth. What John describes in the above verses is a deadly, diabolical amalgamation of Satanic, religio-political, and spiritual forces performing hard-to-deny miracles to influence thought-leaders of our world to unite their resources in warfare against the God of heaven. This alliance is a clear manifestation of the evil intent of the mastermind of deception and destruction, conceived in his selfish, corrupt heart, even before his great fall from grace.

> *"How art thou fallen from heaven, O Lucifer, son of the morning! How art thou cut down to the ground, which didst weaken the nations! For thou hast said in thine heart, <u>I will ascend into heaven</u>, <u>I will exalt</u>*

<u>*my throne above the stars of God: I will sit also upon the mount of the congregation, in the sides of the north: I will ascend above the heights of the clouds: I will be like the most High*</u>."

Isaiah 14:12-14, KJV

A Seed of Resistance

One prolific Christian writer has insightfully explained that through the fall of man, it was Satan's plan to enter into an alliance with humankind to make war against his Creator; but God specially interposed to stem the tide of the enemy's evil intentions.[20]

> *"And I will put enmity between you and the woman, And between your seed and her seed; He shall bruise you on the head, And you shall bruise him on the heel."*

Genesis 3:15

God took affirmative action at the time of the fall to ensure that Satan was inhibited from exercising complete control over humankind. Therefore, He spoke this word of containment to the serpent (Satan), which offered hope and assurance of victory to the fallen pair through the promised seed (Jesus Christ) of the woman. But until that promised offspring comes, and until dominion is restored to Adam's race, God placed a seed of resistance in man's spirit to check the advances of the evil one. Ellen White confirmed this when she wrote:

> It is the grace that Christ implants in the soul which creates in man enmity against Satan. Without this converting grace and renewing power, man would

continue the captive of Satan, a servant ever ready to do his bidding. But the new principle in the soul creates conflict where hitherto had been peace. The power which Christ imparts enables man to resist the tyrant and usurper. Whoever is seen to abhor sin instead of loving it, whoever resists and conquers those passions that have held sway within, displays the operation of a principle wholly from above.[21]

Such grace was exemplified in the lives and experiences of those who courageously separated themselves from the Church of Rome in order to preserve and practise the truth of the gospel as proclaimed by Jesus and the apostles. Many of these faithful followers paid the ultimate price with their lives, but they also perpetuated a legacy of resistance and resilience that gave new life and power to the gospel of the kingdom.

Throughout the centuries that followed, the commanding witness and testimony of these fallen saints, and the fearless proclamations of their remnant comrades, became the catalyst that unleashed the colossal reformatory wave that shook the foundations and strongholds of the Church of Rome, releasing countless thousands of God's chosen children from its deadly, mystifying grip. The Word of God says:

> *"And they overcame him because of the blood of the Lamb and because of the word of their testimony, and they did not love their life even to death."*
>
> Revelation 12:11

"Galilean, thou hast conquered!"[22] Indeed He has! And His kingdom marches on!

Notes

1. Bruce L. Shelley, *Church History in Plain Language* (Nashville, TN: Thomas Nelson Publishers, 1995), 42.
2. Ibid, 38.
3. Kenneth Scott Latourette, *A History of Christianity, Vol. 1* (New York: HarperCollins Publishers, 1975), 85.
4. Ignatius, *Letter to the Romans* 5.2-3, quoted in Ivor J. Davidson, *The Birth of the Church: From Jesus to Constantine, A.D. 30-312* (Grand Rapids: BakerBooks, 2004), 203.
5. Ibid, 182.
6. *Martyrdom of Polycarp* found in *Early Christian Fathers* edited by Cyril C. Richardson (Philadelphia: Westminster Press, 1953), 141-58.
7. The *Martyrdom of Polycarp* is one of the works of the Apostolic Fathers, giving details of the execution of the 86 year old bishop of Smyrna at the hands of the Romans around AD 155-156.
8. Shelley, 75.
9. Ivor J. Davidson, *The Birth of the Church: From Jesus to Constantine, A.D. 30-312* (Grand Rapids: BakerBooks, 2004), 214-217.
10. Latourette, 89-90.
11. Paul Hutchinson and Winfred E. Garrison, *20 Centuries of Christianity* (NY: Harcourt, Brace and Co., 1959), 44-48, quoted in Bruce L. Shelley, *Church History in Plain Language* (Nashville, TN: Thomas Nelson Publishers, 1995), 93.
12. Ibid, 94.
13. Latourette, 92.
14. Davidson, 345.
15. Shelley, 96.
16. Latourette, 166-169, 203-218. Also Mariology relates to the veneration and invocation of Mary, the mother of Jesus to make intercession to God on behalf of the living.

17. Sainthood refers to the veneration and invocation of the Disciples of Jesus, and devout men and women, so labeled by the Church, to make intercession to God on behalf of the living.
18. Shelley, 96.
19. Wallace K. Ferguson and Geoffrey Bruun, *A Survey of European Civilization*, (Boston: Houghton Mifflin Company, 1969), 246-247.
20. Ellen White, *The Great Controversy*, (Boise, ID: Pacific Press Publishing Association, 1950), 505.
21. Ibid, 506.
22. A legend reports that these were the last words of Julian (called "the Apostate" by Christian historians) who tried in vain to revive pagan cultic worship by infusing it with Christian forms and liturgy. See Wallace and Brunn, 91.

CONFLICTS IN THE KINGDOM

7

The kingdom of heaven may be compared to a man who sowed good seed in his field. [25]But while his men were sleeping, his enemy came and sowed tares among the wheat, and went away. [26]But when the wheat sprouted and bore grain, then the tares became evident also. [27]The slaves of the landowner came and said to him, "Sir, did you not sow good seed in your field? How then does it have tares?" [28]And he said to them, "An enemy has done this!" The slaves said to him, "Do you want us, then, to go and gather them up?" [29]But he said, "No; for while you are gathering up the tares, you may uproot the wheat with them. [30]Allow both to grow together until the harvest; and in the time of the harvest I will say to the reapers, 'First gather up the tares and bind them in bundles to burn them up; but gather the wheat into my barn.'"

Matthew 13:24-30

Tares Among the Wheat

In this 13th chapter of the gospel of Matthew alone, Christ told seven kingdom parables, besides the parable of "The Sower"— the understanding of which is the key to understanding all the parables of Jesus (Mark 4:13). The fact that here, and more than 100 times in the four gospels combined, the great theme of Jesus' teaching was about the kingdom of heaven, is reason enough for His modern-day followers to make kingdom expansion and kingdom proclamation their top priority. Moreover, these kingdom parables ought to be the subject of our constant study, so that we do not become victims of the enemy of our salvation and lose our way in the glitz and glamour of the kingdoms of this world which are passing away.

In light of the current discourse of this volume, no other parable of the kingdom portrays more clearly the subtle, insidious infiltration of the kingdom of heaven by the Prince of darkness than the parable of the tares among wheat. Even while Jesus was speaking this parable, Judas was already a "part" of the inner circle of His kingdom campaign, and clearly represented a living illustration of what Jesus was talking about, though unknown to His disciples—even Judas himself. However, Jesus was completely aware of Judas' dubious character, yet He did not deny him the opportunity to fellowship with the group and to be exposed to the merciful overtures of His divine grace. Later, Jesus would say of him at their last dinner together:

> "*Truly, truly, I say to you, a slave is not greater than his master, nor is one who is sent greater than the one who sent him.* ¹⁷*If you know these things, you are blessed if you do them.* ¹⁸<u>*I do not speak of all of you. I know the ones I have chosen*</u>*; but it is that the Scripture may be fulfilled, 'HE WHO EATS MY BREAD HAS LIFTED UP HIS HEEL AGAINST ME.'* . . . ²⁶<u>*That is the one for whom I shall dip the morsel and give it to him*</u> *So when He had dipped the morsel, He took and gave it to Judas, the son of Simon Iscariot.*"

John 13:16-18, 26

Notwithstanding, Jesus allowed Judas the full benefits of discipleship—giving him an inner-circle seat during all of His discourses. Judas had a close-up view of all His miracles; the privilege to baptize new disciples (John 4:1, 2); the authority to preach the kingdom of God, cast out demons and heal the sick in His name (Matthew 10:1-8; Mark 6:7-13); the olive branch of peace and reconciliation by washing his dusty feet; and the distinct honor to sit with Him at His last table fellowship with His disciples before He departed this life. As a matter of fact, the Bible says that Jesus loved His disciples, including Judas, to the end (John 13:1).

Indeed the tare (Judas) lived and grew among the wheat, nurtured and fed by the same "Rain" from heaven, until the time of harvest. Jesus lived what He taught and gave no occasion to the "Accuser of the brethren" (Satan and all who operate through his influence), to advance any argument against God's character. God is just and the justifier of all who diligently seek Him, giving to all mankind free and equal access to His saving grace. However, in spite of Christ' gracious advances to this fallen disciple, Judas ultimately made his choice and reaped the harvest of his own destruction (Matthew 26:14-16; 27:1-5).

No doubt, the character and final end of the tares are personified in the character and final demise of Judas, the disciple of Jesus. There is very sober instruction here for all who decide to become disciples of Christ, especially those functioning in leadership roles, because the true character of every disciple will be ultimately displayed. Preachers, leaders and teachers of the gospel of Jesus Christ, not everyone who is following you is really with you; for the disciple is not above His Master (Matthew 10:24; John 15:20).

If the ministry of Jesus attracted a "Judas", so will yours; for not all who choose to follow the Master through your ministry is called of God. One may preach the gospel of the kingdom as Judas did, perform miracles and cast out demons in the name of Jesus, baptize new believer into the kingdom family, sup at the fellowship table with fellow-believers, and still be an emissary of the wicked one — a son of perdition, just like Judas (John 17:12). Consequently, Jesus warned His disciples then as He warns us now:

> *"Not everyone who says to Me, 'Lord, Lord,' will enter the kingdom of heaven, but he who does the will of My Father who is in heaven will enter. ^{22}Many will say to Me on that day, 'Lord, Lord, did we not prophesy in Your name, and in Your name cast out demons, and in Your name perform many miracles?' ^{23}And then I will declare to them, 'I never knew you; DEPART FROM ME, YOU WHO PRACTICE LAWLESSNESS.'"*
>
> Matthew 7:21-23

One thing is very certain, and that is, harvest time is coming for every blade of wheat and every tare in the kingdom field, and every man's work would be tested by fire (1 Corinthians 3:13). Through the window of this parable we see a daily outworking of God's purpose in His kingdom. God has not given us the responsibility of rooting out those whom our short-sighted human judgment perceive to be tares among the kingdom wheat, for we are sure to destroy valuable grain in the process. This is a work He reserves only for the angels and Himself at the harvest time (Matthew 13:28-30), when the true character of every man's work will be revealed. Great injury and sorrow are brought repeatedly to innocent souls and the body of Christ through the missteps and ill-advised actions of many who think it is their responsibility to clean up the people of God.

This house-cleaning approach is contrary to the direct instruction of the Master. It is very interesting to note that Jesus never ejected Judas from His fellowship, or ever told any of the other eleven disciples what type of person Judas was. No one knows for sure what sort of reaction or injury such a decision would have caused. Christ so masked the gentle rebuke He gave to Judas when he sat at the last supper that is was completely misinterpreted by the rest of the group.

> *After the morsel, Satan then entered into him. Therefore Jesus said to him, 'What you do, do quickly.' <u>²⁸Now no one of those reclining at the table knew for what purpose He had said this to him. ²⁹For some were supposing, because Judas had the money box, that Jesus was saying to him, 'Buy the things we have need of for the feast'; or else, that he should give something to the poor.</u> ³⁰So after receiving the morsel he went out immediately; <u>and it was night</u>.*
>
> John 13:27-30

The dynamics of Judas' relationship to Christ and his fellow-disciples represented only a microcosm of what was to occur within the larger body of Christ in the kingdom realm. These dynamics were lived out in the daily experiences of the disciples and the early church. The believers were in constant danger with false disciples very much like their Master was in unceasing peril with the pretentious Scribes and Pharisees. These religious leaders followed Him daily, anxiously waiting for any "wrong" word from His lips that they might falsely accuse and judge Him (Luke 20:20, 21). The apostle Paul, in his final message to the leaders of the church in Miletus and Ephesus, reiterated a warning that he had often given to the brethren over a period of three years:

> *"For I know this, that after my departing shall grievous wolves enter in among you, not sparing the flock. ³⁰Also of your own selves shall men arise, speaking perverse things, to draw away disciples after them. ³¹Therefore watch, and remember, that by the space of three years I ceased not to warn every one night and day with tears."*
>
> Acts 20:29-31

In a similar fashion, he wrote letters to the churches in Corinth and Galatia explaining that he was in constant danger because of false brethren among the disciples, some of whom were sent to spy out the liberty of Christ' purchased heritage in an effort to bring them again into bondage of fruitless Jewish tradition (2 Corinthians 11: 26; Galatians 2:3-5).

Without any prevarication, tares among the wheat are a kingdom reality that will always be a part of the life and ministry of the body of Christ till the end of time. It was a prevailing condition that threatened the viability of the apostolic church and came to a head shortly before the turn of the Middle Ages. Through the Constantinian strategy of patronization and institutionalization, and the resulting union of Church and State, the enemy of Christ had effectively sown tares among the wheat in the kingdom field, and had cunningly set the stage for internal conflict, confusion and costly casualties among the saints of the Most High God for ages to come.

In the Shadows of the Reformation

From the early Middle Ages to the Reformation, the Church of Rome, which was the church in the western Empire, wielded its irresistible influence in shaping the thought and life of the Christian world, through the long arm of the State. During the second half of the fifth century, the church in the east, which was predominantly Greek-speaking, had settled all disputes for patriarchal supremacy and had given primacy to the patriarch of Constantinople, the imperial capital.

In the west, the imperial power was severely weakened and finally destroyed under repeated attacks by barbarian invasions. This enormous vacuum was immediately filled by the bishops of the predominantly Latin-speaking Church, who assumed the responsibility for governing both the Church and the State. The authoritative, powerful leadership of the Latin Church fathers (like Ambrose of Milan, Jerome, Augustine of Hippo, and, of course, Pope

Gregory, the Great), combined with Roman institutionalism and Latin organizationalism, brought discipline, order and respectability to the Church and its supporting entities.

Through its well-ordered system of religion, its clerical hierarchy and its authoritative, centralized government, headed by the office of the bishop of Rome (the Papacy), the Western Church expanded rapidly to major countries far beyond Roman borders, spawning a gigantic network of organizations (religious, political and financial) all around the world. The mystifying power of her carefully-crafted liturgy, gifted hymnody, abundance of wealth, and system of indoctrination became a very pervasive influence, leavening all the systems of religion that grew out of her after the Reformation.

By the time of the Reformation, the Church of Rome had outstripped her eastern counterpart in size and religious influence, and had grown to such power and dominance that even kingly and political authorities were bowing to her demands. All who opposed or ignored her teachings and wishes were excommunicated from the Church's fellowship; debarred from the "holy sacraments" and the rite of extreme unction; brutally tortured, maimed, or cruelly executed. While the self-righteous, indulgent bishops and prelates made themselves rich and fat through the policies and practices of a system of religion designed to fleece on the earnings of the fearful, ignorant masses, the Papacy and the universal system over which it presided, extended its global reach and authority. The Church of Rome was indeed building a kingdom, but it was not the kingdom of God.

Ironically, when Jesus stood accused before Pilate, He spoke of a kingdom that was diametrically opposed to the one the govenor represented and the Jewish leaders proclaimed. He told this ambassador of Caesar:

> "*My kingdom is not of this world*. *If My kingdom were of this world, then My servants would be fighting so that I would not be handed over to the Jews; but as it*

is, My kingdom is not of this realm."

John 18:36

Earlier, Jesus also told His followers—the citizens of His kingdom:

> *"The kings of the Gentiles lord it over them; and those in authority over them are called benefactors. ²⁶But not so with you; rather the greatest among you must become like the youngest, and the leader like one who serves. ²⁷For who is greater, the one who is at the table or the one who serves? Is it not the one at the table? But I am among you as one who serves. ²⁸You are those who have stood by me in my trials; ²⁹and I confer on you, just as my Father has conferred on me, <u>a kingdom</u>, ³⁰so that you may eat and drink at my table in my kingdom, and you will sit on thrones judging the twelve tribes of Israel."*

Luke 22:25-30, NRSV

Indeed the kingdom of heaven is not a system of religion defined by hierarchical bureaucracies, institutional trappings, coercion and fear; but a fellowship community characterized by freedom, servant-hood, empowerment, and service of love. The former are hallmarks of the kingdom of darkness and not the kingdom of light, and wherever they exist, there is the manifestation of systematic abuse and exploitation of the human spirit. In the kingdom of heaven, however, the human spirit harmoniously resonates with the Spirit of life, and is freely released to grow and abound in the grace, peace and joy of its Creator, Redeemer and King, Jesus Christ.

Reformation or Redistribution of Neo-Catholicism?

What the Waldenses and early Christian martyrs died to procure, and the honorable cohort of Protestant reformers—like John Wycliffe, John Huss, Jerome, Martin Luther, William Tyndale, Ulrich Zwingli, Conrad Grebel, Felix Manz, John Calvin, and Hugh Latimer, to name a few—risked and gave their lives to defend and proclaim, was the infallibility of the Word of God as the only authoritative rule of faith and practice in matters of conscience. The bold, persuasive stance of these defenders of the Christian faith challenged and repulsed the authority of the institutional church, dispensed through her bishops, priest and prelates. It was this formidable resistance and spirit-filled witness that gave birth to the Protestant Reformation.

However, although the Reformation brought freedom to the body of Christ from the controlling influence of Catholicism, it did not release the minds of the masses completely from everything that was Catholic. While the reformers' points of controversy with the Church of Rome centered mainly on issues of doctrine, the authority of Scripture, and the scandalous, exploitative behavior of many in its priesthood, they did not denounce all Catholic forms, structures and practices. Consequently, many of these institutional trimmings found their way into the Protestant movement in the form of religious feast days and holy days (Easter, Christmas, Sunday sacredness, Lent, etc.), liturgical style, and organizational and hierarchical structures, controlled by a centralized government.[1]

What resulted and continues to exist is what Ernst Troeltsch[2] has insightfully described as a Protestantism that is a "modification of Catholicism," in which Catholic problems remain but different solutions and reasons are given. Modern Christianity is still plagued by the issues of ecclesiastical power and control, exploitation of the masses for pecuniary gain, authority of the clergy, and the church or denomination (via tradition and church policy) usurping the authority of the Scriptures and Christ in the religious experience of followers.

Thus, while the most enduring legacies of the Protestant Reformation were freedom of religious expression and the establishment of the Scriptures as the sole rule of faith and practice for all Christians, it also gave birth, in quick succession, to institutional surrogates of the mother Church—denominations, named after their founders or founded upon some biblical principle or idea. Consequently, western Christianity became completely divided into growing numbers of religious sects, and the body of Christ "so-called" began to adopt new institutional forms— Lutherans after Martin Luther, Calvinist after John Calvin, Mennonite after Simon Menno, Wesleyans after John and Charles Wesley, Anabaptist after Conrad Grebel and Felix Manz, Anglicanism (English Catholicism) after English reformers, and a multiplicity of denominations and religious organizations.

In order to reduce the theological dissonance created by these new expressions and caricatures of the one true body of Christ, theologians and apologists developed the concept of the mystical church—that is, all "true" followers of Jesus scattered about in the ever-increasing religious communities that now comprise post-modern Christianity.

Interestingly, in Nebuchadnezzar's vision of the great image, recorded in the second chapter of the book of Daniel, he saw in the feet of the image an illogical mixture of iron and miry clay (Daniel 2:33, 41-43, KJV). This strange mixture is a clear indication that residue of the image's legs of iron (a symbol of Rome) was quite present in its feet of clay. This phenomenon points to the fact that the influence of the kingdom of Rome, through its religio-political systems, would be present and operable in the political and religious systems that govern the end-time nations of our world.

It is no wonder, then, that John, in prophetic vision, saw the whole world captivated by the mystifying power of the beast (the leadership of the Church of Rome) that was empowered by the dragon (a symbol of Satan and the Roman political system – Revelation 12:7-9; 13:2) to make war with the people of God

(Revelation 13:3, 7-8). Even more astounding is John's description of the Church of Rome and her relationship to her institutional surrogates as she deceptively confused the inhabitants of the earth with her false doctrines. Let us read this in Revelation 17.

> *"And there came one of the seven angels which had the seven vials, and talked with me, saying unto me, Come hither; I will show unto thee the judgment of the great whore that <u>sitteth upon many waters</u>:* ²*With whom <u>the kings of the earth have committed fornication, and the inhabitants of the earth have been made drunk with the wine of her fornication</u>.* ³*So he carried me away in the spirit into the wilderness: and I saw a woman sit upon a scarlet colored beast, full of names of blasphemy, having seven heads and ten horns.* ⁴*And the woman was <u>arrayed in purple and scarlet color</u>, and decked with gold and precious stones and pearls, having a golden cup in her hand full of abominations and filthiness of her fornication:* ⁵*And upon her forehead was a name written, MYSTERY, BABYLON THE GREAT, THE MOTHER OF HARLOTS AND ABOMINATIONS OF THE EARTH.* ⁶*And I saw <u>the woman drunken with the blood of the saints, and with the blood of the martyrs of Jesus</u>: and when I saw her, I wondered with great admiration."*
>
> Revelation 17:1-6

It must be understood that the exiled apostle was making prophetic declarations with regard to the evil work of the corrupt religious system of the Church of the State, while at the same time announcing her ultimate judgment. Obviously, John was using figurative language to veil his very pointed message so that its true import would be hidden from his religious persecutors. He describes the Church of Rome and her deceptive religious system as a "great whore," who sits on many waters, because of her unfaithfulness to her professed Husband, Jesus Christ. John did not leave us to speculate regarding the posture of the great whore. She is sitting upon many waters. These waters upon which she sits are symbolic of peoples, multitudes, nations and languages (Revelation 17:15) over which the Church of Rome exercises absolute control. This description completely harmonizes with the idea of the whole world wandering after the coercive beast power (Papal system of Roman Catholicism) in Revelation 13.

This whore, who is dressed in purple and scarlet—royal color of Rome and also a symbol of her iniquitous life—is an antithesis to the true bride of the Lamb, Jesus Christ, who is dressed in fine linen, clean and white, which represents the righteous acts of the saints (Revelation 19:7, 8). However, the contrast is unmistakable—the adulterous woman of Revelation 17 is the clear depiction of a false religious system that has committed whoredom with political powers (Revelation 17:2) through political favors, doctrinal compromise and incorporation of cultic practices in Christian services. This is not the first place in Scripture that God refers to spiritual apostasy as fornication, adultery or whoredom. God instructed His servant Hosea to marry an adulteress to vividly portray Israel's unfaithfulness to Him when she went whoring after false gods (Hosea 3, 4). In the book of Jeremiah, God instructed the prophet to pay attention to Israel's unfaithfulness toward Him.

> *Then the LORD said to me in the days of Josiah the king, Have you seen what faithless Israel did? She went up on every high hill and <u>under every green tree, and she was a harlot there</u>. ⁷I thought, 'After she has done all these things she will return to Me'; but she did not return, and her treacherous sister Judah saw it. ⁸And I saw that for all the <u>adulteries of faithless</u>*

> <u>*Israel*</u>, *I had sent her away and given her a writ of divorce, yet her treacherous sister Judah did not fear;* <u>*but she went and was a harlot also.*</u> *⁹*<u>*Because of the lightness of her harlotry, she polluted the land and committed adultery with stones and trees.*</u> *¹⁰Yet in spite of all this her treacherous sister Judah did not return to Me with all her heart, but rather in deception, declares the LORD.*

Jeremiah 3:6-10

Following this line of reasoning, therefore, it is not difficult to see why John described the relationship between the Church of Rome and her political allies as spiritual whoredom. Moreover, through this adulterous union, the Church has confused—made drunk—the inhabitants of the earth with the wine of her false teachings (Revelation 17:3). The golden cup borne by the apostate Church contained the "abomination and filthiness of her fornication"—the deceptive, tainted doctrines with which she mesmerized and made drunk the inhabitants of the earth.

The inscription on the forehead of this immoral woman, the apostate Church of Rome, speaks volumes about her deceptive character and far-reaching influence. "MYSTERY, BABYLON THE GREAT, THE MOTHER OF HARLOTS AND ABOMINATIONS OF THE EARTH" (Revelation 17:5). This system of religion is mysterious because of the capricious power (dragon or Satan – Revelation 13:2; 12:9) that supports and works through its worldwide network. It is also mysterious because it professes to belong to the kingdom of light while at the same time exercising the coercive, deceitful influence of the kingdom of darkness.

The name Babylon the Great is an antitypical title borrowed from the great tower of Babel (Genesis 11:1-9) and Nebuchadnezzar's Babylon the great (Daniel 4:30), and represents any system (religious or political) that controls the religious experience of God's children, as well as one that opposes the will and purposes of the Almighty. Just as the city of Babylon sat on the waters of the river Euphrates and held the people of God captive for seventy years; so it is that Mystery, Babylon the Great sits on, or holds sway over, the waters of peoples, multitudes, nations, and languages (Revelation 17:1). Babylon also depicts a state of irreconcilable confusion and disarray (Genesis 11:9), and clearly reveals not only the whore's misrepresentation of the truth of God's Word, but also the debilitating effects that her false teachings, syncretistic practices and human traditions had upon the daughters she so painfully produced through the Protestant Reformation.

The enemy of the kingdom had put in place his masterpiece of deception through the institutionalization of the body of Christ (the ungodly fusion of the Church and State), for more than a thousand years. As a result, the mysterious imprints of the Church of Rome were wholly or partly, already in the psyche of the initiators of the Reformation. This imprint set the stage for this spiritually adulterous and confused woman to give birth to apostate daughters. Through spiritual heredity, these children learned to ply the trade of their powerful, crafty mother, spreading abominations throughout the whole earth.

Indeed the mystery of iniquity was already at work (2 Thessalonians 2:7) for Mystery Babylon the Great to become the Mother of fertile Harlots, and her deceptive legacy could be clearly seen among her children in contemporary Christianity. These include rigid institutional control over Christ's blood-bought heritage; clerical (ministerial) abuse and exploitation of God's children; upscale religious merchandizing with its multiplicity of empty promises; preoccupation with money, wealth and materialism; and external forms and empty piety. Added to these are the exaltation of man-made traditions over God-ordained truth; doctrinal compromise and religious accommodations to attract the secular, the wealthy and the ungodly; emphasis on church membership over committed discipleship, and denominational loyalty over Master-disciple obedience, are all variant manifestations of neo-Catholicism in apostate Protestantism.

Satan's Expansion Strategy

"But the Spirit explicitly says that in later times some will fall away from the faith, paying attention to deceitful spirits and doctrines of demons."

1 Timothy 4:1

"For the time will come when they will not endure sound doctrine; but <u>wanting to have their ears tickled</u>, they will accumulate for themselves teachers <u>in accordance to their own desires</u>, ⁴and will turn away their ears from the truth and will turn aside to myths."

2 Timothy 4:3, 4

In the eyes of unconverted, secular observers, post-Modern Christianity appears to be the most confused religion in the world, daily spawning different perversions of the simple truth of the gospel of Jesus Christ, as salvation-seekers flock to "teachers in accordance to their own desires." This last-day phenomenon is what Paul describes in the above passages of scripture. However, in the midst of this exacerbating religious confusion that currently characterizes apostate Protestantism, the wheat of the kingdom of heaven grows imperceptibly until the time of harvest (Matthew 13:24-30).

Satan already knows that the kingdom of light has triumphed, and will triumph over his kingdom of darkness. Nevertheless, the deceiver hopes that through his expanding strategy of spiritual delusion, via religious confusion and internal conflict, he may succeed in causing believers to lose their way by turning on one another in the name of God. Because of this unhealthy practice, many on-looking, non-Christian observers are alienated from the kingdom altogether.

Religious institutionalism and the multiplication of religious systems constitute two of the major hindrances to kingdom expansion in these closing days of human history. Many kingdom citizens are forging their independence from the kingdom through their various religious colonies (denominations), creating many confusing kingdom disconnects—a form of collective individualism. So many of God's children cannot have a clear view of His kingdom because the institutional church, with its man-made traditions and cluttered agendas, gets in the way.

The messages of kingdom dominance, kingdom imminence, and the glorious return of the King are virtually absent from the vocabulary and from the pulpits, of many contemporary congregations. Institutional survival has influenced the preaching and teaching schedules of modern Christianity to favor subjects that cater to the attraction of followers rather than the conversion of sinners to the gospel of Jesus Christ and His kingdom.

The enemy of Christ has succeeded in using the energy of the Reformation to create new expressions of the one body of Christ, resulting in the denominational and religious confusion that we have today. Amusingly, denominationalism and religious institutionalism, regardless of the profession, are predicated more upon what separates one sect of believers from the body of Christ than upon what unites all believers in Christ, who is the ONLY true Head of His church. Even more ironical is the fact that there is much more that unites these fractions in the body than some of the issues that precipitate the schisms and conflicts that we currently see. So who is really the head of all these conflicting and competing fractions "in the body of Christ"? Surely, Christ is not a schizophrenic Head, and is clearly not the Author of this growing, Babylonic confusion.

Religious sectarianism is truly a scourge of the enemy of the kingdom of heaven and must be seen for what it is. The body of Christ is one and so is His kingdom, *for any kingdom divided against itself is laid waste; and any city or house divided against itself will not stand* (Matthew 12:25). All must be reminded that these are the words of the King, Himself; and neither His church nor His kingdom can be shaped by human hands (Daniel 2:34, 45), for though they are in the world, they are certainly not of this world.

The Shepherd and His Sheep

While the present condition of Christianity appears very frustrating and confusing to the non-Christian observer, the truth about His chosen possession is very clear to the omniscient Lord of all the earth. Just as not all who called Abraham their father belong to Israel, so it is that not all who call the name of Christ are His. Christ once asked the thought-provoking question of the multitudes that thronged to hear Him: "*And why do you call Me 'Lord, Lord,' and do not do what I say?*" The obvious implication of this question is that all true citizens of the kingdom (Lord is a kingdom term) will be obedient to the demands of the King. The love of God and obedience to Christ constitute the divine DNA that resides in the spirit of every kingdom citizen who has been purchased with the precious blood of Jesus.

> "*The one who says, 'I have come to know Him,' and does not keep His commandments, is a liar, and the truth is not in him; ⁵but whoever keeps His word, in him the love of God has truly been perfected. By this we know that we are in Him:*"
>
> 1 John 2:4, 5

Christ knows all who are truly His, and He will call and gather them together at the appropriate time according to His purpose. The true people of God are not a denomination or a church in the sense of its contemporary ecclesiastical usage, but a kingdom movement of committed disciples of Jesus, growing like yeast hidden in the massive lump of the religious confusion still obvious today (Matthew 13:33). Christ reminds us:

> "<u>I am</u> the good shepherd, and I know <u>My</u> own and <u>My</u> own know Me, ^{15}even as the Father knows Me and I know the Father; and <u>I</u> lay down <u>My life</u> for the sheep. ^{16}I have other sheep, which are not of <u>this fold</u>; I must bring them also, and they will hear <u>My</u> voice; and they will become <u>one flock with one shepherd</u>."

John 10:14-16

The issue in the above scriptural text is absolutely clear. It is, without any doubt, not about any denominational claim (who we say or think we are as a believing community), but rather, it is totally and completely about who Christ says are really His. The true weight of what Christ is saying here is not completely captured in the English translation of the text for it omits the emphasis of the Greek textual construction, which is more forceful. It reads: *I myself am* (clearing indicating that no one else is) *the Shepherd, the Good One!*

Even more, the Good Shepherd knows His own, and His own knows Him. The word used for know in both instances is the Gk. ***ginōskō***, which means to know experientially or intimately (as opposed to **oida** or **eidō**, which means to know by outward appearance or intuitively). Christ was very certain and emphatic when He said: *My sheep hear My voice, and I know them, and they follow Me* (John 10:27). This is the heart of Christian discipleship—Jesus inviting His disciples to follow Him as sheep who hear (and understand) the voice of their Master Shepherd and respond in obedience to Him.

Thus, in the midst of all our chaos and confusion—the denominational hair-splitting, the name-calling, back-stabbing and back-biting, truth-claiming, character-smearing and whatever else there is—Christ says that He knows all who truly belong to Him. He has ONE flock and HE is the ONLY GOOD SHEPHERD. Over the centuries, many have tried to get past this truth with their many claims and theories over the "this fold," but the veracity of the Bible does not leave us any room to guess or speculate. "This fold" is not decided upon, or controlled, by humanity. It is identified only by the Good Shepherd, Himself, and it embraces all true believers that have passed the divine scrutiny of Him who is also the ONLY gate to the sheepfold.

"This fold" represents the new Israel that Christ purchased through the shedding of His own blood (John 10:11, 15)—His kingdom citizens, even His general assembly and church of the first-born who are already enrolled in heaven, not just on earth (Hebrews 12:22-24). The Master has not given His blood-bought heritage or its headship to any man or any system of religion. He has retained these ownership rights solely to Himself for He, and ONLY He, understands the gross deceitfulness of the human heart to judge correctly all who do, or do not, belong to Him. Christ does not have other folds; ONLY other sheep. He has ONE fold, and all humanity, including the under-shepherds who help care for Christ's sheep, must come through the ONLY entrance (Jesus) into that ONE sheepfold. All must work in concert with (not apart from) the Good Shepherd to bring His other lost sheep safely into His fold.

Religious institutionalism has attempted to make adjustments to the entrance to the sheepfold by invariably replacing, attaching to, or downsizing the door by man-made inventions such as infant baptism, self-righteous rituals, restrictions and traditions. This is one of the legacies the mysterious whore (Revelation 17) has bequeathed to her fallen daughters. As denominations, organizations and institutions multiply in numbers, so also do the subtle nuances of the prerequisites and requirements for entrance into these communities.

Faith in the Son of God and in His efficacious sacrifice for sin is simply not enough to satisfy institutional demands, and, therefore, cannot stand on its own as the sinner's only means of salvation. The wandering and lost must square up to the institutional standards of men and their religion or must find salvation elsewhere. Human religion does not trust the grace of God that brings salvation to all (Titus 2:11), to transform sinners, let alone mature them. Therefore, is it any wonder why many sinners are left confused and lost in their pursuit to satisfy their heart cries for peace and salvation in Jesus Christ?

However, the Good Shepherd is very cognizant of the plight of His lonely, straying sheep that stand in grave danger of being exploited and hurt by those under-shepherds who are mere thieves and robbers—wolves in sheep's clothing, preying on the innocent and the ignorant. He presents Himself in stark contrast to the man-made doors, protected by human traditions from the destitute seekers after God. "*I am the door*," He says. "*If <u>anyone</u> enters through Me, he <u>shall be saved</u>, and <u>shall go in and out</u> and find pasture*" (John 10:9). Jesus is the open door to all sinners who seek entrance into His kingdom of eternal life. He does not discriminate against any fallen offspring of Adam, regardless of his/her present sinful condition or past actions.

While some professing communities may favor some sinners above others, Jesus openly receives anyone, with the exception of no one, who chooses to enter the kingdom of heaven through Him. Christ does not only promise such a one salvation, but also the freedom (the ability to go in and out) accorded to all citizens of His kingdom. The saved sinner would have equal and full access to all the benefits of the kingdom to meet and satisfy his/her every need. This is what Jesus means when He says that the one who enters through Him shall find pasture.

Consequently, Christ's scathing rebuke to the religious leaders of His day is indicative of His posture against those who make it their self-righteous duty to hedge up the Way (Jesus) to the eternal life by their human restrictions and/or substitutions.

"*But woe to you, Scribes and Pharisees, hypocrites!*

For you lock people out of the kingdom of heaven. For you do not go in yourselves, and when others are going in, you stop them."

Matthew 23:13

Christ Calls His Own

"<u>My sheep</u> hear <u>My voice</u>, and <u>I know them</u>, and they follow Me; ²⁸and I give eternal life to them, and they will never perish; and <u>no one will snatch them out of My hand</u>. ²⁹<u>My Father, who has given them to Me</u>, <u>is greater than all; and no one is able to snatch them out of the Father's hand. ³⁰I and the Father are one</u>."

Verses 27-30

It is extremely important to note how very personal Jesus is in John 10:1-30. Christ, the Good Shepherd, is painstakingly possessive about His sheep, even to the point of laying down His life for them. <u>Fourteen times</u> Christ uses the possessive pronoun "My" in this discourse — <u>four</u> of those in reference to His sheep; <u>four times</u> He uses My Father; <u>three times</u> My life; <u>twice</u> He uses My voice; and <u>once</u> He uses My hand. Listen to Jesus speak:

I am the door (vv. 7, 9) – twice
I am the good shepherd (vv. 11, 14) – twice
I know My sheep (v. 14, 27) – twice
I lay down My life for the sheep (vv. 11, 15, 17, 18) – four times
I have other sheep (v. 16)
I must bring them to the fold (v. 16)
I will give them eternal life (v. 28)
No one shall snatch them out of My hand (v. 28)

Does the Good Shepherd sound like anyone who is willing to relinquish His oversight or control of His chosen heritage by giving it to another? Absolutely not! To the contrary, He speaks more like someone who is so protective over His own that He will not abdicate the responsibility of ownership to anyone else. As a matter of fact, Jesus sounds just as intentional about His sheep as He did about His church when He declared to Peter, in Matthew 16:18: "... *you are Peter, and upon this rock I will build My church...*"[3]

The truth is that this declaration in Matthew and what Jesus is saying in John 10 regarding His personal relationship to His sheep represent one and the same thing—and that is, He is the ONLY true Builder of His church, just as He is the ONLY Good Shepherd of His sheep. These truths are very consistent with Christ's words and actions: "*And I have other sheep which are not of this fold; I must bring them also . . .*" (John 10:16); and *the Lord was adding to their number day by day those who were being saved* (Acts 2:47); and He does so even today! Please notice that the bringing to the fold and the adding to His church are both divine operations—with or without human cooperation.

Additionally, a very careful reading of John 10 reveals that Christ is mirrored in every object in the passage—the door, the good shepherd and even the fold, which is His body. Christ moves His listeners from a relationship of a more general nature (John 10:1-5)—talking about "a thief and a robber" (v. 1), "a shepherd and his sheep" (vv. 2-4), and "a stranger" (v. 5), all in the 3rd person—to a very specific understanding of His personal relationship to His sheep. *I am the door. . . I am the Good Shepherd. . . I know My sheep. . . I lay down My life for My sheep. . . I have other sheep. . . I must bring them to the fold. . . I will give them eternal life. . . No one shall snatch them out of My hand*, all in the 1st person. If there is anything at all that we can learn from this very cogent message of the Good Shepherd it is this: **"Don't mess with My sheep! I have given My life for them and I have the power to take you out if you try to hurt them in any way or pluck them out of My hand!"** (I am speaking colloquially).

When Saul (who became Paul, the apostle) was breathing threats and murder against the early disciples of Christ (Acts 9:1, 2), Jesus personally confronted him on his way to Damascus with the jolting question: *"Saul, Saul, why are you persecuting Me"* (Acts 9:4)? This was a very personal accusation—attacking His sheep was an assault on the Shepherd. Saul answered the question with a question: *"Who art Thou, Lord"* (v. 5)? Saul was obviously confused, not only from being knocked off his horse and by the great brilliance of the blinding light from the sky above, but also by the question itself.

How do you interpret a religious sect as being a "Me"? As far as Saul was concerned, he was persecuting "the Way" (v. 2; Acts 22:4) and not an individual called "the Way." However, the Good Shepherd left Saul no doubt in the answer to his inquiry when he replied: *"I am Jesus whom you are persecuting"* (Acts 9:5). The sect, called "the Way" and Jesus, is one and the same entity. Every sheep in the sheepfold is representative of the literal body of Christ, and any assault on them is an attack on His person.

Through the prophet Isaiah, the Lord, the Good Shepherd, speaks of His relationship to His sheep in this way:

> *"But now, thus says the LORD, your Creator, O Jacob, And He who formed you, O Israel, Do not fear, for <u>I have redeemed you; I have called you by name; you are Mine!</u> ²When you pass through the waters, <u>I will be with you</u>; And through the rivers, they will not overflow you. When you walk through the fire, you will not be scorched, Nor will the flame burn you." ³For <u>I am the LORD your God, The Holy One of Israel, your Savior; I have given Egypt as your ransom, Cush and Seba in your place. Since you are precious in My sight, Since you are honored and I love you</u>,* **⁴I will give other men in your place and**

other peoples in exchange for your life."

Isaiah 43:1-4

It is very important to observe that the nature of the language here in the book of Isaiah is just as personal and forceful as that in John 10. Pay attention to the following parallel statements:

Isaiah 43:1-4	**John 10**
v. 1 – *"I have redeemed you."*	vv. 11, 15, – *"I lay down My life for the sheep."*
v. 1 – *"I have called you by name."*	v. 3 – *he calls his own sheep by name.*
v. 1 – *"you are Mine!"*	vv. 14, 26, 27 – *My own, My sheep.*
v. 2 – *"I will be with you."*	vv. 3, 4 – *He leads them out; he goes before them.*
v. 3 – *"I have given Egypt as your ransom, Cush and Seba in your place."*	vv. 11, 15, – *"I lay down My life for the sheep."*

In this very personal message through the prophet Isaiah, Christ is not only very possessive regarding His blood-bought heritage; He is also very watchful and protective of them. He says: *I will give other men in your place and other peoples in exchange for your life* (Isaiah 43:4). The warning is very clear: Don't "mess" with the Master's Sheep!

Those who serve as under-shepherds and leaders of Christ's heritage must be aware of the fact that this God-given privilege is also a most awesome responsibility. They must be constantly sensitive to the truth that the sheep outside and inside the sheepfold belong to Christ. He is the One who says they are His. He is the One who says He (not us) must bring them to the sheepfold. He was the One who laid down His life for them. He is the One who gives them eternal life. Christ is doing all the work, not us. We are only privileged to be conduits through which His healing, transforming and saving grace flows. Sometimes we try to claim ownership to what does not belong to us and frustrate the free current of the divine grace with our multiplicity of rules and traditions.

However, in the midst of the denominational and religious uncertainty of today, Christ has complete knowledge regarding all those who are His; and He vows by His authority and that of His Father that no one will be able to pry them out of their hands, for He and His Father are one (John 10:27-30). How comforting and reassuring! Men and systems of religion may separate Christ' lambs from their company just as they did in Jesus' day (John 9), but they cannot alienate them from the Good Shepherd (John 9:34-38). Paul asks the question:

> "*Who will bring a charge against God's elect? God is the one who justifies;* ^{34}*who is the one who condemns? Christ Jesus is He who died, yes, rather who was raised, who is at the right hand of God, who also intercedes for us.* ^{35}*Who will separate us from the love of Christ? Will tribulation, or distress, or persecution, or famine, or nakedness, or peril, or sword?"*
>
> Romans 8:33-35

The veteran apostle answers his own question by standing

firmly upon the Word of God that abides forever (Isaiah 40:8; 1 Peter 1:24, 25).

> *"Just as it is written, 'FOR YOUR SAKE WE ARE BEING PUT TO DEATH ALL DAY LONG; WE WERE CONSIDERED AS SHEEP TO BE SLAUGHTERED.' [37]But in all these things we overwhelmingly conquer through Him who loved us. [38]For I am convinced that neither death, nor life, nor angels, nor principalities, nor things present, nor things to come, nor powers, [39]nor height, nor depth, nor any other created thing, will be able to separate us from the love of God, which is in Christ Jesus our Lord."*
>
> Romans 8:36-39

Jesus and the Father work in concert to preserve and protect all who have been redeemed by Christ's blood, and have placed their trust in Him. All glory and praise be to God!

God's Prevailing Will

> *"The owner's servants came to him and said, 'Sir, didn't you sow good seed in your field? Where then did the weeds come from?' 'An enemy did this,' he replied. The servants asked him, '<u>Do you want us to go and pull them up</u>?' [29]'No,' he answered, 'because while you are pulling the weeds, you may root up the wheat with them. [30]<u>Let both grow together</u> until the harvest...'"*
>
> Matthew 13:28-30, NIV

The genuine concern of the slaves over their master's wheat

crop in the opening parable of this chapter motivates them to take preventive action to avoid what they perceive as certain disaster when harvest time arrives. *"Do you want us to go and pull them (the tares) up?"* Although their intentions were good, they came from hearts that were overtaken by fear, and not established by faith in their master. Fear, in most cases, inevitably leads to poor decision-making. These slaves were promptly ready to march through the cultivated field and pull up whatever they perceived to be tares. The wise master knew that, operating from the platform of fear, these servants were certain to destroy precious wheat crops in their fear-ridden, clean-up campaign. Thus, he cautions: *"No, because while you are pulling the weeds, you may root up the wheat with them."*

Let Them both Grow Together. . .

The master's instruction is wise counsel to all who work in the kingdom field today. The enemy of the gospel of Jesus certainly knows that the very chaotic situation of this church age (and kingdom dispensation) has the capacity to create deep-seated fear in the hearts of genuine disciples of Christ. Thus, while we profess abiding faith in God, the enemy of our souls still preys on our fear in order to drive us to make very poor decisions, which in turn create a vicious cycle of fearful decision-making. Quite often, it so easy for many sincere believers to become distracted from their task in the kingdom field because they are preoccupied with what other kingdom workers are (or are not) doing. Such preoccupation reduces the effectiveness of the disciple, and often leads to greater chaos as that disciple tries to relieve his fear and anger (often the product of fear) by taking matters into his own hands. Consequently, we currently have otherwise good people among the churches, denominations, ministries, and religious organizations in the kingdom domain, who are attacking one another—name-calling, backbiting, undermining, etc.—and all in the "name of Jesus."

Sometimes our human perception, based upon our fear-driven, faulty assessment of others, will have us judge them as tares in the kingdom field; but we must allow the counsel of Jesus to guide our human spirit—let them grow together, for harvest time is coming. How many innocent children in the kingdom are destroyed by the hasty actions of others to get rid of "evil-doers" from the body of Christ? On the other hand, it is just simply amazing, nothing short of miraculous, to see how often evil has a way of working itself out of the body of Christ, very much like Judas working himself out of his place among Christ's disciples. The law of harvest, like other laws of God, is immutable, and there is harvest to be reaped in this life as there is one to be reaped at the end of the world.

But it is hard to. . .

At times it is awfully hard to follow the Master's counsel, but we cannot allow our fears to rule over our faith in the Master. One day the disciples saw someone, whom they perceived was not a believer, casting out demons in the name of Jesus and they were filled with "righteous" indignation. What made the matter even more offensive to them was the fact that shortly before this incident occurred, they were unable to cast the demon out of a little boy at the foot of the mount of transfiguration (Mark 9:14-18). Still reeling from their own embarrassment before the multitude who witnessed their spiritual impotence, they were somewhat envious of the person who was doing what they themselves were unable to do as disciples of Jesus. Their fear and envy prompted them to make the decision to try to stop another worker in the kingdom field (v. 38). When John approached Jesus on behalf of all the disciples, they expected Jesus to commend their actions, but the Master only repeated what He was saying all along:

> "*Do not stop him,*" Jesus said. "*No one who does a miracle in my name can in the next moment say anything bad about me, ^{40}for whoever is not against*

<u>us is for us</u>. ⁴¹*I tell you the truth, anyone who gives you a cup of water in my name because you belong to Christ will certainly not lose his reward...*"

Mark 9:39-41

This was a precious lesson for the early disciples of Jesus, as much as it is for us; for their attitude reflects very much what is happening among 21st century disciples of Jesus Christ. Here is a typical scenario: Church members of one denomination or ministry may see someone from another denomination performing miracles in the name of Jesus. Instead of praising the name of the Lord, they are overcome by suspicion and anger. These members would voice their "concern" to their minister or church leader, and instead of guiding these believers by the wise counsel of Jesus, he offers them one of his/her own: "Don't you go to those meetings!" "Switch your television station, or turn it off!" "Those miracle-workers are operating by the powers of Satan!" These and other negative, derogatory comments are made regarding the one through whom the miracles were effected, or the ministry or denomination to which such a one belongs.

The last of the above statements is very familiar and interesting, for it was also used against Jesus when He performed the miracle of healing upon the demon possessed man who was not only blind, but also mute. This episode is quite instructive, so read it very carefully:

> "*Then a demon-possessed man who was blind and mute was brought to Jesus, and He healed him, so that the mute man spoke and saw.* ²³*All the crowds were amazed, and were saying, 'This man cannot be the Son of David, can he?'*
> ²⁴*But when the Pharisees heard this, they said,* '<u>This man casts out demons only by Beelzebul the</u>

ruler of the demons.' ²⁵And knowing their thoughts Jesus said to them, <u>Any kingdom divided against itself is laid waste; and any city or house divided against itself will not stand</u>. ²⁶If Satan casts out Satan, he is divided against himself; how then will his kingdom stand?

²⁷If I by Beelzebul cast out demons, <u>by whom do your sons cast them out? For this reason they will be your judges</u>. ²⁸But if I cast out demons by the Spirit of God, <u>then the kingdom of God has come upon you</u>. ²⁹Or how can anyone enter the strong man's house and carry off his property, unless he first binds the strong man? And then he will plunder his house.

³⁰He who is not with Me is against Me; and he who does not gather with Me scatters. ³¹<u>Therefore I say to you, any sin and blasphemy shall be forgiven people, but blasphemy against the Spirit shall not be forgiven</u>. ³²Whoever speaks a word against the Son of Man, it shall be forgiven him; but whoever speaks against the Holy Spirit, it shall not be forgiven him, either in this age or in the age to come."

Matthew 12:22-32

Leaders and teachers of God's people bear an awesome responsibility with regard to the instruction they offer those under their spiritual care. It is very significant to observe in the above passage of scripture that while the people were enamored by the miracle of Jesus, their leaders were filled with envy and anger. Consequently, they used their positions of power to influence the minds of the people against the Son of David, by attributing to the devil the wonderful work that God had wrought through Him. They themselves were not performing any miracles because they were destitute of the power of God. The kingdom of heaven was manifesting itself right before their eyes and they could not discern it because they were blinded by their self-righteous arrogance. Therefore, they were completely cut off from the Source of its power.

As it was then, so it is today. The kingdom of heaven is operating all around us and professed keepers of God's people cannot even discern it, because they are preoccupied with their personal or institutional agendas. However, Christ's words must serve as a serious rebuke and warning to all those who take it upon themselves to judge the works of others in the kingdom and thereby perpetuate feelings of ill-will among believers in the body of Christ. If we cannot speak good regarding the work and ministry of others, we should not speak evil, lest we find ourselves fighting against God Almighty (blaspheming the Holy Spirit by attributing His work to the Devil) and not against puny man or the evil one.

Moreover, we must always remember that the kingdom and its powers are not ours to control. These operate only by the divine prerogatives of the King who graciously dispenses their blessings upon whomsoever He wills. Our authority and power are never inherent, but always transferred—that is, from Christ and His Spirit to us. How many zealous, misguided and self-opinioned believers spend their days upon earth tearing down the works of others instead of building up the kingdom of heaven with their God-given gifts and talents? Instead of trusting in the wisdom of the Master, they go about seeking to establish their own criteria for setting the church and the kingdom right. God is only too wise to commit such an awesome task to erring humans.

We must discipline ourselves to perfect our divine assignment in the kingdom field and leave the results of our work up to the King. During His closing days with His disciples, Jesus presented Peter with his second commission of shepherding His flock (John 21:15-17). The first was that of making disciples. After giving Peter this assignment, Christ instructed Peter to follow Him. Peter began following, but when he turned around, he also saw John following them. He, therefore, asked Jesus: *"Lord, <u>what about him</u>?"* Jesus answered, *"If I want him to remain alive until I return, <u>what is that to you</u>? You must follow me"* (John 21:19-21).

The preoccupation with what others are doing continues to be a major hurdle to cross over for many well-meaning believers, and the enemy of our souls uses this tool of distraction and deception to maximize his advantage in his warfare against Christ's kingdom. We must discipline ourselves to follow Jesus and allow Him to handle whatever appears to be amiss (in our eyes) in His kingdom.

The apostle Paul, more than any other Bible writer, understood this very well, for he had to deal with many distractions and opposition in his ministry.

> *"Some, to be sure, are preaching Christ even from envy and strife, but some also from good will; [16]the latter do it out of love, knowing that I am appointed for the defense of the gospel; [17]the former proclaim Christ out of selfish ambition rather than from pure motives, thinking to cause me distress in my imprisonment. [18]What then? <u>Only that in every way, whether in pretense or in truth, Christ is proclaimed</u>; and in this I rejoice. Yes, and I will rejoice."*
>
> Philippians 1:15-18

What the apostle is saying here, echoes very much what Jesus said to His disciples (through John) when they complained about someone else healing in their Master's name. Christ's words were: *"do not stop them,"* or simply *"leave them alone."* Paul says *"what then?"* or in today's language, *"big deal!"* The message here is very clear for the many self-righteous judges who go out of their way to prove that their way of preaching the gospel of Jesus is right, while condemning others: *"What is that to you? Follow thou Me!" "Leave them alone!" "Big deal!"*

Certainly, there are many who are out and about in the world preaching "strange" gospels, and others who are preaching Christ from mixed motives; but Paul is not distracted by these ambitious, self-serving, self-proclaimed preachers of Christ. His position is very simple: As long as Jesus Christ is being proclaimed, it's all good (so to speak); for it is Christ who says: *"And I, if and when I am lifted up from the earth* [on the cross], <u>*will draw and attract*</u> *all men* [Gentiles as well as Jews] *to Myself"* (John 12:32, The Amplified Bible).

Be assured of this very thing: Salvation is not the work of men. It is the work of God. It is the grace of God that draws (brings) men to salvation (Titus 2:11; Romans 2:4). Humankind may enjoy the privilege of being co-laborers with God in the proclamation of the gospel. But make no mistake about it: it is the power of God alone that draws sinners to Christ—not the voice, antics or charisma of the preacher. The name and the cross of Jesus Christ are the divine magnets to draw all types of sinners to the presence of God, irrespective of the channel through which the gospel is proclaimed.

There is absolutely nothing that can be done to hurt the Name that has already conquered every other name under heaven and on earth—be they names of angels, preachers, organizations, denominations, churches or any other. Praise the Lord! At the name of JESUS every knee MUST bow and every tongue MUST confess that JESUS IS LORD, INDEED! He has not surrendered His control over His kingdom field, nor will He change the words that have gone out of His mouth—the wheat and tares will grow together until harvest time. Remember?

Do not be distracted by the enemy, for we fight not against flesh and blood; but our struggle is against rulers and powers of darkness, evil spirits operating in the unseen realm. The real issue in the warfare against the kingdom of darkness is not whether that person, church, ministry, or organization is doing right according to our judgment; but whether or not we are focused on what Christ has called us to do in His kingdom. There is a wise, old adage that says: *"When you mind someone else's business, your own business goes astray."* Christ will hold us responsible for the task He has assigned to us; not for what He has assigned (or did not assign) to someone else.

Paul never lost focus on what God had called him to do. Hence the reasons why at the end of his life he was able to say with confidence: "*I have fought a good fight, I have finished the course, I have kept the faith...*" (2 Timothy 4:7). This veteran apostle understood the Christian warfare and did not use his God-given talents and resources to stone the devil's dogs (as a matter of speaking), but to proclaim the gospel of the kingdom where it had never been preached before (Romans 15:18-21). It is this servant of God who tells us that we must "*fight the good fight of faith. . .*" Not every fight is a good fight. Whenever we fight out of our fears instead of our faith it is more likely to be a bad fight. Fear produces torment which short-circuits our spiritual sensitivity and impairs our better judgment. The Bible is very clear when it says that "*God has not given us a spirit of timidity, but of power and love and discipline*" (2 Timothy 1:7).

Fear then, is of the evil one. The root of all our fears lies in the enemy's ability to turn our attention away from God and to have us focus our minds on the situations or sources of our fears. Once that occurs, fear is unavoidably produced through our instant (or sometimes prolonged) logical assessment of our situation, which we perceive is outside the realm of our ability to control. However, when we focus our minds on God and away from our distresses, we soon realize that He is much bigger that all our puny situations. Faith wells up in the heart and we are able to face our battles as mighty conquerors through our Lord, Jesus Christ. We have this sure word from the prophet Isaiah:

> "*Thou will keep him in perfect peace <u>whose mind is stayed on thee</u>: because he trusteth in thee. ⁴Trust ye in the Lord for ever: for in the Lord Jehovah is everlasting strength.*"

Isaiah 26:3, 4, KJV

As we work in the kingdom field, let us remain focused on our Master, who says to all: "Stop worrying about what others are (or are not) doing; you must follow Me" (John 21:22, my paraphrase). Of course, the religious confusion in the world, especially among Protestants, sometimes makes it very difficult to do so; but we must maintain our spiritual equilibrium by keeping our eyes on Jesus. Some wheat in the field may look likes tares, and some tares may really resemble wheat; but we are not called to be judges over another man's field or servant (Romans 14:4; Matthew 7:1-5).

Christ calls us all to be co-workers with Himself, to prepare His field for the final harvest. Do not be distracted by the religious conflicts in the kingdom. They are indicative of the truthfulness of Christ's words—that is, not only must the wheat and the tares grow together, but also that harvest time is coming. Be comforted by the very fact that through all the confusion that surrounds us, God is working out His eternal purpose and will ultimately reap a bountiful harvest. Be diligent, therefore, about your assigned task! *Be ye also patient; stablish your hearts: for the coming of the Lord draweth nigh* (James 5:8)!

Notes:

1. Read Frank Viola, *Pagan Christianity: The Origins of Our Modern Church Practices* (Present Testimony Ministry, 2002) for additional information on this matter.
2. Ernst Troeltsch, *Protestantism and Progress: A Historical Study of the Relation of Protestantism to the Modern World* (Boston: Beacon Press, 1912), 59.
3. See chapter 4 of this volume, *The Church and the Kingdom*, for a more detailed explanation of this powerful statement.

PRELUDE TO THE PRESENCE

8

"There will be signs in the sun and moon and stars, and on the earth dismay among nations, in perplexity at the roaring of the sea and the waves, ^{26}men fainting from fear and the expectation of the things which are coming upon the world; for the powers of the heavens will be shaken. ^{27}Then they will see THE SON OF MAN COMING IN A CLOUD with power and great glory. ^{28}But when these things begin to take place, straighten up and lift up your heads, because your redemption is drawing near."

Luke 21:25-28

Return of the Forerunner

At the beginning of His ministry, Jesus gave one essential message to His disciples to preach to the nation of Israel (the Jews first) and the world (Matthew 10:5-8). It was the same message that was given to His forerunner and wilderness-dweller, John the Baptist, who proclaimed it fearlessly to the leaders and people of Israel (Matthew 3:1-8). This was the same message Jesus began preaching after John was placed in prison and later beheaded by Herod (Matthew 4:12-17). The message: *"Repent, for the kingdom of heaven is at hand"* (Matthew 3:2; 4:17; 10:7).

The imminence and the immediacy of the kingdom of heaven were to be the ever present reality in the life and teaching of the believing community. However, over the centuries, this core message of the kingdom became increasingly muted as the body of Christ succumbed to the overtures of Roman institutionalism during and after the Constantinian era. This phenomenon gave birth to diverse forms of a post-Reformation Christianity driven by organizational agendas rather than by kingdom priorities. Like Israel of old, we have allowed institutional demands to dictate our interpretation and approach to our kingdom assignment, and wallow in the deception that our organizational expansions have the seal and approval of our Commissioner, Lord and King.

It was not without reason that Jesus told His disciples to preach the message of the imminence and immediacy of His kingdom first to the lost sheep of the house of Israel and not the Gentile world. It was God's wake-up call to the backslidden nation to refocus the minds of His chosen people on the true purpose and reason for their existence. The good news of the risen Christ and His kingdom was not only the heart and soul of the ministry of the early church, but also the cornerstone of the preaching and teaching of one of its greatest leaders—Paul, the apostle to the Gentiles. As a matter of fact, the book of Acts ends with this exemplary testimony concerning the ministry of the imprisoned servant of God:

> "And he stayed two full years in his own rented quarters and was welcoming all who came to him, *³¹<u>preaching the kingdom of God and teaching concerning the Lord Jesus Christ</u>* with all openness, unhindered."
>
> Acts 28:30, 31

We do not know exactly how long after his two-year house arrest that Paul was executed, but his letters bear witness to the fact that he never deviated from the gospel theme of Christ and His kingdom. What a sterling example for professed believers today! We have strayed very far away from the central task of preaching and building the kingdom of God, and have allowed the bureaucracies of organized religion to place "more pressing," alternative demands in our path.

However, the time is now at hand for the last-day return of the "spirit" of John the Baptist. God is giving His last rallying call for faithful forerunners of the soon-coming King and His glorious kingdom. He is not looking for, nor moved by, bureaucratic religious and political endorsements, but is seeking anointed vessels, emptied of selfish ambitions and full of the faith and the Holy Spirit. He is not interested in ostentatious labels and self-righteous claims, but only in humble, fearless voices that are willing to cry aloud in the wilderness of these post-Modern days: *"Prepare ye the way of the Lord, make His paths straight"* (Matthew 3:3, KJV).

The anointed King is urgently calling His present-day disciples to follow His directive to preach the kingdom of God first to His house, so that an awakened body of Christ will abandon the multiplicity of man-made lists of to-do's and unite in one voice to proclaim to the dying world the timeless message: *"Repent, for the kingdom of heaven is at hand."* This message must first do a reformatory work within the believing community before it could have any significant effect in the world, readying a prepared people for the return of the King. We must return to the spirit that drove the apostolic believers to preach only Christ crucified! Christ resurrected from the dead! Christ coming again in power and great glory, to redeem His own!

Signs of the Approaching King

As it was at the beginning of His ministry, so it was at the ending—the Savior kept the centrality of the kingdom before the men He had chosen to finish the work which He begun. However, as the time of His departure was quickly approaching, Jesus began focusing the attention of His disciples not so much on the imminence of the kingdom that was already unfolding before them, but on the certainty of His return to receive that very kingdom. His parting promise to them was: *"If I go... I will come again to receive you to Myself; that where I am there you may be also"* (John 14:3).

Of course, Christ's disciples were very anxious about this promise, and one day they asked Him the million-dollar question: *"Tell us, when will these things happen, and what will be the sign of Your coming, and of the end of the age"* (Matthew 24:3)? In other words, what will be the prelude to your presence? While it is not my intention to explore the details of every sign Christ enumerated in the 24th chapter of Matthew, I will simply review some of them to show the accuracy of the fulfillment of the King's predictions.

Messianic Imposters and False Prophets

The very first sign Christ gave to His disciples regarding the nearness of His return was the appearance of messianic impersonators and false prophets. As a matter of fact, He gave this warning twice in this one chapter—once in verse 5 and then again in verses 23-27. Let's briefly look at these:

> *"For many will come in My name, saying, 'I am the Christ,' and will mislead many."*

Matthew 24:5

> *"Then if anyone says to you, 'Behold, here is the Christ,' or 'There He is,' do not believe him.* [24]*"For false Christs and false prophets will arise and will show great signs and wonders, so as to mislead, if possible, even the elect.* [25]*"Behold, I have told you in advance.* [26]*"So if they say to you, 'Behold, He is in the wilderness,' do not go out, or, 'Behold, He is in the inner rooms,' do not believe them.* [27]*"<u>For just as the lightning comes from the east and flashes even to</u>*

<u>*the west, so will the coming of the Son of Man be.*</u>"

Matthew 24:23-27

The first thing to observe in these verses is that Christ did not only speak of a few impersonators and false prophets, but warns of many. These agents of evil are not simply preachers or teachers of the gospel, but also dubious impersonators of Christ, claiming to be the Messiah, or to have been appointed by heaven to act in His stead. In order to authenticate their claim, these charismatic personalities will operate under the influence of the prince of darkness to perform very powerful signs and wonders, with the intention to gain authority and control over the minds and actions of believers. Jesus says that the performance of these impersonators will be so convincing that "IF" it were possible, they would deceive even the very elect of God (Matthew 24:24).

This statement is a very clear indication that our natural senses alone (seeing, hearing, feeling, tasting, and smelling) will be utterly insufficient to discern the veracity of the signs and wonders that will be performed in the name of Christ in the last days. The believer's ability to invalidate the miraculous claims of these false Christs will rest solely upon his personal relationship with the Master, supported by his knowledge of, and complete faith in, His Word which stands firm forever.

It is only those sheep who walk daily with the Shepherd who will be able to discern His voice amid the deceptive, confusing voices of the ravenous wolves let loose from the pit of hell in order to devour inattentive, straying lambs of the flock. One inspired writer has rightly said: "None but those who have fortified the mind with the truths of the Bible will stand through the last great conflict."[1]

Regarding deceivers and false prophets, Jesus said: *"you will know them by their fruits"* (Matthew 7:20). A thorough knowledge and understanding of the Word of God will not only enhance our capability to identify correctly the fruits of false prophets, but also give us the ability to examine their roots long before there are any fruits on the tree of their religious claim or profession. This is diagnosis 101—*you will know them by their roots*. Any system of religion that does not have Jesus Christ and the Word of God as the dominant center of its core beliefs and practices is certainly not of God.

Secret Rapture?

The other issue in the preceding verses of Scripture deals the secret appearance of Jesus. Christ makes it abundantly clear that His coming will not be a secret catching away of His church—not when He is coming to put and end of sin, death and the grave; not when He is coming in the clouds with power and great glory (Luke 17:27). Christ says that His coming would be gloriously observable, *as the lightning comes from the east and flashes even to the west*. Many use the two verses in Matthew 24: 40, 41 to build an entire teaching on a secret rapture without paying careful attention to everything else that Jesus and the Bible say about the King's return. Let us read the context of these two verses of Scripture:

> "*For the coming of the Son of Man will be just like the days of Noah*. ³⁸*For as in those days before the flood they were eating and drinking, marrying and giving in marriage, until the day that Noah entered the ark*, ³⁹*and they did not understand until the flood came and took them all away;* so will the coming of the Son of Man be. ⁴⁰*Then there will be two men in the field; one will be taken and one will be left.* ⁴¹*Two women will be grinding at the mill; one will be taken and one will be left*."

> Matthew 24:37-41

Please observe that verse 37 forms the thesis statement that provides the context for everything else that follows. It reads: *"For the coming of the Son of Man will be just like the days of Noah."* What were the people doing in Noah's day prior to the flood? They were preoccupied with the demands and festivities of their everyday lives—eating, drinking, marrying and being given in marriage—while, at the same time, scoffing at the word of truth regarding the imminence of the world-wide deluge. The antediluvians were engrossed in their daily rounds of activities and secular carousing *until the day Noah entered the ark* (v. 38). Their rejection of the truth had completely clouded their understanding of its reality *until the flood came and took them all away* (v. 39). Jesus then concluded His scenario with a confirmation of His opening thesis statement: *"so will the coming of the Son of Man* be" (v. 39). This is the context for the two verses that follow.

> "*Then there will be two men in the field; one will be taken and one will be left.* ⁴¹*"Two women will be grinding at the mill; one will be taken and one will be left.*"

Verses 40, 41

These two verses simply stress the fact that prior to the return of Jesus, people will be doing just as the people of Noah's day did—ignoring or even scoffing at the truth of Christ's return, busy in their pursuit of pleasure and the everyday demands of life. The apostle Peter wrote:

> "*Know this first of all, that in the last days mockers will come with their mocking, following after their own lusts,* ⁴*and saying, Where is the promise of His coming? For ever since the fathers fell asleep, all continues just as it was from the beginning of*

> *creation. ⁵For when they maintain this, it escapes their notice that by the word of God the heavens existed long ago and the earth was formed out of water and by water, ⁶through which the world at that time was destroyed, being flooded with water. ⁷But by His word the present heavens and earth are being reserved for fire, kept for the day of judgment and destruction of ungodly men."*
>
> 2 Peter 3:3-7

These last-day scoffers would rather believe lies about the return of Jesus in order to maintain a measure of comfort with their ungodly, pleasure-seeking lifestyle. They choose to ignore the truth of God's Word so that they can follow the inclinations of their deceitful hearts. This they will continue to do until Christ actually punctures the azure skies with His glorious presence to receive His waiting saints—His beloved bride, His church and citizens of His kingdom. This is the scene that the apostle Paul described when he wrote:

> *"For the Lord Himself will descend from heaven with a shout, with the voice of the archangel and with the trumpet of God, and the dead in Christ will rise first. ¹⁷Then we who are alive and remain will be caught up together with them in the clouds to meet the Lord in the air, and so we shall always be with the Lord."*
>
> 1 Thessalonians 4:16, 17

It is in this context that two people may spend their lives working at the same place, or even sleeping in the same bed; and one of them will be saved, or taken, and the other will be lost, or left behind. The heart-breaking point of Jesus' message here, and what happened in Noah's day, is that the close association between people, whether common-law or conjugal, corporate or industrial, familial or relational, communal or personal, has absolutely no correlation with their personal salvation and final destiny. Paul clearly agrees with Jesus' description of the inhabitants of our world immediately prior to His return.

> *"For you yourselves know full well that the day of the Lord will come just like a thief in the night. ³<u>While they are saying, 'Peace and safety!' then destruction will come upon them suddenly like labor pains upon a woman with child, and they will not escape</u>. ⁴But you, brethren, are not in darkness, <u>that the day would overtake you like a thief</u>; ⁵for you are all sons of light and sons of day. We are not of night, nor of darkness; ⁶so then let us not sleep as others do, but let us be alert and sober. ⁷For those who sleep do their sleeping at night, and those who get drunk get drunk at night. ⁸But since we are of the day, let us be sober, having put on the breastplate of faith and love, and as a helmet, the hope of salvation. ⁹For God has not destined us for wrath, but for obtaining salvation through our Lord Jesus Chris."*
>
> 1 Thessalonians 5:2-9

How much clearer can the Word of God be? When we examine carefully the body of scriptural evidence regarding the powerful, cataclysmic, visible, return of Jesus, we will readily see that the verses of Matthew 24:40, 41 give absolutely no indication of Jesus secretly snatching away believers from the earth.

John, on the isle of Patmos, had a glimpse of his Master's return, which he described in the following terms:

> *"Look, he is coming with the clouds, and <u>every eye</u>*

> _will see him_, even those who pierced him; and _all the peoples of the earth will mourn because of him_. So shall it be! Amen."

Revelation 1:7, NIV

What John saw is exactly what Jesus revealed to His disciples while sitting on the temple mount shortly before His humiliation, resurrection and ascension.

> "*At that time the sign of the Son of Man will appear in the sky, and _all the nations of the earth will mourn_. They _will see_ the Son of Man coming on the clouds of the sky, _with power and great glory_.*"

Matthew 24:30, NIV

John even gave a more detailed description in the book of Revelation. In apocalyptic vision he saw:

> "*The sky was split apart like a scroll when it is rolled up, and every mountain and island were moved out of their places. [15]Then the kings of the earth and the great men and the commanders and the rich and the strong and every slave and free man hid themselves in the caves and among the rocks of the mountains; [16]and they said to the mountains and to the rocks, Fall on us and hide us from the presence of Him who sits on the throne, and from the wrath of the Lamb; [17]for the great day of their wrath has come, and who is able to stand?*"

Revelation 6:14-17

What we read here does not sound like a secret, does it? Rest assured then, that our only source of safety to withstand the great delusions of the last days is our abiding faith in the unfailing Word of God. Only those who make the study of the Scriptures the mainstay and compass of their lives will be able to repulse the artful deceptions of the enemy in earth's climactic season. Paul warns us that if we refuse to receive the truth of the Word of God, and of our Lord's return, God will allow us to be deluded by false teachings.

> "Then that lawless one will be revealed . . . ^{9}that is, the one whose coming is in accord with the activity of Satan, with all power and signs and false wonders, ^{10}and <u>with all the deception of wickedness for those who perish, because they did not receive the love of the truth so as to be saved</u>. ^{11}<u>For this reason God will send upon them a deluding influence so that they will believe what is false</u>, ^{12}in order that they all may be judged who did not believe the truth, but took pleasure in wickedness."
>
> 2 Thessalonians 2:8-12

We must be faithful stewards of the truth. We must be hearers and doers of the Word, so that we do not become spiritual casualties of the satanic agencies that are cranking up their deceptive activities as the great day of the Lord approaches.

Wars, Political and Social Unrest

Jesus went on to describe the deterioration of international relations between nations prior to His return.

> "*You will be hearing of wars and rumors of wars. See that you are not frightened, for those things must take*

> *place, but that is not yet the end. ⁷For nation will rise against nation, and kingdom against kingdom, and in various places there will be famines and earthquakes. ⁸But all these things are merely the beginning of birth pangs."*
>
> Matthew 24:6-8

We do not have to look very far to see the fulfillment of this prophecy of Jesus. Escalating political tension and unrest have become a part of the societal framework of major nations across the world. The reality of war and nuclear annihilation are constant threats to humanity's survival, as nations like North Korea and Iran dance with nuclear energy in their efforts to gain international recognition and acceptance. Nations that profess to be united on paper are at war in the real world, because the glue of trust and confidentiality that should hold them together often loses its cohesiveness at the negotiation table. Fragile peace accords are broken at will as one nation seeks to gain political and military advantage over another.

Today, we are not only hearing about war; but we are at war. America's ongoing war against the Taliban in Afghanistan, and the counter-insurgency by coalition forces against disgruntled Iraqi extremists have become magnets for major terrorist organizations that have deep-seated hatred for the United States. When will these end, or will they ever end? No one knows for sure. We do not know if we can trust all the political rhetoric and empty promises that ride the emotions of those who have stakes in these wars.

In other parts of the Middle-East, the situation is no different. The nation of Israel continues to fight for its right to exist peacefully, while its displaced blood relatives, the Palestinians, fight equally for their right to have a place they call home. This catch-22 situation has made the track of land from the Gaza strip all the way up to the Golan Heights the most unstable and volatile region in the world. Moreover, regular fighting and skirmishes among Israel's neighbors also contribute to the growing insecurity of the area, leaving political rivals at their wits' end as they struggle daily to procure, protect, and preserve land and resources for their people.

Beside the political instability and the constant threat of war that breathe heart-stopping fear and apprehension with regard to our future existence on this planet, there are the growing waves of social unrest that roll threateningly over the nations. Angry, dissatisfied citizens continually seek to express their increasing frustration with the governments they have appointed to provide for their freedom, their welfare and their safety.

Protests and protest marches, supporting one cause or another, inundate the landscape of our modern societies, while wily politicians perform balancing acts, trying to keep their political future alive through their peace offerings of empty promises. Fearful, frustrated, exhausted and unfulfilled, depressed and bewildered masses roam our planet, going through their daily grind in search of the dreams that have eluded them. On the other hand, those who have exploited them and their resources, live in revelry and wantonness. James aptly describes this sad state of affairs as a prelude to the return of the Lord of all the earth.

> *"Come now, you rich, weep and howl for your miseries which are coming upon you. ²Your riches have rotted and your garments have become motheaten. ³Your gold and your silver have rusted; and their rust will be a witness against you and will consume your flesh like fire. It is in the last days that you have stored up your treasure!*
>
> *⁴Behold, the pay of the laborers who mowed your fields, and which has been withheld by you, cries out against you; and the outcry of those who did the harvesting has reached the ears of the Lord of Sabaoth. ⁵You have lived luxuriously on the earth and led a life of wanton pleasure; you have fattened your*

> *hearts in a day of slaughter. ⁶You have condemned and put to death the righteous man; he does not resist you.*
> *⁷Therefore be patient, brethren, until the coming of the Lord. The farmer waits for the precious produce of the soil, being patient about it, until it gets the early and late rains. ⁸You too be patient; strengthen your hearts, for the coming of the Lord is near."*

James 5:1-8

Waiting for deliverance becomes a very difficult thing to do in a fast-paced age like ours, where technology has gotten us used to such amenities as instant messaging, fast foods, express travel, overnight delivery and even just-in-time services. Patience is definitely not one of the favored character traits of our time, but the promises of God stand sure. Now, more than ever, we must not lose faith in the God who cannot lie (Titus 1:2) and does not change (Malachi 3:6; Hebrews 13:8); but we must strengthen our hearts through the daily study of His Word, for the coming of the King is certainly very near.

Environmental Signs

> *"For nation shall rise against nation, and kingdom against kingdom: <u>and there shall be famines, and pestilences, and earthquakes, in divers places</u>."*

Matthew 24:7, KJV

Deteriorating environmental conditions and the unpredictable increase in global disasters are also very clear indications that the prophecy of Jesus regarding His return is right on target. Many major nations of our world are now "going green"[2] in their efforts to slow down, or possibly turn back, the threatening results of "global warming"[3] precipitated by mankind's wanton exploitation, pollution and destruction of the natural environments of land, air, sea and waterways. We are already reaping the "first fruits" of the harvest produced by our indiscriminate use of our natural resources. For example, growing world hunger, coastal erosions, inland flooding in untold proportions, increasing hurricanes of G-5 magnitude, multiplicity of earthquakes and tsunamis in different places, mutation of old and the outbreak of new types of diseases are altogether breathing fear and discomfort everywhere. Indeed, the earth is crying out under the unbearable yoke of human destruction and environmental frustration.

> "*How long is the land to mourn And the vegetation of the countryside to wither? For the wickedness of those who dwell in it, Animals and birds have been snatched away, Because men have said, He will not see our latter ending.*"

Jeremiah 12:4

> "*The creation waits in eager expectation for the sons of God to be revealed.* [20]*For the creation was subjected to frustration, not by its own choice, but by the will of the one who subjected it, in hope* [21]*that the creation itself will be liberated from its bondage to decay and brought into the glorious freedom of the children of God.* [22]*We know that the whole creation has been groaning as in the pains of childbirth right up to the present time.*"

Romans 8:19-22, NIV

The apostle Paul says that not only mankind is tired and

frustrated over the deteriorating conditions of human existence and longs for deliverance from this planet that seems destined for destruction; but that the entire creation cries under the decaying bondage of human exploitation and yearns for liberation and redemption as well. Paul describes the whole of creation as groaning like a woman in childbirth, anxiously waiting for release and vindication; for indeed God will destroy those who destroy the earth (Revelation 11:18). The return of Jesus is the ultimate solution to our irreversibly crumbling environment and to the impending doom of every form of life on planet earth.

Spiritual Declension and Increased Immorality

> ". . . and because lawlessness is increased, most people's love will grow cold. ^{13}But the one who endures to the end, he will be saved."
>
> Matthew 24:12, 13, NASB

The King James version says:

> ". . . and because iniquity shall abound the love of many shall wax cold. ^{13}But he that shall endure to the end the same shall be saved."

It is an incontrovertible fact that our secular age has become the breeding ground for lawlessness; for it produces a form of individualism that places "the self" and its lustful desires at the center of the human experience. Undeniably, secularism is a last-day phenomenon that displaces God as the ultimate source of truth, authority and accountability, and creates a pluralistic environment in which each individual becomes his own arbiter of truth, authority and accountability. As a direct result, respect, responsibility and answerability are fast losing their cohesive strength to hold the humane fabric of our society together, because the individual has become a law unto himself.

The exponential increase of lawlessness, extreme violence and horrendous crimes have lost their ability to shock a generation that has grown used to steeling its nerves to the repetitious display of the flowing of blood and the wanton destruction of human life. Even from a very early age, the children of our generation have learned to experience ecstatic joy and delight in their ability to spill the guts and blood of their electronic opponents while playing their video games. As this affinity toward lawlessness abounds, and the inhumanity of humankind toward one another increases, so it is that hatred, revenge and fear erode the love and peace of God in the human heart. For certain, we have come to the perilous times that Paul talks about in his letter to Timothy:

> *"But mark this: There will be terrible times in the last days.* ²*People will be <u>lovers of themselves</u>, <u>lovers of money</u>, <u>boastful</u>, <u>proud</u>, abusive, <u>disobedient to their parents</u>, <u>ungrateful</u>, <u>unholy</u>,* ³<u>*without love*</u>*, unforgiving, slanderous, <u>without self-control</u>, brutal, <u>not lovers of the good</u>,* ⁴*treacherous, rash, <u>conceited</u>, <u>lovers of pleasure rather than lovers of God</u>—*⁵<u>*having a form of godliness but denying its power*</u>*. Have nothing to do with them.* ⁶*They are the kind who worm their way into homes and gain control over weak-willed women, who are loaded down with sins and are swayed by all kinds of evil desires,* ⁷*always learning but never able to acknowledge the truth."*
>
> 2 Timothy 3:1-7, NIV

We are living witnesses of these times right here, and right now! Paul's list of human characteristics and behaviors are so accurate in its reference to our times, that it is impossible for the average reader to review this list and not come away with the sense that the apostle is speaking directly to our age. Does not our society glamorize evil, immorality, materialism and pride, while, at the same time, look with indifference upon anyone who is bold enough to take a stand in favor of moral codes of conduct?

How quickly the well-trained camera-operators and news-reporters shy away from athletes and celebrities who attempt to acknowledge God for their successes and accomplishments? Even the names of God and Christianity are relegated like the "*N*-word" in the public arena, under the pretense that people ought to be "politically correct" and sensitive to the feelings of the ungodly in our pluralistic society—the atheist, the agnostic and other non-Christian religions. What a sad and unholy state of affairs! Could Paul be any more accurate when he characterized the last-day generation as being *unthankful, unholy ...haters of those that are good...proud, arrogant, lovers of pleasure more than lovers of God*?

What is even more shocking, is the fact that Paul's description does not only portray the attitude of an ungodly, secular society, but also a brand of Christianity that has become absorbed by the culture that surrounds it. In contemporary Christianity, church-seekers are allowed to transfer practically anything associated with their former lifestyle—short of maybe sex and drugs, so to speak—into professed Christian communities without any major problems.

The crossover to Christianity is no longer harnessed by the virtues of self-denial, self-sacrifice or cross-bearing, but by "user-friendly" adoptions, accommodations and glossing over of the worldly and secular. Many churches are yielding to the pressures and influences of a post-Modern, secular society in order to assimilate more members while simultaneously losing their dumbfounded, disappointed and disenchanted dissenters.

Secularism[4] and the post-Modern culture have made unholy inroads into church life, blurring the line of distinction between the sacred and the profane. These twin forces have confused and corrupted societal value systems, elevating the twin-god of self and human reason above the God of creation. The over-abounding desire to please "the self" has become the subversive motive force that drives human thoughts and actions, influencing many God-seekers to search for a god they can make into their own image, instead of denying themselves to be transformed into the image of God.

Therefore, what obtains is the current form of Christianity that the apostle Paul most accurately describes as a significant, last-day phenomenon: *"a form of godliness but without any power"* (2 Timothy 3:3). God, in the midst of this perverse generation, is defined by whatever the individual decides that He should be in his life experience—that is, Creator by creature-design, and Potter by clay-portrayal.

It is no wonder, therefore, that our world is in such spiritual darkness and gross wickedness, while immersed in a promising sea of academic brilliance and human genius. It is also not surprising that while we claim that mankind is living in his best days, humanity is set on edge by living through its worst fears with confusion of faces. Isaiah prophesied that *"darkness shall cover the earth and gross darkness the people"* (Isaiah 60:2). The truth is that the current spiritual and moral declension of our world registers the scathing testimony that this last phase of the church age, with its multiplicity of conflicting religions and impotent "sacred" forms, has failed to deliver to humanity a powerful witness for the kingdom of God. Both humanity and the King are disenchanted by the lukewarm religion of this soon-to-pass-away generation.

Kingly Indictment

In the third chapter of the book of Revelation, verses 14 through 22, Christ addresses the misguided religious insipidity that characterizes the Christianity in these last days. His message comes at the end of a seven-letter series (beginning with Revelation 2:1 and ending at chapter 3:22), written to the seven historical churches of Asia Minor.[5] These letters also bore pointed testimony and application to the seven distinct periods of church history—beginning with the Apostolic Age of the church and ending with our last-day era. The letter addressed to the last of these seven churches, Laodicea, is the one that bears very serious import to the body of Christ in these last days. The message reads:

> "To the angel of the church in Laodicea write: <u>The Amen</u>, <u>the faithful and true Witness</u>, <u>the Beginning of the creation of God</u>, says this: [15]'<u>I know your deeds</u>, that you are neither cold nor hot; I wish that you were cold or hot. [16]So because you are lukewarm, and neither hot nor cold, I will spit you out of My mouth. [17]'<u>Because you say</u>, 'I am rich, and have become wealthy, and have need of nothing,' and you do not know that you are wretched and miserable and poor and blind and naked, [18]'<u>I advise you to buy from Me gold refined by fire</u> so that you may become rich, and <u>white garments</u> so that you may clothe yourself, and that the shame of your nakedness will not be revealed; and <u>eye salve to anoint your eyes</u> so that you may see. [19]'Those whom I love, I reprove and discipline; <u>therefore be zealous and repent</u>.
>
> [20]'Behold, I stand at the door and knock; if anyone hears My voice and opens the door, I will come in to him and will dine with him, and he with Me. [21]He who overcomes, I will grant to him to sit down with Me on My throne, as I also overcame and sat down with My Father on His throne. [22]He who has an ear, let him hear what the Spirit says to the churches.'"

Revelation 3:14-22

Although Laodicea was a literal church in Asia Minor, it was also a symbolic representation of the last era of the Church of Christ before His glorious return. The name is derived from a compound Greek word **Laodikeia**—from **laos** meaning people, and **dikē** meaning judgment—which yields the meaning of "people adjudged" or "people in judgment." Thus, the Laodicean church age is the last phase of the body of Christ, living in a time of impending judgment. Consequently, this makes what Jesus says to this last-day church a matter of supreme importance.

This letter begins with three descriptions of the Author (Jesus Christ)—namely, the "Amen", the "faithful and true Witness", and the "Beginning of the creation of God." The title "Amen" (which means *so let it be*) indicates the finality, certainty and inalterability of what Christ is about to say to His professed followers. Whatever Christ has to say is already the settled truth in heaven.

The description "faithful and true Witness" is very amenable to Laodicea's judgment-bound situation, and portrays the sterling character of the testimony Christ bears regarding the reputation and boastful claims of those who profess His name. This testimony is, in every way, brutally honest and uncompromisingly true.

As the "Beginning of the creation of God", Christ also has absolute knowledge and understanding regarding the issues He is about to address with Laodicea. In other words, Christ's testimony about Laodicea is not based on hear-say from any secondary source. He is the Alpha and Omega, the omniscient, omnipresent One, who is the inscrutable Eye-witness of all that goes on in His body—the church. He is the ultimate Source.

I Know Thy Works!

The very first word Christ has for His church in this end-time season is very sobering. *I know your deeds* (Revelation 3:15). I have a complete understanding of who you really are and what you are really doing. I see and hear of your profession, but I also know your true reputation. *I know you!* Doesn't this truthful statement appear very familiar? This is déjà vu—*I am the Good Shepherd and I know My own, and My own know Me* (John 10:14)—for the Good Shepherd is now the faithful and true Witness of His judgment-bound people.

What does Christ know about this last church age? He says He knows all about our mediocre, tasteless religion. Our pretentious, tepid Christianity is a repulsive turnoff that makes Him sick to the stomach. He would have preferred if we were not Christians at all, for then He may have been able to lead us to repentance. Additionally, Christ would have rather if we were consecrated, spirit-filled disciples, for then He would have been able to use us for His glory. But since we are neither, our spiritual indifference makes us useless to Him. We are like salt that has lost its savor, good to be thrown out and trampled under the foot by men (Matthew 5:13).

This very critical situation described by the "Amen" demands our notice and our immediate, soul-searching response. Laodicea represents an age of the church in which many professed believers are grossly self-deceived, yet spiritually indifferent and self-satisfied. It is a church age that is characterized by wealth and materialism (falsely appraised as spiritual prosperity and blessing); religious form and charismatic hype without spiritual power (2 Timothy 3:1-5); and spiritual poverty, wretchedness, blindness and nakedness (Revelation 3:14-17). These deceptive maladies are the root cause of the misguided ignorance that produces our short-sighted, self-righteous assessment of our distasteful Christianity that says "*we are rich and increased with goods and have need of nothing*" (Revelation 3:17).

However, in this very uncomfortable scenario, what really matters is not how we see, or what we think about ourselves, but only what Jesus sees and thinks about us. He presents us with the scathing reality check that our religion is impotent and worthless. Our form of godliness has no serious impact on the culture that is bent on shaping and defining our religious experience. *I know your works!*

Listening to Wise Counsel

Christ challenges our selfish, ignorant preoccupations with the call to come back to Him as the ultimate solution to our spiritual dilemma. "Buy of Me," He says, "gold refined by fire, that you may become rich," for there is no one else who can supply our need, (Revelation 3:18). "Buy of Me" is really an invitation of Jesus to all who will give heed to His counsel. Christ uses the word "buy" as a conversational device to express the transactional relationship between an individual and Himself. This transaction involves a real exchange, not so much of goods, services and money (although these may be included), but of life and philosophies. It is an exchange of Christ's life and philosophy for ours. One song-writer captures this transaction in the following way:

> Cover with His life, whiter than snow
> Fullness of His life then shall I know
> My life of scarlet, my sin and woe
> Cover with His life, whiter than snow[6]

The same idea is expressed in the Isaiah 55 when God invited the nation of Israel into a renewed relationship with Himself.

> *"Ho! Everyone who thirsts, come to the waters; And you who have no money come, buy and eat. Come, buy wine and milk without money and without cost.* [2]*"Why do you spend money for what is not bread, and your wages for what does not satisfy? Listen carefully to Me, and eat what is good, And delight yourself in abundance.* [3]*Incline your ear and come to Me. Listen, that you may live; And I will make an everlasting covenant with you . . ."*

Isaiah 55:1-3

Jesus invites Laodicea to "buy gold refined by fire." This gold represents a genuine faith in Christ that has been purified by fiery trials from pride, selfishness, greed, and every kind of inordinate affections. The human heart is so deceitful and desperately wicked (Jeremiah 17:9) that it is only the grace of God that can purify it from its entrails of fleshly dross, and infuse it with sterling faith and love toward God. Gold portrays a faith that has complete reliance on Jesus as our only Surety and Source of Salvation. Our sufficiency is not our education or economic situation; not our flamboyant preachers, and not our religious organizations or denomination. That faith is also driven by a love that flows out of a genuine union with the living Christ, embracing all people regardless of race, ethnicity, lifestyle, or religion. The spring of such love is the abiding presence of Christ in the heart. As our faith accepts and embraces the relationship with the King of kings, we are given full access to the true riches His kingdom affords.

The transaction continues as Christ also counsels us to replace our filthy, earthly rags of self-righteousness and self-approbation with the genuine righteousness which only He can provide—the spotless, white garment of His righteous character. Nothing else will ever suffice. His righteousness and greatness alone must be manifested in, and must be proclaimed by, His people. These are not just externally woven garments that easily conformed to the pressures of a *denominational or institutional social culture*. They are internal life characteristics reproduced by the very mind and spirit of the living Christ abiding in the soul. This is the legacy of the new covenant, and totally represents God's work; not man's.

> *"FOR THIS IS THE COVENANT THAT I WILL MAKE WITH THE HOUSE OF ISRAEL AFTER THOSE DAYS, SAYS THE LORD: <u>I WILL PUT MY LAWS INTO THEIR MINDS, AND I WILL WRITE THEM ON THEIR HEARTS</u>. AND I WILL BE THEIR*

GOD, AND THEY SHALL BE MY PEOPLE. [11]AND THEY SHALL NOT TEACH EVERYONE HIS FELLOW CITIZEN, AND EVERYONE HIS BROTHER, SAYING, 'KNOW THE LORD,' [12]FOR <u>ALL WILL KNOW ME</u>, <u>FROM THE LEAST TO THE GREATEST OF THEM</u>. FOR I WILL BE MERCIFUL TO THEIR INIQUITIES, AND I WILL REMEMBER THEIR SINS NO MORE."

Hebrews 8:10-12

Christ says that if we "buy" the white garment of His righteousness, He will not reveal the shame and nakedness of the vain profession which we hold so dear (Revelation 3:18). This purchase is without money or price for we are spiritually poor and can never earn enough to pay for what Christ offers. Such a revelation would have a most devastating effect upon the self-righteous, holier-than-thou image we portray to the world around us. Our hollow profession will become so apparent to the on-looking world that it will humble our religious pride and precipitate a broken, contrite community that embraces Christ as the *only* source and assurance of their righteousness; the *only* hope and security of their salvation; and the *only* reason and focus of their boast.

How often our un-converted, un-believing secular world looks on in horror at the unmasking of prominent "righteous" believers as their nakedness is paraded for all to behold? Such misfortunes should be ample warning for us to heed Christ's counsel to put no confidence in deceitful flesh, especially our own. The righteousness of Christ must be our security and sufficiency.

Additionally, Christ wants to clear our spiritual vision by cleansing our hearts and renewing our spirits. Experience has shown that what a person sees does not depend so much on what is in his line of vision, but on what he has stored up in his spirit and mind. A person's mind can color any situation. We tend to see people and situations not as they are, but as we are. In contemporary Christianity communities, believers and un-believers are still viewed through the opaque lenses of race and ethnicity, color and creed, sex and social standing, education and economics, prejudice and preferences.

Therefore, Jesus wants to clear our vision by changing our hearts, and this can only happen as we keep our eyes focused on His righteous character and yield our wills to the powerful, converting influence of His Spirit. Christ promises to anoint our eyes with celestial eye-salve to counteract our spiritual blindness regarding ourselves, our mission, and the lost world (Revelation 3:18). This heavenly anointing will give us clear spiritual revelation and discernment to accomplish the following:

(1) *See* ourselves in the light of the righteous character of Jesus Christ, for without His righteousness we are utterly worthless.
(2) *See* God's mission as Christ saw it, not as a vehicle to glorify ourselves and our institutions; but to glorify Him as we seek to win the lost.
(3) *See* all men and women as Christ sees them—as people in need of His love and salvation, regardless of their life situation, color, race, ethnicity, or any other human distinction.

Zealous, Corporate Repentance

"Those whom I love, I reprove and discipline; therefore be zealous and repent. [20]Behold, I stand at the door and knock; if anyone hears My voice and opens the door, I will come in to him and will dine with him, and he with Me."

Revelation 3:19, 20

Although Christ's message to Laodicea is one of reproof and discipline, it is delivered in mercy and love. Self-righteous pride makes it very difficult to handle such a straightforward testimony as this, and it is altogether much easier to think that this word is meant for someone else. However, if you are a part of the body of Christ in the 21st century, this message is addressed directly to you, and it comes to you wrapped in the love of Jesus. The faithful and true Witness says *"those whom I love. . ."* I believe that I am included in *those*; so are you and all who profess the name of Christ.

It is extremely significant to understand that this call to repentance has very strong and pointed corporate overtones. While it is important and necessary for the individual believer to hear and obey this message from Jesus, the nature of the delivery of this letter takes the form of a corporate address to the end-time body of Christ. Moreover, this address is given through the angel (Greek ***aggelos***, for messenger or leader) of the body. Consequently, Christ expects the corporate leadership of His people to pioneer the delivery of, and response to, His message to Laodicea—to lead them into an unprecedented season of repentance and reformation, in preparation for the final move of God to make ready a people for the return of the King.

Therefore, get on with it and repent! The Master does not want a lethargic response from His lukewarm followers. He is trying to induce them with a new spirit of promptitude and earnestness that will lead to positive action on their part. "Turn away," He says, from your self-centered preoccupations—your religious forms and empty professions, your public performances and private fantasies, your material display and subtle merchandising, your blinded prophesying and wretched people-pilfering, your miserable weekly living and Sunday/Sabbath morning "Holy Ghost" fixing—turn away!

"Turn to Me in true humility of soul and brokenness of spirit, and I would heal your backsliding and make you a real blessing in this soon-to-perish earth." This, in essence, is what Christ means by the phrase "buy of Me." It is a spiritual transaction involving humble repentance and beneficial exchange—a giving up the filthy rags of our self-righteous religion for the glorious righteousness and riches of heaven.

Barrier to Blessings

In His urgent attempt to arrest the attention of His last-day people, Christ portrays Himself as standing outside *the bolted door* of the church of Laodicea (Revelation 3:20). This is a very striking and disturbing posture—Christ being locked out of His church, knocking in an attempt to gain entry. The bolted door stands as a barrier between Christ and His people, and represents an attitude of avoidance, independence and self-sufficiency. Laodicea is the church age that does not want Christ to interfere or disturb the course of activities and events that are taking place within the body. The bolted door is a mere reflection of the mind-set that says: *"We are rich and we have a lot of 'good things' going on. We don't really need You to come in and alter the way we do things in and around here."* The very subtle message is: *"Leave us and our systems alone!"*

It is very significant to observe that at the very beginning of Christ's letters to the seven churches, that the Son of man was walking in the midst of the seven golden candlesticks (Revelation 1:13). These candlesticks represented the seven churches (v. 20), and Christ was at the heart of the worship and community experience of His body during the apostolic (or first) church period. However, during the ensuing centuries, the presence and authority of Christ was slowly displaced by the traditions of men and the authority of the church, especially during and after the Constantinian era. After the Reformation, the new expressions of the church (denominations and religious organizations) adopted the religious culture of the Church of Rome, in which the authority of the institution usurped the authority of Christ in the life and experience of the believer.

Are We Listening?

The Laodicean dilemma is a déjà vu experience for the faithful and true Witness, for this is not the first time Christ came knocking on the door of His house—the church. As it was in the beginning so it is now in the end of the church age. Christ came knocking on the door of the house of Israel, but the corporate leadership of His people refused to open the door and give the Messiah full control of His house. Moreover, they blocked access to the door from the masses and stood ready to cast out anyone who "breeched" the entrance in order to have fellowship with the Savior (John 9:1-34). These religious leaders had firm control over the minds and resources of the people of God and would stop at nothing to protect their lucrative turf from any "intruder"—even the Heir of the vineyard of Israel (Matthew 21:33-43). Hence, they diabolically engineered false witnesses against Him, and set up a kangaroo court to condemn Him to death.

At the beginning of the existence of the Nation it was not so. Christ was the very heart and soul of the economy of Israel, just as He was the living centerpiece among the seven candlesticks (or churches) at the beginning of the church age, during the days of the apostles. When Israel was wandering through the wilderness, the Messiah was mirrored in every aspect of their holy sanctuary and its services, very much as the resurrected Christ and His kingdom were the glorious theme on the lips of the early disciples.

However, with the passing of time, the people of God went in and out of apostasy and captivity, and lost their vision of Christ and their sense of purpose and mission in the world. In order to compensate for this loss and to avert the possibility of going into exile in the future, the leadership of Israel assumed a very rigid, ritualistic control over the Nation, meticulously multiplying and imposing new religious requirements on the people. These they preserved and rigorously protected and kept in place even during the time of Christ.

The experience is not very different for the Church of Christ—the reconstituted Israel (Galatians 3:27-29), from the apostolic age through to the time of Laodicea, the last stage of the Church. As we read the seven letters of Christ, addressed to the seven periods of church history, we can sense a checkered journey of faithfulness and apostasy from Ephesus through to Laodicea (Revelation 2 and 3). This apostasy came to a head during the Middle Ages and continued to escalate until the time of the Reformation.

Like Israel coming out of captivity, a new expression of the church emerged, yielding a multiplicity of different denominations and religious organizations, with a proliferation of rituals, rules, policies, and traditions to govern and control the people of God. This is the detestable situation that Christ now encounters in Laodicea—a confused, institutionalized people under the corporate control of a religious leadership that has usurped Christ's authority over His blood-bought heritage.

Thus, Christ is knocking at the door of Laodicea, because He desires to regain the full allegiance and commitment of His body. He wants IN on all that goes on in His church. He is not satisfied to be just its figurehead Savior and Lord. He wishes to be the ONLY HEAD and controlling influence over His blood-bought heritage, to be the central spot in the heart of His church. Every thought, every decision, and action that occur in the body must be controlled by Him, and bring glory ONLY to Him.

However, it is not easy for the corporate leadership of God's people to relinquish the control they possess over the minds and resources of Christ's inheritance. While individuals within the believing community will hear and respond to the Savior's knocking on the door, corporate leadership in many quarters will resist and even restrict access to Christ, for fear that He would set these dear ones free from their manipulative control. Nevertheless, they will not maintain this control for very much longer, for the King is getting ready for His imminent return, and He will reclaim His chosen heritage before He puts in His appearance.

A Doomed System

> "*After this I saw another angel coming down from heaven. He had great authority, and the earth was illuminated by his splendor. ²With a mighty voice he shouted: Fallen! Fallen is Babylon the Great! She has become a home for demons and a haunt for every evil spirit, a haunt for every unclean and detestable bird; ³for all the nations have drunk the maddening wine of her adulteries. The kings of the earth committed adultery with her, and the merchants of the earth grew rich from her excessive luxuries.*"

Revelation 18:1-3, NIV

It is quite obvious from the above scripture that John is making the connection between the fall of Babylon and the great whore of Revelation 17—that is, Babylon the Great, the mother of harlots and abomination of the earth (Revelation 17:5). Besides using the feminine gender pronoun, she, to describe Babylon, John uses the same description here, as he did in Revelation 17:2, for the activities of the whore with the kings and merchants of the earth. Whereas in chapter 17, the exiled apostle portrays the sins of the great whore, in chapter 18, the angel from heaven reiterates those sins and pronounces judgment upon her.

In the previous chapter of this volume we identified the great whore and mother of harlots who sits on many waters, as the Church of Rome—modern Roman Catholicism. This insidious religious system of Babylon has usurped the authority of God in the earth and exercises devious and coercive control over its inhabitants, including unwary, weak citizens of Christ's kingdom. However, God has remembered her sins and iniquities and is ready to execute His judgment against her, just as He did with Nebuchadnezzar's Babylon for its domination and exploitation of His people Israel (Jeremiah

51:5-10, 34, 35). John was invited by one of the seven angels who was commissioned to pour out seven deadly plagues upon rebellious sinners on the earth to come and see this judgment of the great whore (Revelation 17:1; 15:1).

Babylon and Laodicea

The sins[6] for which Babylon is being brought to judgment can be summarized as follows:
  (1) Adultery and whoredom with the kings and merchants of the earth—that is, spiritual apostasy through political alliance, doctrinal compromise and syncretistic practice (18:3).
  (2) Unabashed materialism and wanton luxury—for example, religious merchandising, clerical extortion and abuse, and luxurious living (18:3, 7).
  (3) Pride and arrogance—self-glorification and self-exaltation (18:7).
  (4) Artful deception—through her religious and political sorcery (18:23).
  (5) Religious persecution—drunk with the blood of the prophets and the saints (18:24).

This laundry list of transgressions does not only depict the iniquitous lifestyle of Mystery Babylon the Great, but also reflects the influence she has had on the thinking and behavior of her apostate daughters, who are a part of those professing Christianity in the Laodicean church age.

While Laodicea (historical and figurative) is distinctly not Babylon, her lukewarm religion certainly bears the marks of Babylon's sinister influence at work in her midst. There are marked similarities between the sins of Babylon and the charges brought against Laodicea by the faithful and true Witness. Pay careful attention to the comparison of Revelation 3:14-22 and 18:3-24 in the table below.

Charges Against Laodicea	Charges Against Mystery Babylon the Great
(a) "Being rich and have become wealthy" (3:17)—that is, materialistic and living luxuriously.	(1) Unabashed materialism and wanton luxury (18:3, 7).
(b) "Having need of nothing" (3:17)—pride and arrogance indeed!	(2) Pride and arrogance—self-glorification and self-exaltation (18:7).
(c) "Practising a tasteless Christianity" (3:15, 16)—a form of deceptive godliness, but without God's power.	(3) Artful deception—through her religious and political sorcery (18:23).
(d) "Self-worship or idolatry, which is a form of spiritual adultery" (3:18)—that is, replacing faith in the righteousness of Christ with faith in human works, forms and ceremonies.	(4) Adultery and whoredom with the kings and merchants of the earth—that is, spiritual apostasy through political alliance, doctrinal compromise and syncretistic practice (18:3).
(e) "Spiritual persecution" (3:20)—holding the heritage of Christ hostage behind closed doors, while the Master stands outside knocking.	(5) Religious persecution—drunk with the blood of the prophets and the saints (18:24).

Truly, the real problem with the church of the Laodicean age is not her lukewarm religion, but her spiritual self-deception and extreme ignorance. Her Lukewarm condition is merely the symptom or result of her gross misconception of her true spiritual standing before the Judge of all the earth—a reflection of the mystical hallmark of Babylon.

The religion of Babylon is a religion of works and of systematic control over the minds and religious experience of God's people and the inhabitants of the earth. It is a religion that usurps not only the authority of Christ over the salvation of His children, but also exalts human traditions, rituals and ceremonies above the righteous merits of Christ's efficacious sacrifice on behalf of all sinners. Such a religion imprisons the human spirit; minimizes the work of the Holy Spirit and the power of God's grace to convert and transform sinners; and shuts up the kingdom of God against men and women.

However, God has a time of reckoning with the doomed apostate system. Through His "angelic messengers,"[7] He announces the fall of the great whore and the destruction of her evil empire. This fall involves both the uncovering of Babylon's pretentious piety, which masquerades her hideous nakedness, and the complete dismantling of her corrupt religious system that has aligned itself with the kingdom of darkness to deceive the leaders and nations of the world. In these closing days of this earth's history, the mysterious stone of Daniel 2 (vv. 34, 44-45) is about to crush all the kingdoms of men, including Babylon the great, as the King of kings stands ready to set His citizens free and unite them under the one banner of Prince Emmanuel.

The King's Final Call

> *"Then I heard another voice from heaven say: Come out of her, <u>my people</u>, so that you will not share in her sins, so that you will not receive any of her plagues;*

> *⁵for her sins are piled up to heaven, and God has remembered her crimes."*
>
> Revelation 18:4, 5

It is very important to distinguish the voice in the above verses from the voices of the angels that preceded this announcement. The use of the Greek ***allos*** (which means another of the same kind, as opposed to ***heteros***, indicating another of a different kind), to describe the voice of the one making the announcement, may lend to the idea that this was the voice of another angel. However, the use of ***allos*** here can very well mean another voice of the same authoritative quality—since all the messages came from the same authoritative source—and not necessarily the same person or by the same means.

Additionally, all the angels who preceded this voice spoke with reference to the third person, while this voice speaks with reference to the first person, saying: *"Come out of her <u>my people</u>. . ."* (Revelation 14:6-12; 18:1-3). Moreover, the phrase, *my people,* matches the one spoken by God through the prophet Zechariah with regard to the very same scenario—that is, the shaking and the plundering of Babylon to gather a people to Himself. *And <u>many nations shall be joined to the LORD</u> in that day, and shall be <u>my people</u>:* (Zechariah 2:11).

Thus, this voice of Revelation 18:4, has to be the voice of God, Himself, as is the case every time the phrase "a voice from heaven" is used in the book of Revelation (See 10:4, 14:2, 13). There are other places in Scripture that reflect this identification with the phrase—namely, God's judgment on Nebuchadnezzar (Daniel 4:31); the baptism and transfiguration of Jesus (Matthew 3:17; 17:5); and the Father's answer to the request of Jesus (John 12:28).

What is rather certain about this voice is that it delivered a very clear, authoritative "press" release that originated from the divine throne room. It declared God's intention not only to destroy

Babylon, but also to show His compassionate desire to recover and save His people from spiritual captivity. This merciful act of God is demonstrated repeatedly throughout the course of redemptive history. When God called Lot out of Sodom, the angel of the Lord said to him:

> *"Up, take your wife and your two daughters who are here, or you will be swept away in the punishment of the city. ¹⁶But he hesitated. So the men seized his hand and the hand of his wife and the hands of his two daughters, for the compassion of the LORD was upon him; and they brought him out, and put him outside the city."*

Genesis 19:15, 16

God spoke with the same sense of urgency to Israel when He was about to judge literal Babylon for its inhumanity towards His people during the time of their captivity. Through the prophet Isaiah, He said:

> *"<u>Go forth from Babylon</u>! <u>Flee from the Chaldeans</u>! Declare with the sound of joyful shouting, proclaim this, Send it out to the end of the earth; Say, "the LORD has redeemed His servant Jacob."*

Isaiah 48:20

The very same call is repeated by the prophet Jeremiah: "<u>Flee out of Babylon; leave the land of the Babylonians</u>, and be like the goats that lead the flock" (Jeremiah 50:8, NIV). Then again: "<u>Flee from Babylon! Run for your lives</u>! Do not be destroyed because of her sins. It is time for the LORD'S vengeance; He will pay her what she deserves. And: "<u>Come out of her, my people! Run for your lives</u>!

Run from the fierce anger of the LORD (Jeremiah 51:6, 45, NIV). These two verses reflect the prophetic symbolism of God's call in Revelation 18:4; and the overall destruction of literal Babylon in 538 B.C. was a figurative representation of God's final judgment against mystical Babylon the great, near the close of earth's history.

Jeremiah, chapters 50 and 51 bear marked similarities to Revelation 18. For example, even as *"the wall of Babylon has fallen down"* (Jeremiah 51:44), in a similar fashion, *"fallen, fallen is Babylon the great"* (Revelation 18:2). Just as all the nations of old lamented over the utter destruction of ancient Babylon (Jeremiah 50:46), so will all those who have associated with or profited from the activities of the ill-fated whore (Revelation 18:9-19).

A People of God's Choosing

Despite the unimaginable corruption, wickedness, and bold-faced arrogance of this doomed city, God still has a people in Babylon. He calls them His people, and the truth of the matter is only God knows who they really are. Humanity may attach labels and lay claims of identification with reference to being the true people of God, but these mean absolutely nothing until God gives His final word. He alone can make that decisive call. In this context, Babylon is more than just some physical location. It is also a spiritual condition, characterized by a mind that is in rebellion against the principles of God's government and kingdom. Any person or system of religion, who partakes in the sins of Babylon, is considered to be a part of Babylon—hence the reason why the angel warns: *"Come out of her, my people, so that you will not share in her sins . . ."* (Revelation 18:4).

While many professing Christianity may not be in physical Babylon (Roman Catholicism), and may even speak against or decry her abominable condition, they may still be victims of her spiritual intoxication and moral corruption. Their religious experience has been tainted by the wine (false teachings, traditions, and practices) from the blasphemous cup of the great whore (Revelation 17:2, 4). It is the wine of spiritual deception that has infiltrated the body of Christ at the end of the age and that is partly, or wholly, responsible for the self-deception and lukewarm condition of Laodicea.

However, there is still hope for Laodicea. Before the inevitable demise of Babylon, and the subsequent destruction of the kingdoms of this world in the battle of Armageddon (Revelation 16:13-16 and 19:16-21), the Majesty of heaven will again recover and gather a people to Himself. He says through the prophet Zechariah,

> *"Deliver thyself, O Zion, that dwellest with the daughter of Babylon. ⁸For thus saith the LORD of hosts; After the glory hath he sent me unto the nations which spoiled you: <u>for he that toucheth you toucheth the apple of his eye</u>. ⁹For, behold, <u>I will shake mine hand upon them</u>, and they shall be a spoil to their servants: and ye shall know that the LORD of hosts hath sent me. ¹⁰Sing and rejoice, O daughter of Zion: for, lo, I come, and I will dwell in the midst of thee, saith the LORD. ¹¹And <u>many nations shall be joined to the LORD</u> in that day, and shall be <u>my people</u>: and I will dwell in the midst of thee, and thou shalt know that the LORD of hosts hath sent me unto thee."*
>
> Zechariah 2:7-11

God has a personal score to settle with Babylon and her surrogates for their enslavement of Christ's chosen heritage, the apple of His eye, and the inhabitants of the earth. He plans a mighty shaking among the structures of these mystical institutions until He has recovered the last one of His imprisoned children. In that day, says the prophet, nations will gather themselves to the Lord, Himself—not to any system of religion or institution; for the Lord,

Himself, will dwell in the midst of them, and they shall be called His people. This is indeed an end-time representation of Christ, the King and His kingdom citizens. Christ will have the last say regarding all those who really belong to Him. In that day, there will be, indeed and in truth, one fold and one Shepherd—Christ, the Lord.

Many professed believers, who have been mesmerized by the intoxicating doctrines and traditions of Babylon, will hear the knock of Christ and open the door of their souls to Him. These are they who would receive fresh revelation and empowerment by the angel (messengers of mercy) who lightens the earth with the glory of God through the revelation of the truth of Christ and His kingdom (Revelation 18:1). They would recognize the voice of the Good Shepherd and, through the power of Holy Spirit, break free from all the restraining influences of Babylon—religious systems, spiritual, physical and emotional addictions, false teachers and leaders, friends, family and relatives, and all entrapments. Nothing would be more precious than their love for Christ and the truth that drives them.

On the other hand, those who refuse the counsel of the faithful and true Witness, and prize the approval of men and their human systems more than the truth as revealed by Christ, will yield their full allegiance to Babylon and be a part of her fall and destruction. These will not be able to recognize the voice of the Good Shepherd, for only His sheep will hear His voice and follow where He leads (John 10:3, 4, 27). They would join with like-minded professors in their campaign to restrain, persecute and even destroy those who are leaving the ranks of the self-deceived to take their stand with Christ and the revelation of truth.

We are living in grand and awful times, on the verge of these momentous events. Now is the day of opportunity for professed believers in this judgment-bound church age, because Christ is still knocking at the door. The letter to Laodicea does not reveal whether or not *the door* was opened for Jesus to gain entrance and access to the heart of His church, but it does convey His willingness to hold sweet communion with those in the body who choose to open the door of their hearts to Him. The hour is very late, and the Savior is seeking to bring His final blessings that would empower His church for its end-time mission, but worldliness and materialism, spiritual insipidity and a false sense of security, have bolted this door of opportunity. However, Christ is willing to dispense His blessings upon anyone who is ready and willing to respond to His gracious overture. He says:

> *"He who overcomes, I will grant to him to sit down with Me on My throne, as I also overcame and sat down with My Father on His throne."*

Revelation 3:21

Let us, through the grace of God, overcome every inclination of our own hearts, and the influence of others, that would reduce our capability to respond positively to the counsel of the true and faithful Witness. We are living in the prelude to His presence and we must throw open the door of our hearts to Him now. When He does appear, He will throw open the doors of His kingdom to us, and grant us the wonderful privilege and indescribable joy to sit on His everlasting throne.

Notes

1. Ellen White, *The Great Controversy* (Boise, ID: Pacific Press Publishing Association, 1950), 593.
2. *Going green* is the phrase used to describe nature-friendly ways to produce, consume and dispose of all products and services in the global effort to reduce the emission of carbon dioxide and other greenhouse gases that can contribute to and accelerate global warming.
3. *Global warming* is the phenomenon that describes the ongoing

increase of the average temperature of the Earth's near-surface air and oceans. If this phenomenon is not placed in check it will adversely affect global eco-systems and will precipitate a multiplicity of catastrophic disasters all over the world—for example, massive flooding, hurricanes, earthquakes and untold destruction of plants and wildlife.
4. *Secularization* has to do with the orientation of a society that increasingly relates to life without any overt reference to God. It is a process that progressively places the human being at the center of the universe, and human thought as the ultimate authority of the human life and experience.
5. The seven churches of Asia Minor were located in Ephesus, Smyrna, Pergamum, Thyatira, Sardis, Philadelphia, and Laodicea, in that order. These churches were also symbolic representations of seven distinct periods of church history, beginning with apostolic times and ending with the period of the church prior to the end of the age and the return of Jesus in the clouds of heaven.
6. F. E. Belden, *Cover With His Life*, published in *The Church Hymnal* (Washington, D.C.: Review and Herald Publishing Association, 1941), 477.

.

ONE DAY WITH THE KING

9

"Know this first of all, that in the last days mockers will come with their mocking, following after their own lusts, ⁴and saying, Where is the promise of His coming? For ever since the fathers fell asleep, all continues just as it was from the beginning of creation. . .

⁸But do not let this one fact escape your notice, beloved, that with the Lord one day is like a thousand years, and a thousand years like one day. ⁹The Lord is not slow about His promise, as some count slowness, but is patient toward you, not wishing for any to perish but for all to come to repentance.

¹⁰But <u>the day of the Lord</u> will come like a thief, in which the heavens will pass away with a roar and the elements will be destroyed with intense heat, and the earth and its works will be burned up.

¹¹Since all these things are to be destroyed in this way, what sort of people ought you to be in holy conduct and godliness, ¹²looking for and hastening the coming of <u>the day of God</u>, . . ."

2 Peter 3:3-12

A few years ago, in October 2006, Gener8Xion Entertainment Incorporated produced a best-selling movie on the life of Esther (a Jewish girl who became queen in a Gentile kingdom) that grossed some $4.3 million at the box office. This movie, "One Night with the King," attracted movie-goers, Christians and non-

Christians alike, from everywhere across North America and around the world. Many who were familiar with the biblical account of the Esther story probably attended the showing to see if the movie maintained the integrity of Scripture, while others may have just wanted to be entertained by the silver screen production of the same. On the other hand, the movie's riveting clips also attracted many, many people who just wanted to find out what it would be like to spend one night with the king. Of course, many of these people were not thinking of spending that one night with the King of kings, the Lord, Jesus Christ, but the handsome screen actor portrayed in the movie clips, or with any other such earthly figures for that matter. Whatever the motives for attending, "One Night with the King" captured a world-wide audience and made the box office, video stores and retail outlets very, very happy.

The Bible also dramatizes another scenario with a King—not any king, but the King of all kings. He is Jesus, the King of David, whose kingdom is not of this world (John 18:36, 37), but actively operates within it. This kingdom is destined to bring to naught the kingdoms of men, and establish its eternal reign and righteous rule forever. However, this biblical drama is not a silver screen production. It is more like reality television. It is a real life, one-day encounter between all humanity and the King of glory, being played out live on the stage of this earth. Anthony Emrold Phillip (alias, Brother Valentino) once tried to capture this idea about life in one of his most memorable performances as a calypsonian (sic)—"Life is a Stage." In the very first verse of the calypso he explains:

> "Life is a stage
> And we are the actors
> And everybody has a part to play
> Like a never ending movie
> With all different characters
> Each one has a role to portray..."[1]

However, while Brother Valentino portrays all of life as a stage, "One day with the King" represents the final scene on the stage of life. Unlike the Queen Esther movie, this live drama will permanently decide the destiny of every human being who ever lived on this planet. Absolutely no one will be able to escape the outcome of this awesome, climatic encounter; for this day with the King is a day of reckoning and judgment for all mankind. "One day with the King" is often spoken of by the prophets of old as the "great day of the Lord". The phrase is used at least 15 times in the Old Testament and 5 times in the New, and in each case, it carries the idea of God executing decisive judgment against those who live in rebellion to His will. Listen to the prophet Isaiah:

> "*Wail, for <u>the day of the LORD</u> is near! It will come as destruction from the Almighty. . . ⁹Behold, <u>the day of the LORD</u> is coming, Cruel, with fury and burning anger, To make the land a desolation; And He will exterminate its sinners from it."*
>
> Isaiah 13:6, 9

The prophet Ezekiel expresses the same thoughts twice in his book (Ezekiel 13:5; 30:3); Joel, five times (Joel 1:15; 2:1, 11, 31; 3:14); Amos, twice (Amos 5:18, 20); Obadiah, once (Obadiah 1:15); and Zephaniah, twice (Zephaniah 1:7, 14). Hear these awesome words from Zephaniah:

> "*Near is <u>the great day of the LORD</u>, near and coming very quickly; listen, <u>the day of the LORD</u>! In it the warrior cries out bitterly. ¹⁵<u>A day of wrath is that day</u>, <u>A day of trouble and distress</u>, <u>A day of destruction and desolation</u>, <u>A day of darkness and gloom</u>, <u>A day of clouds and thick darkness</u>, ¹⁶<u>A day of trumpet and battle cry</u> against the fortified cities and the high*

> *corner towers. ⁱ⁷I will bring distress on men so that they will walk like the blind, because they have sinned against the LORD; and their blood will be poured out like dust and their flesh like dung. ¹⁸Neither their silver nor their gold will be able to deliver them on <u>the day of the LORD'S wrath</u>; And all the earth will be devoured in the fire of His jealousy, for He will make a complete end, indeed a terrifying one, of all the inhabitants of the earth."*
>
> Zephaniah 1:14-18

However, of all the Old Testament prophets, the words of Malachi have the most direct connection to the body of Christ living through the last scenes of the drama of the ages, before the return of the King. He wrote:

> *"Behold, I am going to send you Elijah the prophet before the coming of <u>the great and terrible day of the LORD</u>. ⁶<u>He will restore the hearts of the fathers to their children</u> and the hearts of the children to their fathers, so that I will not come and smite the land with a curse."*
>
> Malachi 4:5, 6

This prophecy concerning Elijah, the prophet, found its fulfillment in the life and ministry of John the Baptist, the forerunner to the Messiah. The historical Elijah lived during the evil reign of King Ahab, who, under the influence of his domineering wife and Baal worshipper, Jezebel, encouraged rebellion and great wickedness among the people of God. Elijah, the Tishbite, mysteriously appears on the scene of Israel's history to bring revival and reformation to the nation and to turn the heart of the people back to their God. In describing the mission of John the Baptist to his father Zacharias, the angel Gabriel said:

> "*For he will be great in the sight of the Lord; and he will drink no wine or liquor, and he will be filled with the Holy Spirit while yet in his mother's womb. ¹⁶And he will turn many of the sons of Israel back to the Lord their God. ¹⁷It is he who will go as <u>a forerunner before Him in the spirit and power of Elijah</u>, <u>TO TURN THE HEARTS OF THE FATHERS BACK TO THE CHILDREN</u>, and the disobedient to the attitude of the righteous, so as to make ready a people prepared for the Lord.*"
>
> Luke 1:15-17

Jesus also clearly identifies John the Baptist as the returning Elijah, after the imprisoned prophet sent some of his followers to authenticate his (John's) belief regarding the person and ministry of the Messiah. "*As these men were going away, Jesus began to speak to the crowds about John, "What did you go out into the wilderness to see? A reed shaken by the wind? ⁸But what did you go out to see? A man dressed in soft clothing? Those who wear soft clothing are in kings' palaces! ⁹But what did you go out to see? A prophet? Yes, I tell you, and one who is more than a prophet. ¹⁰This is the one about whom it is written, '<u>BEHOLD, I SEND MY MESSENGER AHEAD OF YOU, WHO WILL PREPARE YOUR WAY BEFORE YOU</u>.' . . . ¹⁴And if you care to accept it, <u>he himself is Elijah, who was to come</u>*" (Matthew 11:7-10, 14).

Like his prototype, Elijah, John the Baptist suddenly appears, from the wilderness, on the landscape of Judaism with the very strong, uncompromising message: "*Repent, for the kingdom of heaven is at hand*" (Matthew 3:2). When questioned by the priests and Levites about his identity and credentials, the prophet simply said: "*I am a voice of one crying in the wilderness, make straight the way of the Lord*" (John 1:23). This statement of John was an allusion to the prophecies of Isaiah—"*A voice is calling, clear the way for the Lord in the wilderness*" (Isaiah 40:3)—and Malachi—"*Behold I am going to send My messenger, and he will clear the way before Me*" (Malachi 3:1).

Disciples and D-Day

Although the prophecy of Malachi regarding the coming of Elijah before *the great and terrible day* of the Lord met its initial fulfillment in the life and ministry of John the Baptist, there is a secondary and final revelation of this prophecy in the life and work that Christ has committed to His disciples. It is quite obvious that the *great and terrible day* described by Malachi and all the prophets of the Old Testament did not occur during the time of Christ, but is reserved until the end of the age. Consequently, the disciples of Christ, living in these last days, are the modern-day Elijahs and John the Baptists, commissioned by Jesus to proclaim the message of His kingdom and prepare a people for His glorious return to judge the living and the dead. Jesus once told His disciples: "*And this gospel of the kingdom shall be preached in the whole world for a witness to all the nations, and then the end shall come*" (Matthew 24:14).

Obviously, *the end* referred to here is D-Day (Deliverance or Destruction Day) for the inhabitants of planet earth. It is that *great and terrible Day of Judgment* for all those who rejected the witness of the kingdom's gospel. Now is not the time for the church of Christ to preach a conciliatory, compromising gospel of user-friendliness and non-offense, for the eternal destiny of humankind is at stake. The gospel of the kingdom that was preached by both John and Jesus, Himself, was a gospel that called for heart-felt repentance for one's sins, and a complete turning toward God and away from a life of iniquity. The operative word of that gospel was *Repent! Turn away! Turn around!*

Far too many professed believers are allowed to feel very comfortable with marrying elements of their old life with those of their new experience in Christ, without bearing the full cost of discipleship that the Master and His kingdom demand—that is, complete self-denial, cross-bearing and unqualified obedience to will of Christ. But D-Day—that "One day with the King"—is silently, but quickly approaching, and it will test the quality of every man's work to see whether it was true service toward God or vain religious profession to please men. The apostle Paul says that that *<u>day of the Lord</u> will come as a thief in the night; in the which the heavens shall pass away with a great noise, and the elements shall melt with fervent heat, the earth also and the works that are therein shall be burned up* (2 Peter 3:10, KJV). What did Jesus have to say about that day?

> "Many will say to Me on <u>that day</u>, '<u>Lord, Lord, did we not prophesy in Your name, and in Your name cast out demons, and in Your name perform many miracles</u>?' ²²*And then I will declare to them, '<u>I never knew you</u>; DEPART FROM ME, YOU WHO PRACTICE LAWLESSNESS.'"*
>
> Matthew 7:22, 23

"One day with the King" is a day of revelation, when the truth about the character and work of every human being shall be made known. Profession of faith means absolutely nothing. An authentic relationship with the King is everything. On *that day* there will be, as there are now, many people who purportedly spent their entire lives working for the King but never took the time to really know Him. They are busy with the work of the Lord, they say; but obviously too busy to take the time to know the Lord who called them to work. Like Martha, these conscientious workers for God have their priorities mixed up. In their estimate, they consider the time spent sitting at the feet of Jesus inconsequential when compared to the great task He has called them to do. What these well-intentioned believers fail to realize is that with regard to sinner and salvation, Christ is the one who does all the work, all the time. We may try to work apart from Him, and even then, He will still accomplish His purpose in spite of us. Nevertheless, it is only the power of God that can draw and convert the sinner (John 6:44).

The erroneous reasoning of the workers for God in the above scripture is that they thought they were doing the work and, therefore, doing God a favor. Listen to them: "*We prophesy... We cast out demons... We perform miracles...*" Can humanity perform these functions apart from supernatural influences—either from God above, or from satanic forces from beneath? Certainly not! Now, if their claims were true, they were operating under one of the two supernatural influences. Only the King has the right to judge, for He knows all those who truly belong to Him. *I never knew you* would be the saddest words any human ears would ever hear on *that day*, and no human works would be able to change the outcome of those fatal words. What an awful day that would be!

Panoramic Display

When Jesus stood before Caiaphas and his kangaroo crew that the Jewish leadership had assembled together in order to put the Savior to death, they sought to justify their wicked intentions by manipulative coercion. Caiaphas said to Jesus: "*I charge you under oath by the living God: Tell us if you are the Christ, the Son of God*" (Matthew 26:63, NIV). By placing the Savior under oath in the name of the living God, whom Caiaphas, himself, did not know, Jesus could no longer maintain His silence. "*Yes, it is as you say...*" (v. 64). He did not only confirm the words that came out of Caiaphas' mouth, but went on to speak with Messianic authority: "*But I say to all of you: In the future you will see the Son of Man sitting at the right hand of the Mighty One and coming on the clouds of heaven*" (v. 64).

Later, Jesus would authenticate this declaration through the prophetic revelation He gave to His servant John, the disciple whom He loved. John wrote: *"BEHOLD, <u>HE IS COMING WITH THE CLOUDS</u>, and <u>every eye will see Him</u>, even those who pierced Him; and <u>all the tribes of the earth</u> will mourn over Him. <u>So it is to be. Amen</u>"* (Revelation 1:7).

Notice that John's prophecy ends with a double confirmation—so it is to be, so it is to be (interpretation of Amen). Moreover, Jesus Christ—the Alpha and the Omega, the First and the Last, the Christ of all history, the everlasting God who is, and was, and is to come; even the Almighty—stands behind what John has written. This prophecy is certain. D-Day (that "One day with the King") will be a panoramic display of Christ's power and glory for the entire world to see.

Snapshots of D-Day

Throughout the book of Revelation, the apostle John gives us snapshots of different scenes that will transpire in this last episode of human history as we know it. Using limited but graphic human language, John said he saw:

> *"The sky receded like a scroll, rolling up, and every mountain and island was removed from its place. ¹⁵Then the kings of the earth, the princes, the generals, the rich, the mighty, and every slave and every free man hid in caves and among the rocks of the mountains. ¹⁶They called to the mountains and the rocks, Fall on us and hide us from the face of him who sits on the throne and from the wrath of the Lamb! ¹⁷For <u>the great day</u> of their wrath has come, and <u>who can stand</u>?"*
>
> Revelation 6:14-17

John's rhetorical question at the end of his message is simply for effect, because the answer is quite obvious. The wicked and rebellious shall not stand at the end of D-Day. It is only those who have washed the robes of their characters, and made them white through the blood of the Lamb, who would be able to stand in that last great day (Revelation 7:14). Isaiah saw this in prophetic vision and wrote: "*And it shall be said in <u>that day</u>, Lo, this is our God; we have waited for him, and he will save us: this is the LORD; we have waited for him, we will be glad and rejoice in his salvation*" (Isaiah 25:9). On that fatal day there will be only two classes of people on the earth—those who will be waiting to receive Him and those who will be running away from His presence.

In another scene, John sees Christ as a mighty warrior (not a wounded Lamb), coming with the armies of heaven to wage war against the wicked, deceptive alliance of the beast, the false prophets and the political powers of the earth. This is the battle previously described in Revelation 16:13, 14 as the battle of Armageddon—the war of *the great day of God* Almighty. John wrote:

> "*And I saw heaven opened, and behold, <u>a white horse</u>, and He who sat on it is called <u>Faithful and True</u>, and in righteousness He judges and wages war. [12]His eyes are a flame of fire, and on His head are many diadems; and He has a name written on Him which no one knows except Himself. [13]He is clothed with a robe dipped in blood, and His name is called <u>The Word of God</u>.*
>
> *[14]<u>And the armies which are in heaven, clothed in fine linen, white and clean</u>, were following Him <u>on white horses</u>. [15]From His mouth comes a sharp sword, so that with it He may strike down the nations, and He will rule them with a rod of iron; and He treads the wine press of the fierce wrath of God, the Almighty. [16]And on His robe and on His thigh He has*

a name written, 'KING OF KINGS, AND LORD OF LORDS...'
[19]And I saw the beast and the kings of the earth and their armies assembled to make war against Him who sat on the horse and against His army. [20]And the beast was seized, and with him the false prophet who performed the signs in his presence, by which he deceived those who had received the mark of the beast and those who worshiped his image; these two were thrown alive into the lake of fire which burns with brimstone."

Revelation 19:11-20

There is so much that could be discussed from all the facts and symbolisms of these prophetic verses, but to devote such time and space to pursue these details would defeat the straight-forward purpose of this volume. Consequently, I will stick to the basic theme of the passage, which, in my estimate, is the global war between the forces of good and evil—the armies of Christ and the armies of Satan. There are some who hold to the view that this battle, Armageddon, is a political warfare of global proportions that will be fought in the valley of Megiddo, in Palestine of the Middle-East. However, the scriptural harmony of Revelation 16 and 19 suggests quite a different scenario.

However, this battle is much more than a political warfare between enemy nations. Rather, it is more a supernatural battle between the kingdom of God and the kingdom of darkness, which will ultimately incorporate all the nations of earth who have been deceived by the dragon (Satan), the beast (Papal system) and the false prophet (apostate Christianity). John said he saw this in apocalyptic vision:

"*And I saw coming out of the mouth of the dragon*

and out of the <u>mouth of the beast</u> and out of the <u>mouth of the false prophet</u>, three unclean spirits like frogs; ¹⁴<u>for they are spirits of demons, performing signs, which go out to the kings of the whole world, to gather them together for the war of the great day of God, the Almighty</u>."

Revelation 16:13, 14

In Revelation 19:19 we read: "<u>And I saw the beast and the kings of the earth and their armies assembled to make war against Him who sat on the horse and against His army</u>." When we compare these passages of Scripture with what John so aptly describes in Revelation 19:11-21, we can readily see that the battle of Armageddon, the great day of God the Almighty, and the war between the King of kings with armies of heaven and the satanic alliance of the beast, false prophet, and the kings of the earth are all referring to one and the same event.

John makes use of quite an array of descriptors to give his readers clear insight into many distinctive features of this great battle, namely:

- Christ's character and His eternal godhead—Faithful and True, eyes of flames of fire, name is Word of God (vv. 11-13).
- His kingship and majesty—many diadems on His head, riding a white horse, name on His robe and thigh (vv. 11-12, 16).
- His dominion and power—smite and rule the nations with a rod of iron (v. 15).
- His wrath and righteous judgment—robe dipped in blood, judges and make war in righteousness (vv. 11, 13, 15; also compare Isaiah 63:1-6).

The apostle's overall portrayal of Christ on D-Day is that of a conquering warrior and not of a suffering, bleeding Lamb. The King of kings is coming not only to redeem the citizens of His eternal kingdom, but also to put an eternal end to sin and sinners in the earth. "One day with the King" is a day of glorious redemption for the people of God on the one hand, and a day of disastrous retribution for rebellious sinners on the other.

Guess Who is Coming to Supper?

As the Satanic alliance arrays itself against the armies of heaven in this penultimate battle of the ages, the hosts of this kingdom of darkness are destroyed by the sharp sword—the Word (vv. 15, 21; Hebrews 4:12)—which proceeds out of the mouth of Christ. Just as the whole of creation came into being by the word of the Lord (Psalm 33:6, 9), even so the wicked will be cut down by the word of judgment from Christ's mouth. However, the beast and false prophet are thrown alive into the lake of fire and brimstone (v. 20).

In anticipation of this utter destruction of the armies of the evil one, an angel, clothed in the effulgent glory of his supreme Commander, issues an invitation to the great supper of God Almighty. The strange menu of this extravagant feast is the dead carcasses of humankind and beasts, slain through the powerful words of the King. An even greater peculiarity about this is the types of guests who are invited to dine at God's table. They are every imaginable kind of bird which flies in the mid-heaven. They are the ones who are invited to partake of the flesh of all the dead, strewn across the face of the whole earth.

> *"Then I saw an angel standing in the sun, and he cried out with a loud voice, saying to all the birds which fly in mid-heaven, "Come, assemble for <u>the great supper of God</u>, ¹⁸so that you may eat the flesh of kings and the flesh of commanders and the flesh of*

mighty men and the flesh of horses and of those who sit on them and the flesh of all men, both free men and slaves, and small and great. . . ²¹And the rest <u>were killed with the sword which came from the mouth of Him who sat on the horse</u>, and all the birds were filled with their flesh."

Revelation 19:17, 18, and 21.

What a terrible scene! Jeremiah prophesied that *the slain of the LORD shall be at <u>that day</u> from one end of the earth even unto the other end of the earth: they shall not be lamented, neither gathered, nor buried; they shall be dung upon the ground* (Jeremiah 25:33, KJV).

Dress Rehearsal

Every movie, every play, has a dress rehearsal, in which the actors review their scripts, pace through their scenes, and make dry runs of the entire production. The same is true with "One day with the King." Every human being is in dress rehearsal right now for D-Day, and the way we relate to the King now will determine the outcome of our response to Him in that great day—ecstatic joy or ice-cold fear. The psalmist David clearly understood what dress rehearsal, in relation to "One day with the King," was all about. Hence he wrote: *"Who knows the power of your anger? For your wrath is as great as the fear that is due you. Teach us to number our days aright, that we may gain a heart of wisdom* (Psalm 90:11, 12, NIV).

A heart (or mind) of wisdom is developed through reverence and respect for God and His will and purpose for our lives. It was David, himself, who said that *the fear of the Lord is the beginning of wisdom; and all who follow His precepts have good understanding* (Psalm 111:10). Making wise choices with regard to how we live is the most important thing we can do during this time of dress rehearsal for D-Day.

In his letter to Titus, Paul refers to our period of dress rehearsal as a time of grace through which we are to (as it were) master our life-script in preparation for this "One day with the King." He wrote: *"For <u>the grace of God has appeared</u>, bringing salvation <u>to all men</u>, ¹²<u>instructing us to deny ungodliness</u> and <u>worldly desires</u> and <u>to live sensibly, righteously and godly</u> <u>in the present age</u>, ¹³looking for the blessed hope and the appearing of the glory of our great God and Savior, Christ Jesus. . ."* (Titus 2:11-13).

Perfecting this dress rehearsal is a humanly impossible, for *the way of man is not in himself: it is not in man that walketh to direct his steps* (Jeremiah 10:23, KJV). *For there is a way that seemeth right unto a man, but the end thereof are the ways of death* (Proverbs 16:25, KJV). It is for this reason that God has made available to all mankind an abundant supply of His grace, through the Holy Spirit, to instruct all humanity how to deny ungodliness and worldly lusts; and how to live wisely, righteously and godly during dress rehearsal, while keeping D-Day in view. These instructions come through the revelation of His word—the master script for governing all human life, which, if clearly understood and followed, will prepare the obedient for the great day of the Lord.

Follow the Cue Line

> *"For the Son of man is as a man taking a far journey, who left his house, and gave authority to his servants, and to every man his work, and commanded the porter to watch. ³⁵<u>Watch ye therefore: for ye know not when the master of the house cometh, at even, or at midnight, or at the cockcrowing, or in the morning</u>: ³⁶Lest coming suddenly he find you sleeping. ³⁷<u>And what I say unto you I say unto all, Watch</u>."*
>
> Mark 13:34-37

It is very customary that during a staged play or movie-shoot that the producer or director of the production gives verbal, written or even signaled cues to the cast so that the timing and sequence of their various parts synchronize harmoniously to deliver a stunning performance. If important cues are missed, improperly timed, or interpreted wrongly, they can spell disaster for the entire production. It is for this reason that dress rehearsals are conducted in order to minimize or completely eradicate any major glitches during the final screen or stage performance.

Since we are living in dress rehearsal time for D-Day, it is very important for us to pay very close attention to the cues that the King has delivered to us in His word. If we miss them, it can be disastrous for us when the final curtain falls on the stage of this world. While time and space do not allow me the luxury to itemize all these cues, a careful reading of Matthew 24 and 25, Mark 13, Luke 17 and 21 will provide a direct and adequate frame of reference to awaken, and possibly satisfy, anyone's interest on the subject. When Jesus gave these cues, He was actually talking to His disciples about dress rehearsal and D-Day.

> *"And there shall be signs in the sun, and in the moon, and in the stars; and upon the earth distress of nations, with perplexity; the sea and the waves roaring; ²⁶men's hearts failing them for fear, and for looking after those things which are coming on the earth: for the powers of heaven shall be shaken. ²⁷And then shall they see the Son of man coming in a cloud with power and great glory. ²⁸<u>And when these things begin to come to pass, then look up, and lift up your heads; for your redemption draweth nigh</u>."*

Luke 21:25-28, KJV

The Master also told His disciples that in order for them to observe the cues He sends them, they must be on the alert. He warns: "<u>Watch</u> *therefore: for ye know not what hour your Lord doth come...* *⁴⁴Therefore be ye also ready: for in such an hour as ye think not the Son of man cometh*" (Matthew 24:42, 44, KJV)

In our post-Modern age, we are constantly bombarded by multitudes of distractions from an equally staggering number of known and unknown sources. This makes it increasingly difficult for an individual to keep faithful watch over his soul. If one is not very careful and prayerful, the daily grind of this earthly life can obscure his/her vision of the signaled cues the Word and the Spirit are trying to deliver in these closing scenes of earth's history. Jesus cautioned His disciples and us to:

> *"Be careful, or your hearts will be weighed down with dissipation, drunkenness and the anxieties of life, and that day will close on you unexpectedly like a trap. ³⁵For it will come upon all those who live on the face of the whole earth. ³⁶<u>Be always on the watch</u>, and pray that you may be able to escape all that is about to happen, and that you may be able to stand before the Son of Man."*
>
> Luke 21:34-36

One day the King of glory, our Lord and Savior, Jesus Christ, will return to receive the citizens of His kingdom. What a day that will be! While we wait for His appearing, we ought not become weary, but watchful; for the cues all around us indicate that it will not be much longer. Let's encourage one another to follow the advice of the King:

> "<u>Watch ye therefore</u>: *for ye know not when the master of the house cometh, at even, or at midnight, or at the cockcrowing, or in the morning: Lest coming*

suddenly he find you sleeping. <u>And what I say unto you I say unto all</u>, <u>Watch</u>."

Mark 13:35

And remember: It would be worth living, waiting and watching for "One day with the King."

Notes

1. Anthony Emrold Phillip, *Life is a Stage*, 1971 calypso music, adopted from William Shakespeare's *As You Like It, Act II, Scene VII*.

GODS' GLORIOUS MOUNTAIN

10

"... <u>But the stone that struck the statue became a great mountain and filled the whole earth</u>... ⁴⁴<u>In the days of those kings the God of heaven will set up a kingdom which will never be destroyed</u>, and that kingdom will not be left for another people; <u>it will crush and put an end to all these kingdoms</u>, but <u>it will itself endure forever</u>. ⁴⁵Inasmuch as you saw that a stone was cut out of the mountain without hands and that it crushed the iron, the bronze, the clay, the silver and the gold, <u>the great God has made known to the king what will take place in the future</u>; so the dream is true and its interpretation is trustworthy."

Daniel 2:35, 44, 45

More than 26 centuries have passed since God declared His hand to a proud heathen king concerning the future of his kingdom and the remaining history of the human race. Through the prophetic voice of His servant, Daniel, the Lord, Jehovah, outlined the rise and fall of earthly kingdoms and the emergence of the everlasting kingdom of heaven—symbolized by the *stone that was cut out of the mountain without hands*. The Divine Watcher did not allow one word of His servant to fall to the ground, but fulfilled every letter with immaculate accuracy.

Now the fullness of time has come, and the future reaches back to embrace the past as the "stone" grows into the complete image and likeness of the "mountain" from which it was divinely hewn. As it was in the beginning, so shall it now be in the end—the everlasting kingdom of heaven, bequeathed to man at creation, wrested by Satan through deception, and restored by Christ (the true "stone") through redemption, shall be delivered to the saints at His return.

Daniel said that the kingdom of heaven shall not be left to another people (Daniel 2:44), but for the saints of the Most High God. They shall take the kingdom, and possess it forever, even forever and ever (Daniel 7:18). This possession is initiated at the return of Jesus and is consummated at the "Marriage Supper of the Lamb." At that time, Christ will speak gently to His bride—His ransomed church—saying: *"Come, you who are blessed by my Father; take your inheritance, the kingdom prepared for you since the creation of the world* (Matthew 25:34).

The apostle John describes the celebrative atmosphere that attends this most glorious, royal occasion. He said he heard a fourfold hallelujah chorus celebrating the salvation, glory, power, true and righteous judgment, and the omnipotent reign of the Lord, God, Almighty. Three of those hallelujahs came from a great multitude in heaven, possibly all the redeemed and the heavenly hosts. The other came from the twenty-four elders and four living creatures who worship before the throne of God (Revelation 19:1-6).

The reason for all this celebration was not only the awesome majesty, power, salvation, victory and reign of the King of kings and Lord of lords, but also the delightful honor to be counted worthy to share in this once-in-an-eternal-lifetime experience at the celestial marriage table. John heard the saints and the heavenly hosts saying:

> *"Let us rejoice and be glad and give the glory to Him, for the marriage of the Lamb has come and His bride has made herself ready." ⁸It was given to her to clothe herself in fine linen, bright and clean; for the fine linen is the righteous acts of the saints. ⁹Then he said to me, "Write, 'Blessed are those who are invited to*

the marriage supper of the Lamb.'"

Revelation 19:7-9

What a breath-taking, awe-inspiring event to witness! It was so moving and transcendent that John felt compelled to bow in worship to the angel that brought this panoramic revelation to him; but the celestial messenger had to restrain John and redirect his worship to the enthroned God of the universe.

When Christ initiated His church, He made a promise to Peter, the other disciples, and to all who, by faith, would embrace Him as the Son of the Living God and Savior of humanity. In that promise He pledged to His bride: *The gates of hell shall not prevail against you!* (Matthew 16:18); *I will be with you till the end of the age* (Matthew 28:20). Throughout her long history of warfare against hardships and heresies, punishments and persecutions, artful deceptions and bitter disappointments, imprisonment and institutionalization, Christ, the faithful husband, stood by His betrothed bride, bringing her safely to her palace of rest and rejoicing in His glorious, everlasting kingdom. The King fulfilled his pledge to His Queen (the church) and gave her full and complete victory over the gates of hell and the kingdom of darkness. The exiled apostle saw the triumphant bride, standing on what he described as "a sea of glass mixed with fire," rejoicing in her victory over the enemy.

> *"And I saw something like a sea of glass mixed with fire, and those who had been victorious over the beast and his image and the number of his name, standing on the sea of glass, holding harps of God. ³And they sang <u>the song of Moses, the bond-servant of God, and the song of the Lamb</u>, saying, 'Great and marvelous are Your works, O Lord God, the Almighty; Righteous and true are Your ways, King of the nations!' ⁴Who will not fear, O Lord, and glorify Your name? For You*

alone are holy; For ALL THE NATIONS WILL COME AND WORSHIP BEFORE YOU, FOR YOUR RIGHTEOUS ACTS HAVE BEEN REVEALED."

Revelation 15:2-4

It appears that the song of Moses and the Lamb is a song of salvation and redemption, a song of experience. Consequently, it is only those that have experienced the joy of deliverance from sin's bondage and oppression that would be able to sing this song. It is also a song of victory that gives honor and glory to God who was, and is, the active, omnipotent Overseer (really Over Seer) that orchestrated the deliverance of Israel out of Egypt. He is the One who will deliver His church—Israel reconstituted—out of this sinful world (a figure of Egypt under the despotic rule of Satan).

This is why the song is about Moses and the Lamb. It is a song that connects type (Moses) with anti-type (Christ, the Lamb). Indeed, God's *"righteous acts have been revealed"* in these related experiences. Therefore, He is worthy of all glory, praise and worship.

Answer to Prayer

"*. . . Thy kingdom come. Thy will be done on earth as it is in heaven . . .*"

Matthew 10:6

When the Master prayed this prayer, the will of God, pertaining to the kingdom, was already a settled fact in heaven. Now, through the apocalyptic vision of John, the earth has completely caught up with heaven, and there is a remarkable display of celestial harmony, celebrative praise and continuous, heart-felt worship. To have heard about the kingdom from the very lips of Jesus must have been a most thrilling and precious adventure; to have proclaimed the kingdom's gospel must have been a most joyous and rewarding privilege; but now to experience the kingdom's reality, even only in vision, must be the indescribable zenith of the life of this lowly fisherman—Christ's beloved apostle and kingdom witness to earth's last generations. It is this John who gives us a glorious, but restricted, view of the kingdom that has come in a world that has been reborn through the power of the gracious, omnipotent will of a loving God. Listen to him:

> "Then <u>I saw</u> a <u>new heaven and a new earth</u>; for the first heaven and the first earth passed away, and there is no longer any sea. ²And <u>I saw</u> <u>the holy city, New Jerusalem</u>, coming down out of heaven from God, made ready as a bride adorned for her husband. ³And <u>I heard</u> <u>a loud voice from the throne</u>, saying, Behold, the tabernacle of God is among men, and <u>He will dwell among them</u>, and <u>they shall be His people</u>, and God Himself will be among them, and ⁴He will wipe away every tear from their eyes; and there will no longer be any death; there will no longer be any mourning, or crying, or pain; <u>the first things have passed away</u>. ⁵And He who sits on the throne said, Behold, I am making all things new." And He said, "Write, for these words are faithful and true."
>
> Revelation 21:1-5, NIV

The word, '*then*', at the beginning of Revelation 21 indicates that something transpired before the introduction of the events of this chapter. A quick review of chapter 20 reveals that these events were the millennial reign of Christ and the saints (v. 4, 6), the binding of Satan during the millennium (vv. 1-3), the resurrection of the wicked dead who were slain at the return of Jesus (v. 5), judgment of all the wicked before God's great white throne, which actually takes place during Christ's millennial reign (vv. 4, 11-15), and the complete eradication of every trace of sin in the lake of fire and brimstone—the second death (vv. 6-10; Revelation 21:8). Included in the lake of fire and brimstone are Satan, the beast, the false prophet, rebellious sinners, death and the grave. Moreover, it is this lake of fire and brimstone—which annihilates sin, sinners, and the kingdom of darkness—that will also purify the entire planet of everything associated with the former creation.

The Coronation of the Stone

It is out of the ashes of this global chaos that the celestial phoenix of a regenerated[1] cosmos—the new heaven and the new earth which John sees—arises. This is the eternal reward of the saints, for the meek shall inherit the earth (Matthew 5:5). As the new heaven and the new earth emerge, John also sees the holy city, New[2] Jerusalem, coming down from God out of heaven as a bride exquisitely dressed for her husband. This is matrimonial language. The old Jerusalem in the land of Palestine as we know it today, perished with the heaven and earth of the former creation, and now a whole new order appears.

John sees the New Jerusalem and the new heaven and earth as a match made out of heaven (so to speak). He also heard the voice of God from the throne room pronouncing the nuptial blessing on the glorious reunion: *"Behold, the tabernacle of God is with men, and he will dwell with them, and they shall be his people, and God himself shall be with them, and be their God"* (Revelation 21:3, KJV). This New Jerusalem is the mother (an allegory of Sarah) of the children of promise, who, through Jesus, have lived a life of faith and obedience to God (Galatians 4:21-28).

When the Jews built the tabernacle in the city of Jerusalem to house the presence of God in the holy of holies, God's true purpose was always to dwell in the hearts of His people, for He does not dwell in temples made by human hands (Acts 7:48-50). The Jews missed this critical and eternal truth even when God was dwelling, in the person of His Son, in the midst of them. We also stand in the gravest danger of missing the same truth if we allow ourselves to become distracted and absorbed by the magnificent, sprawling structures we profess to erect in the name of God. Be reminded of the fact that just as the old tabernacle, which was truly a world wonder, was destroyed by the Roman army under General Titus in AD 70, so will the current tabernacle, the city of Jerusalem and the whole earth be destroyed at the return of Jesus.

However, what the apostle John saw and heard was what was intended to occur all along since the creation of humanity. Here, the tabernacle is not a structure in the city of Jerusalem, but the entire New Jerusalem is the tabernacle of the Most High God. John said that he did not see any temple in the city for the Lord God, the Almighty, and the Lamb are its temple (Revelation 2:22). The psalmist David calls the New Jerusalem the city of our God, the mountain of His holiness, and the city of the great King. This is the "glorious mountain" of the kingdom of heaven, the divine coronation of the "mysterious stone" that has laid to waste all the kingdoms of men.

> "*Great is the LORD, and greatly to be praised in <u>the city of our God</u>, in <u>the mountain of his holiness</u>. ²Beautiful for situation, <u>the joy of the whole earth</u>, is mount Zion, on the sides of the north, <u>the city of the great King</u>.*"
>
> Psalm 48:1, 2, KJV

The voice from the throne room (God) says that the tabernacle is not only in the midst of the redeemed, but that God, Himself, shall dwell among them and be their God, and they shall be His people. To dwell means to live permanently, to take up an abiding resting place. God can live permanently among the redeemed because He is already living in the eternally transformed body temples of these kingdom citizens. This theocratic occupation offers an everlasting sense of security, peace, protection and goodwill to the ransomed multitudes of the new world, for God

> *"will wipe away every tear from their eyes; and there will no longer be any death; there will no longer be any mourning, or crying, or pain; the first things have passed away. And He who sits on the throne said, Behold, I am making all things new." And He said, "Write, for these words are faithful and true."*
>
> Revelation 21:4, NIV

This is the inheritance of the overcomers (Revelation 21:7), the one which Peter calls *imperishable, undefiled* and *will not fade away* (1 Peter 1:4). It is imperishable because the kingdom is unshakeable and stands forever; undefiled because nothing that defiles shall enter there (Revelation 21:27); and unfading because of the ever present glory of the Son of Righteousness (Revelation 21:23). Peter says that the overcomers are protected by the power of God through faith for salvation that is ready to be revealed in the last day (1 Peter 1:5). It is this revelation that John's feeble human tongue tries so eloquently to describe, a revelation which I will not even attempt to modify or embellish. Let the prophet speak:

> *"And he carried me away in the Spirit to a great and high mountain, and showed me the holy city, Jerusalem, coming down out of heaven from God, [11] having the glory of God. Her brilliance was like a very costly stone, as a stone of crystal-clear jasper. [12] It had a great and high wall, with twelve gates, and at the gates twelve angels; and names were written on them, which are the names of the twelve*

tribes of the sons of Israel.

[13]There were three gates on the east and three gates on the north and three gates on the south and three gates on the west. [14]And the wall of the city had twelve foundation stones, and on them were the twelve names of the twelve apostles of the Lamb.

[15]The one who spoke with me had a gold measuring rod to measure the city, and its gates and its wall. [16]The city is laid out as a square, and its length is as great as the width; and he measured the city with the rod, fifteen hundred miles; its length and width and height are equal. [17]And he measured its wall, seventy-two yards, according to human measurements, which are also angelic measurements.

[18]The material of the wall was jasper; and the city was pure gold, like clear glass. [19]The foundation stones of the city wall were adorned with every kind of precious stone. The first foundation stone was jasper; the second, sapphire; the third, chalcedony; the fourth, emerald; [20]the fifth, sardonyx; the sixth, sardius; the seventh, chrysolite; the eighth, beryl; the ninth, topaz; the tenth, chrysoprase; the eleventh, jacinth; the twelfth, amethyst.

[21]And the twelve gates were twelve pearls; each one of the gates was a single pearl. And the street of the city was pure gold, like transparent glass. [22]I saw no temple in it, for the Lord God the Almighty and the Lamb are its temple. [23]And the city has no need of the sun or of the moon to shine on it, for the glory of God has illumined it, and its lamp is the Lamb.

[24]The nations will walk by its light, and the kings of the earth will bring their glory into it. [25]In the daytime (for there will be no night there) its gates will

never be closed; ²⁶*and they will bring the glory and the honor of the nations into it;* ²⁷*and nothing unclean, and no one who practices abomination and lying, shall ever come into it, but only those whose names are written in the Lamb's book of life.*

²²⁽¹⁾*Then he showed me a river of the water of life, clear as crystal, coming from the throne of God and of the Lamb,* ²*in the middle of its street. On either side of the river was the tree of life, bearing twelve kinds of fruit, yielding its fruit every month; and the leaves of the tree were for the healing of the nations.*

³*There will no longer be any curse; and the throne of God and of the Lamb will be in it, and His bond-servants will serve Him;* ⁴*they will see His face, and His name will be on their foreheads.* ⁵*And there will no longer be any night; and they will not have need of the light of a lamp nor the light of the sun, because the Lord God will illumine them; and they will reign forever and ever.*

⁶*And he said to me, "<u>These words are faithful and true</u>"; and the Lord, the God of the spirits of the prophets, sent His angel to show to His bond-servants <u>the things which must soon take place</u>.* ⁷*"<u>And behold, I am coming quickly. Blessed is he who heeds the words of the prophecy of this book</u>."*

Revelation 21:10-27; 22:1-7

Although John falls very short in his description of the glories of the capital city of the kingdom of heaven, yet he gives us enough insight to stimulate our imaginations with the most joyous dreams our puny minds can handle. Such preoccupations fill us with unabated desire, glorious hope and eager anticipation. Who in his right mind would not want to be a part of what John describes? The beloved apostle also leaves us with the blessed assurance that what he describes is a faithful representation of all that was presented to him, and that all these things will shortly come to pass.

Jesus did not only endorse the truthfulness of John's testimony, but also reiterated the fact that His return is very near. He said: "... *behold, I am coming quickly. Blessed is he who heeds the words of the prophecy of this book* (Revelation 22:7); and again "*behold, I am coming quickly, and My reward is with Me, to render to every man according to what he has done* (v. 12); and finally, "*yes, I am coming quickly*" (v. 20).

Surely, the return of Jesus is the blessed hope of all the ages for those who have washed their robes in the precious blood of Calvary's Lamb, through repentance of their sins and faith towards God. This faith yields a life of obedience to His perfect will. It is these precious ones who will have the right to the tree of life and may enter by the gates into the city (Revelation 22:14). The privilege is theirs now, not only to live and pray daily, *"Thy kingdom come;"* but also to say with bold assurance of faith, *"Even so, come, Lord Jesus!"*

These faithful ones shall stand one day on the sea that looks like glass, sparkling with fire, and shall sing the triumphant song of Moses and the Lamb (Revelation 15:2, 3). They are God's trophies of grace, the shining jewels in His "Unshakeable Kingdom," which shall stand fast forever, and ever.

Notes:

1. The adjective, new, used to described heaven and earth in Revelation 21:1 is the Greek ***kainos***—which means new in nature, form or quality when contrasted with the old, suggesting that it was the same heaven and earth, but in a completely renewed state, of a better nature, form and quality. It is not only eternal, but *imperishable, undefiled* and *will not fade away* (1 Peter 1:4). John

did not use the word ***neos*** (for new), because it carries a slightly different meaning. ***Neos*** denotes the idea of recent, or new in time, like a brand new car or baby that never existed before.

2. Again, the word ***kainos*** is used to describe Jerusalem, suggesting that the holy city, New Jerusalem, is not simply a replacement of the old, but its celestial and eternal upgrade as well. It is the same idea that is present when the bible speaks of the old covenant and new or better covenants (Hebrews 8 and 9). They were one and the same covenant, but the new was better because it was ratified by the best Sacrifice, administered by the best Priest, and God was doing the work in the heart of men (Hebrews 8:10-12) and not man trying to save himself.

Conclusion

Dear reader, be assured that the unfailing, prophetic Word of God, through His servant Daniel, is hastening to its dramatic, unalterable end. The "mysterious stone,"[1] unseen by the natural, unregenerated eye (John 3:3), is growing progressively into the "everlasting mountain"[2] of God—linking it eternally with the great mountain (God's eternal kingdom) from which it was cut (Daniel 2:34, 35, 44, 45). Through many earthly distractions, the god of this world[3] has blinded the visions of this heedless, last-day generation from the grand and dreadful events soon to take place on this planet.

The Bible warns that while the great minds of our age try hopelessly to calm global pandemic fear by predicting peace and safety, sudden destruction will overtake the inhabitants of earth. Absolutely, nothing will be able to protect humanity from the deadly judgments that shall precede the great and terrible day of the Lord (1 Thessalonians 5:2, 3).

In the light of these inescapable truths, it is critically important for you, through faith in Christ, to pursue the surrendered life of the born-again child of God now, so that your present and future place in His eternal kingdom is guaranteed. Do not allow yourself to be distracted by the traditions of men, situations of life, or the things of this corrupt world. Be assured the kingdom of God is much bigger than the very narrow confines of the religion and systems of humanity.

While the church—the assembly of born-again believers—was called to proclaim the kingdom's gospel, inviting people of every earthly description to enter into kingdom life, the assembly itself is not the kingdom. The church does not, and cannot, contain the kingdom, but the kingdom the church. The kingdom of God exists on one eternal continuum, but the church exists only in time. It is the assembly of God's children, ransomed from among men; and is in transition from an existence in time to abundant life in eternity.

It is worthwhile to remember that God, not men, is the only One who determines your legitimate kingdom citizenship. Therefore, live a life of obedience to Him, and of loving service to humanity (Micah 6:8). Stand courageously as a faithful steward of God's grace, for very soon, the Holy One who shook Mount Sinai in the days of Moses, shall once more shake the heavens and the earth (Hebrews 12:26). When this occurs, the crumbling kingdoms of men will give way to the eternal kingdom of His dear Son and our Savior, Jesus Christ. It is my prayer that you may be found firmly planted among those things which cannot be moved (Hebrews 12:27), waiting patiently and prayerfully for the grand reception of your Father's "Unshakeable Kingdom."

> *Therefore, since we are receiving a kingdom that cannot be shaken, let us be thankful, and so worship God acceptably with reverence and awe.*
>
> Hebrews 12:28

Notes

1. God's kingdom of grace—the invisible, dynamic image of Christ's incorruptible seed life (1 Peter 1:23) which silently grows within every believer, in tandem with His kingdom forces at the work in His church and in the world.
2. God's kingdom of glory—the transcendent, eternal kingdom of God that restores its reign over the earth through the glorious, triumphant return of Christ as King of kings and Lord of lords.
3. One of the many aliases of Satan — 2 Corinthians 4:4. See also John 12:31; 14:30; 16:11 (prince of this world), and Ephesians 2:2 (prince of the power of the air).

About The Author

Ruthven J. Roy is a pastor, teacher and disciple-maker, whose powerful ministry has impacted the lives of countless numbers of God's children around the world. He is the founder and president of Network Discipling Ministries, an equipping organization that has trained thousands of believers to become fruit-bearing disciples of Christ. Dr. Roy holds degrees from Andrews University and Western Michigan University, and has authored several life-transforming books, including: *The Explosive Power of Network Discipling; The Samson Xfile* and the deeper-life masterpiece, *Imitating God* (text and study guide). He resides in Berrien Springs, Michigan, USA, with Lyris, his dear wife and partner in ministry.

More Exciting Titles
by Dr. Ruthven J. Roy

The Samson Xfile

The Samson Xfile is the intriguing review of the most misunderstood faith-hero in the Bible—Samson. Christian tradition has perpetuated a negative view of this God-warrior; but the mysterious Xfile (Judges 14:4) of God's providence paints an amazingly very different picture. See your life reflected in God's dealing with Samson.

ISBN: 978-0-9717853-1-1 (Hardcover)
       978-0-9717853-2-8 (Paperback)

The Explosive Power of Network Discipling

"Every Christian is called to be a disciple of Jesus; and every disciple is called to be a fisher, not just a member!" In this volume Dr. Roy clearly explains Christ's master plan for growing His kingdom. Christ calls everyone to discipleship, not membership.

ISBN: 978-0-9717853-4-2

Imitating God

Imitating God is not only possible, but it is also guaranteed. This book will make available to you the key to your true identity, and will show you, in very simple steps, how to unleash the power of God's life from within you. Get ready to enter into the **God-zone**.

ISBN: 978-0-9717853-3-5

Study Guide: Imitating God

Do not forget this companion Study Guide to go along with this magnificent text. It would greatly enhance your understanding of all the vital issues that pertain to your spiritual identity and living victoriously. Moreover, this Study Guide will provide you with an exciting, hands-on way to share this good news with others.

ISBN: 978-0-9717853-6-6

Available at your local Christian bookstore

For more information, visit www.networkdiscipling.org, or write to Rehoboth Publishing, P.O. Box 33, Berrien Springs, MI 49103

Contact Information

Dr. Ruthven J. Roy

NETWORK DISCIPLING MINISTRIES
P.O. Box 33
Berrien Springs, MI 49103

Tel: (301) 514-2383
Email: ruthvenroy@networkdiscipling.org
Website: www.networkdiscipling.org

www.ingramcontent.com/pod-product-compliance
Lightning Source LLC
Chambersburg PA
CBHW031945080426
42735CB00007B/273